American Flower Garden Directory

Containing Practical Directions for the Culture of Plants

Robert Buist

APPLEWOOD BOOKS
Bedford, Massachusetts

American Flower Garden Directory
was originally published in

1845

9781429014854

Thank you for purchasing an Applewood book.
Applewood reprints America's lively classics—
books from the past that are still of interest
to the modern reader.
For a free copy of a catalog of our
bestselling books, write to us at:
Applewood Books
Box 365
Bedford, MA 01730
or visit us on the web at:
awb.com

Prepared for publishing by HP

AMERICAN

FLOWER GARDEN DIRECTORY:

CONTAINING

PRACTICAL DIRECTIONS FOR THE CULTURE OF PLANTS

IN THE

FLOWER GARDEN, HOT-HOUSE, GREEN-HOUSE, ROOMS, OR PARLOUR WINDOWS,

FOR EVERY MONTH IN THE YEAR.

WITH

A DESCRIPTION OF THE PLANTS MOST DESIRABLE IN EACH, THE NATURE OF
THE SOIL, AND SITUATION BEST ADAPTED TO THEIR GROWTH,
THE PROPER SEASON FOR TRANSPLANTING, ETC.

WITH INSTRUCTIONS FOR ERECTING A

HOT-HOUSE, GREEN-HOUSE, AND LAYING OUT A FLOWER GARDEN.

THE WHOLE ADAPTED TO EITHER LARGE OR SMALL GARDENS,

WITH INSTRUCTIONS FOR PREPARING THE SOIL, PROPAGATING,
PLANTING, PRUNING, TRAINING AND FRUITING THE

GRAPE VINE.

WITH DESCRIPTIONS OF THE BEST SORTS FOR CULTIVATING IN THE OPEN AIR.

THIRD EDITION, WITH NUMEROUS ADDITIONS.

BY ROBERT BUIST,
NURSERYMAN AND FLORIST.

PHILADELPHIA:
CAREY AND HART.
1845.

PHILADELPHIA:
T. K. & P. G. COLLINS,
PRINTERS.

PREFACE

TO THE FIRST EDITION.

THIS volume owes its existence principally to the repeated requests of a number of our fair patrons and amateur supporters, whose inquiries and wishes for a practical manual on Floriculture, at last induced us to prepare a work on the subject. That now offered is given unaffectedly and simply as a plain and easy treatise on this increasingly interesting subject. It will at once be perceived that there are no pretensions to literary claims—the directions are given in the simplest manner—the arrangement made as lucidly as was in our power—and the whole is presented with the single wish of its being practically useful. How far our object has been attained, of course our readers must judge. Nothing has been intentionally concealed; and all that is asserted is the result of minute observation, close application, and an extended continuous experience from childhood. We pretend not to infallibility, and are not so sanguine as to declare our views the most perfect that can be attained. But we can so far say, that the practice here recommended has been found very successful.

Some, very probably, may be disappointed in not having the means of propagating as clearly delineated as those of culture; but to have entered into all the minutiæ connected therewith, would have formed materials for two volumes larger than the present. We might have described that branch, as it has already been done in works published

both on this continent and in Europe. In one of the former
it is said, "You may now propagate many kinds (*Exotic
Plants*) by suckers, cuttings and layers, which should be
duly attended to, particularly such as are scarce and difficult to be obtained." And the directions given in one of
the most extensive works in Europe on the propagation of
an extensive genus, varied in character and constitution,
run thus: "Cuttings of most kinds will strike root. From
the strongest growing kinds, take off large cuttings at a
joint, and plunge them in a pot of sand under a hand-glass
in the bark bed. Of the smaller kinds, take younger kinds
and put them under a bell-glass, also plunged in heat. The
sooner the plants are potted off after they are rooted the
better."

Such instructions to the inexperienced are imperfect
and unavailing, which, we flatter ourselves, is not the
character that will attach to the present work. We are
well aware that there are persons who, to show their own
superior abilities, may cavil and say that there is nothing
new. To such critics it may be answered, if arranging,
simplifying, digesting and rendering Floriculture attainable
by the humblest capacity, with useful lists and tables on a
plan quite novel, as we believe, offer nothing new, it may
at least be called an improvement. However, we submit
all to a generous public, to whom we are already under
many obligations.

HIBBERT & BUIST.

PHILADELPHIA, *April* 18*th*, 1832.

INTRODUCTION.

We are again called upon to present to the Public the Third Edition of this popular Work on the Culture of Flowers—a taste that is now widely disseminating itself; in fact, a knowledge of which is requisite before a refined education is completed. We boldly and fearlessly say, that no country has made such rapid advancement in the art and science of Horticulture in so short a period, as these United States. Wherever the taste prevails, it diffuses a peace and harmony among its participants without either symbol or mystery. In this edition a feast of new material has been served up; entire lists have been canceled and replaced with those of newer and finer forms and habits; extraneous matter and plants of indifferent character are dropped, and every improvement in the art up to this present time introduced.

True, we have not dilated on the wonderful effects of *electricity* upon vegetation, nor have we been extravagant in the results of *guano* in the growth of plants. With regard to the former, the capability of its reduction to general practice has yet to be proven—and the latter has to be cautiously used, and even then its beneficial effects are not universal. However, it can in a liquid state be used to advantage on almost any plant, especially those of strong habits, such as the *Rose, Geranium, Fuchsia, Heliotrope, Chrysanthemum*, &c. To such, the following proportions will be very beneficial: 1 lb. of guano to 5 galls. of water; after standing 12 or more hours, can be used in the routine of watering once a week or even once in two weeks ; but to plants that have more delicate and silky rootlets, such as *Epacris, Erica, Azalea*, &c., the liquid must be reduced one half.

Our descriptions of plants have been conveyed more with the view of giving an idea of their character to the

1*

general reader, than an accurate botanical synopsis, which would have been known to the botanist alone. All that we have described and recommended have, with a few exceptions, passed under our own observation, and are such as are worthy of cultivation, either for beauty of flower, foliage or habit, together with those celebrated in arts and medicine. Many may, possibly, have passed unobserved, either from their being very generally known or difficult to obtain; but in no case has there been suppression from business prejudices. Where the words "our collections," occur, they are meant for those of the county generally.

All our observations have been guided by dint of practice; and, although others may differ, this is designedly and professedly given as the result of our own experience. The plan laid down is our own routine of culture; the soils are those which we adopt; but, at the same time, conceding that every art and profession is subject to improvement, and none more so than American horticulture. The table of soils was originally constructed at the expense of much investigation and labour, and has, also, in this edition, undergone considerable improvement. To every one that has but a single plant, it will be found invaluable. Although the publications in Europe on Gardening and Floriculture are profuse, yet many of their directions, when practised in the United States, prove almost a dead letter,—not so with their architectural and horticultural designs. The estates of the wealthy are susceptible of great improvement; they want more of the picturesque, and (to use the word of the veteran pioneer of horticulture) gardenesque effect, to relieve their premises from the monotonous erections and improvements which seem to govern all. On culture, a work adapted to the climate must (and no other can) be the guide in this country: on this account, a work like the present has been a desideratum to aid the very rapid advancement of the culture of flowers among the intelligent of our flourishing republic.

R. BUIST.

PHILADELPHIA, *July*, 1845.

TABLE OF CONTENTS.

AMERICAN FLOWER GARDEN

DIRECTORY.

ON LAYING OUT A FLOWER GARDEN.

THE Flower Garden is chiefly devoted to the cultivation of showy flowering plants, shrubs and trees, either natives of this country or those of a foreign clime : it is a refined appendage to a country seat, " suburban" villa, or city residence ; every age has had its principles of taste, and every country its system of gardening. Our limits do not permit us to enter minutely into the details of any of these systems, but a few hints may not be out of place to those whose design is the laying out or improvement of the garden. The Italian style is characterized by broad terraces and paralléle walks, having the delightful shade and agreeable fragrance of the orange and the myrtle. Terraces may be advantageously adopted to surmount steep declivities ; and, if judiciously laid out, would convert a sterile bank into a beautiful promenade, or choice flower garden.

The French partially adopt the above system, interspersing it with parterres and figures of statuary work of every character and description. When such is well designed and neatly executed, it has a lively and interesting effect ; but now the refined taste says these vagaries are too fantastic, and entirely out of place. A late writer says of Dutch gardening, that it "is rectangular formality :" they take great pride in trimming their trees of yew, holly, and other evergreens, into every variety of form, such as mops,

2

moons, halberds, chairs, &c. In such a system it is indispensable to order that the compartments correspond in formality, nothing being more offensive to the eye than incongruous mixtures of character.

The beauty of English gardening consists in an artful imitation of nature, and is consequently much dependent on aspect and locality. It is a desideratum where wood and water can be combined with the flower garden, and the practical eye can dispose of an object to advantage by interspersing shrubbery and walks, that the combined objects form an agreeable whole. They are not to be disposed with a view to their appearance in a picture, but to the use and enjoyment of them in real life.

We will now endeavour to give an explicit exposition of a system adapted to our variable climate of extreme heat and excessive cold. Where choice of aspects can be obtained, preference should be given to a south-east or east; but, if not, south or south-west, and, if possible, sheltered by rising ground or full grown woods from the north-west and north. But to lay down directions for a flower garden is not a little difficult, seeing that there cannot be any given area or any description of local circumstances applicable to all situations. A good soil is the sure foundation on which to rear the grand floral superstructure, and the most genial is a sandy loam: I mean by sandy loam a soil which contains from one-sixth to one-tenth of sand; and if on a gravelly or sandy bottom, so much the better. Where the general surface is gently undulating, it will greatly add to the beauty of arrangement; if access to a spring can be obtained, it will prove a desideratum in completing the whole: it can be available for a fish-pond or an aquarium, or can be converted into a swamp for the cultivation of many of our most beautiful and interesting native plants, such as Habanaria, Lilium, Sarracenia, Dionea, &c., and on the margin of which (if partially shaded) can be planted the beautiful varieties of Azaleas, and the splendid flowering Rhododendron, which, by the by, are almost entirely neglected in all our floral decorations. With many, the arrangement of a flower garden is rather a matter for the exercise of fancy, than one calling for the application of refined taste: true, it may be said there is no mathematical law to guide the designer, so that if he avoid incongruity of arrangement the end is accomplished. But, in commencing these operations, a design should be kept in view that will tend to expand, improve and beautify the situation ; not, as we too frequently see it, the parterre and borders with narrow walks up to the very household entrance: such is decided- ly bad taste, unless compelled for want of room. For per- spicuity, admit that the area to be enclosed should be from one to three acres, a circumambient walk should be traced at some distance within the fence, by which the whole is enclosed ; the inferior walks should partly circumscribe and intersect the general surface in an easy serpentine and sweeping manner, and at such distances as would allow an agreeable view of the flowers when walking for exercise. Walks may be in breadth from three to twenty feet, although from four to ten feet is generally adopted ; and, to have these dry and permanent, those that are to be much used should have six to eight inches of the bottom soil dug out in a concave manner, and in the centre of the concave dig out a trench of about nine inches square to form a drain, which may be made with brick or filled with rough stone, and the concave may be filled with refuse of buildings or broken stone within three inches of the desired height, which should be covered with gravel, and then firmly rolled with a heavy roller. Where the gravel cannot be obtained sand may be used, mixed with a few small stones to bind it, but such needs very repeated rolling. Walks, such as described, when completely finished, will last for ages ; but many will not be disposed to go to such expense : to those we say use tanner's bark, which is very cheap and ac- cessible to all. The outer margin of the garden should be planted with the largest trees and shrubs : the interior ar- rangement may be in detached groups of shrubbery and parterres. In order that the whole should not partake of an uniform and graduated character, it should be broken and diversified by single trees planted in the turf, or aris- ing in scattered groups from a base of shrubs. In some secluded spot rock-work or a fountain, or both, may be erected ; the foundation of the former should consist of mounds of earth, which will answer the purpose of more solid erections, and will make the stones go farther : rocks of the same kind and colour should be placed together, and the greatest possible variety of character, size and form, should be studied, the whole showing an evident and well-defined connection. These erections generally are stiff artificial disjointed masses, and often decorated with plants having no affinity to their arid location. The undertaking, when well completed, will present a field of varied and interesting study, and more than compensate for the labour and expense bestowed upon it. If it is desired that the flower garden should be a botanical study, there should be some botanical arrangement adopted.

The *Linnean* system is the most easily acquired. A small compartment laid out in beds might contain plants of all the twenty-four *classes*, and a few of all the hardy *orders* which do not exceed one hundred. Or, to have their natural characters more assimilated, the *Jussieuean* system could be carried into effect by laying down a grass plat to any extent above one quarter of an acre, and cut therein small figures to contain the natural families, which of hardy plants we do not suppose would exceed one hundred and fifty. The difficulties of this arrangement are, that many of the characters are imperfectly known even to the most scientific. (*Professor Lindley* has given additional light on the subject by his last publication.) All the large divisions should be intersected by small alleys, or paths, about one and a half or two feet wide. When there is not a green-house attached to the flower garden, there should be at least a few sashes of framing or a forcing pit to bring forward early annuals, &c., for early blooming. These should be situate in some spot detached from the garden by a fence of Roses, trained to trellises, Chinese Arbour vitæ, Privet, or even Maclura makes excellent fences; and, when properly trimmed, are very ornamental: they require to be neatly and carefully clipped with shears every September. In the southern states Noisette and China Roses, with a profusion of Sweetbriar, would make the most beautiful of all fences, and could be very easily obtained: a fence three hundred feet long would only cost about one hundred and twenty dollars. Frames for forcing should be made of plank two inches thick, and well put together; the sash should be from five to seven feet long, and from three to four feet wide, and filled with six by eight glass. In the framing ground should be kept the various soils required for plants, and also various characters of manure at all times ready for use, the whole in regular heaps, and kept free from weeds. Having given these brief outlines of a flower garden, we now proceed to give monthly directions for planting and keeping the same in order.

JANUARY.

IF the covering of the beds of choice bulbs, herbaceous plants, or tender shrubs, has been neglected last month, let it be done forthwith. The season is now precarious and delays are dangerous. For particular directions, see *December*. Any bulbous roots that have been kept out of the ground should be planted immediately, according to directions in *October*. Some writers have recommended keeping some of the bulbs until this month, in order to have a continued succession. Experience will prove the inefficacy of the plan, and will satisfactorily show that the difference is almost imperceptible, while the flowers are very inferior and much degenerated; and in place of having " a long-continued succession of bloom," there appear, along with your finest specimens, very imperfect flowers, calculated to discourage the admirers of these " gaudy" decoratives of our flower gardens. Whereas, every art employed should be to the advancement and perfection of nature.

OF FRAMING, &c.

The plants and roots that are in frames, should be protected with straw mats and boards, and the frame surrounded with litter, or leaves, or, what is more advisable, banked with turf—the former being a harbour for mice and other vermin. For full directions, see *December*. Under this head the plants, such as *Auriculas, Polyanthus, Daisies, Carnations, Pinks, Pentstemons, Campanula pyramidalis, Double rocket, Double stock, or Stockgillys, Double*

2*

Wall-flower, *Anemone*, *Ranunculus*, &c., as previously
enumerated as frame plants, will require very little water,
and be sure to give none while they are in a frozen state.
If snow should cover them, the plants will keep in a fine
state under it, so never remove snow from covering cold
frames, even suppose it should lie for weeks,—nature will
operate here herself.   But when framing cannot be obtained, they will in this latitude keep tolerably, if gently covered with leaves or litter, using means to secure them
from being blown over the garden.

OF PRUNING.

It is not advisable to carry on a general system of pruning in this month, in whatever state the weather may be.
The severest frosts generally are yet to come, and too frequently what is done now in this operation has to be
repeated in the spring, causing, at that time, work to a
disadvantage ; because, if pruning, when done just now,
is accomplished judiciously, whatever more is requisite to
be done in the spring on the same bush, will be injudi-
cious.   Hence, it is far preferable to delay it till the frost
is nearly over, when all can be done to advantage.   There
are, undoubtedly, hardy trees and some shrubs, that may
be pruned and thinned out at any time from the first of
November to the first of March ; such as Cratœgus, Sor-
bus, Spirea and even Althea, in the middle states ; (the
Double white Althea is very tender and requires to be covered.)   The tying together the loose branches of Juniper,
Cedar and Arbour vitæ should be particularly attended to,
as heavy snow frequently destroys the shape of those handsome shrubs by breaking down the branches, &c.—When
the snow is heavy, the precaution of shaking it off should
be resorted to.   In many seasons, the beginning of this
month is open and admits of the operation of digging in
open quarters, which if not done, as advised last month,
ought not to be delayed.   The fruits of it will appear in
the mellowed state of your soil in spring.
If there is any spare time, tallies, straight sticks or stakes,
may be prepared for summer use.   Tie them up in neat
bundles, which will be of great service during the hurried

period of the year. An opportunity of this kind should
always be laid hold of; the beneficial results will in season
be displayed.

FEBRUARY.

WHEN the borders and various compartments were dug
in the autumn, and compost, or a thin coating of well decomposed manure given, the advantage will now, in part,
be experienced. If the weather is open about the end of
the month, the pruning should be done with the utmost
despatch, that all may be prepared for a general dressing
next month, and let nothing be delayed which can now properly be accomplished, under the idea that there is time
enough.

OF PRUNING, &c.

Generally, about the end of the month, the very severe
frosts are over, and when none need be apprehended that
would materially injure hardy shrubs, they may be freely
pruned, and the points cut of such shoots as may have been
damaged by the winter. Most of shrubs require nothing
more than to be thinned of straggling, irregular and injured
branches, or of suckers that rise round the root, observing,
that they do not intermingle with each other. Never trim
them up in a formal manner; regular shearing of shrubs,
and topiary work, have been expelled as unworthy a taste,
the least improved by reflections on beauty, simplicity and
grandeur of nature.

In fact, the pruning of deciduous hardy shrubs, should
be done in such a manner as not to be observable when the
plants are covered with verdure. It may frequently be observed in flower gardens, that roses and shrubs of every
description are indiscriminately cut with the shears, the
Amórphas, Viburnums and *Althèas* sharing the same fate.
Robinias, Colùteas, Cyticus, Rhús, Genistas, with seve-

ral of the *Viburnums*, and many others, bear their flowers
on the wood of last year, and when thus sheared afford no
gratification in flowering. And those shrubs that thus
flower on the shoots of last year, are perhaps worse to keep
in regular order than those to which the knife can be
freely applied; but good management while young will
ensure handsome free flowering plants.

Climbing shrubs, and others that are trained against out-
buildings, walls, or such as are sheltered thereby, and not
now in danger of suffering by frost, may be pruned and
dressed. These should be neatly trimmed, and the branches
moderately thinned out, tying in all the shoots straight and
regular. Avoid, at all times, the crossing of any shoots.

There is not a shrub in the garden that agrees so well
with close cutting, as the *Althèa*, and all its varieties.
These can be made either bushes or trees, and kept at any
desired height. Where the wood of last year is cut to
about two or three inches from the wood of the former year,
the young shoots of the coming season will produce the
largest and finest flowers, and likewise more profusely.
When they have attained the desired height, let them be
kept in the most natural and handsome shape that the taste
of the operator can suggest. They will bear cutting to any
degree.

Honeysuckles of every description may, with all freedom, be trimmed, providing the frost is not very severe.
These are very frequently allowed to become too crowded
with wood, and then superficially sheared or cut. The
flowers would be much finer, and the brush handsomer, if
they were regularly thinned out, divesting them of all naked and superfluous shoots. Of those that remain, shorten
the shoots of last year. Where any of the honeysuckle
kind has become naked at the bottom, and flowering only
at the top of the trellis, or extremities of the shoots, one
half of the bush should be cut to within four inches of the
ground. It will throw out plenty of fine young wood, which
give room for, and train them straight, and to the full extent, during summer. These shoots will flower profusely
the following season, and in like manner, when thought
proper, the other half can be cut.

Roses of the hardy kinds (termed garden roses) that
were not attended to in November, should, if the weather

permit, be dressed and pruned forthwith. In small gardens, where these are generally attached to the walls and fences, neatness should be a very particular object. If any of such bushes have got strong and irregular, the most proper method to bring them to order, will be to cut down each alternate shoot of the bush to within a few inches of the surface, thereby renovating it, and, in part, preserving the flowers. Those that are cut down will put out several luxuriant shoots, which must be regularly tacked in, spreading them in a fan shape. These, in another year, will flower well, when the others may go through the same operation. Thus, in two or three years, the bushes will have resumed a different, and more agreeable aspect. By the above treatment, these ornaments of the garden will always have a neat and healthful appearance, and the roses will be much finer. Where they are intended for the borders, they should never be allowed to get too high. In a border from four to six feet, they ought never to exceed four feet at the back of the border, and in front one foot, after being pruned; they can be kept down by the above method. It is not advisable to cut down rose bushes all at once, unless no regard is paid to flowering. The roses that are in grass plats, and interspersed through the garden, would have a superior appearance in every respect, if they were kept and trimmed like small trees. They may be of different sizes and heights, according to the distance they are from the walk. A single stem may arise from six inches to six feet, with a head in proportion to the height of the stem. Where it is necessary to have them above two feet, and likewise to carry a good head, inoculation must be resorted to, which, in the months of July and August, will be fully treated of. All under two feet (except the weak growing kinds) will do on their own stems, taking care not to allow shoots to arise from the bottom during the summer. For directions for pruning climbing roses, see March and April.

OF PLANTING SHRUBS, &c.

As soon as the frost is out of the ground, these should be planted if the soil is not too wet. Where soil is binding, upon no consideration plant it while wet, rather defer it until the end of March.

Trees and shrubs, if they are well arranged, are the chief ornaments, give the most pleasure, and afford the greatest delight that we enjoy in our gardens. Although they give no sort of nourishment, nor produce any edible fruits, yet they are particularly grateful and conducive to our enjoyments. Our walks in summer would be oppressive, but for their agreeable shade; in the fall and winter, we would be left exposed to the chilling winds, but for the shelter they afford.

Likewise they produce a great variety of flowers, a varied foliage, and are standing ornaments that give no great trouble. In the character of screens they are particularly useful, whether to hide disagreeable objects, or as a guard against the weather; or, if they are planted in masses at a distance, they soon become agreeable objects, frequently very much improve the scenery of the place, become objects of utility as well as ornament, and, in such case, afford the highest satisfaction. When formed so as to exclude offices from the view of the house, or for sheltering the latter, or for connecting the house with the garden, orchard, or any similar purpose, shrubs are both useful and interesting.

Where many shrubs are to be planted, the disposing of them properly is a matter of considerable importance to the future welfare of the whole; and, whether deciduous or evergreens be mixed or grouped, that is, indiscriminately planted together, or the evergreens planted by themselves, as is frequently done, a regular and natural arrangement is indispensable for establishing ornament.

Arranging, no doubt, depends very much on fancy; still, there ought always to be plenty of evergreens planted, that the whole may be more cheerful in winter.

If shrubberies were made to a great extent, the scenery would be much more varied and characteristic by grouping judiciously than by indiscriminately planting.

However, in small flower gardens and shrubberies, the latter has to be adopted. In such places, tall growing kinds should never be introduced, unless merely as a screen from some disagreeable object, for they crowd and confuse the whole. The dwarf and more bushy sorts should be placed

nearest to the eye, in order that they may conceal the naked
stems of the others. Generally when shrubs are planted,
they are small; therefore, to have a good effect from the beginning, they should be planted closer than they are intended to stand. When they have grown a few years, and
interfere with each other, they can be lifted, and such as
have died, or become sickly, replaced, and the remainder
can be planted in some other direction. Keep them always
distinct, one from another, in order that they may be the
better shown off. But if it is not desired that they should
be thicker planted than it is intended to let them remain,
the small growing kinds may be six or eight feet apart; the
larger, or taller sorts, ten to twenty feet, according to the
condition of the soil.

Thick masses of shrubbery, called thickets, are sometimes wanted. In these there should be plenty of evergreens. A mass of deciduous shrubs has no imposing
effect during winter; and, as this is not the proper season
for planting evergreens, (April, and the end of September,
or first of October being best,) small stakes can be placed
in the destined spot. Planting in rows, or in any plan of
a formal character, should at all times be avoided.

In planting at this season, observe that the roots are not
much exposed to the air, especially if the wind be high and
sharp; but it is always better, if possible, to defer the business until good, mild weather. According to directions in
November, the ground will be well prepared, and only requires a hole dug for the reception of the roots, which must
be considerably larger, that the roots may not be in the
least confined. Break the earth well at bottom, put in as
much as will receive the plant from one to two inches (according to its size) lower than it has previously been in the
Nursery. If any of the roots are bruised or broken, cut
them off; then place the plant in the centre of the hole,
breaking fine all the soil that is put in, at the same time
shaking the stem a little, that the earth may mix with the
roots; when full up, press all the soil down with the foot,
that it may, in some degree, consolidate about the roots,
and support the plant. Tall plants should have a good
stake for support, and place a small bandage between the
stake and stem of the shrub or tree, where the tie is made,
to prevent the bark from suffering by friction. Observe,

always, before planting, if the soil is not suitable, to supply that which is congenial to the nature of the intended plant. When shrubs or trees are to be carried to any distance, the roots should be carefully kept from air, by tying damp moss, straw or mats about them, as circumstances will admit: the success, in part, depends on due attention being paid, to prevent the roots drying before planting. Although we have given the above directions for planting in this month, it will frequently occur, that they can only be put into practice during the next, as this month is often the severest of the season.

OF HYACINTH AND OTHER BULBS.

Towards the end of the month, if the weather proves favourable, the covering should be partially taken off from the Hyacinths, Tulips and other bulbous roots. It sometimes occurs, that, by careless planting in the autumn, they are thrown above ground by the frost, especially if the ground is inclined to moisture, and they not being deep enough planted: if such is the case, cover them with decayed leaves, old tan, or soil, whichever is most convenient; if not done, the sun and air will overpower the bulbs, and although the fibres have hold of the ground, the flowers will be miserably weak.

MARCH.

As soon as the frost is entirely gone, uncover all plants or shrubs that have been protected, preserving carefully such of the materials as will answer the same purpose next season. Cut off all decayed shoots, or such as have been hurt by the frost. The Lagerstrœmias will flower in greater perfection, if they are pruned closely; that is, cut the shoots of last year, to within two or three eyes of the wood of the previous year, at the same time having regard to the regular and natural shape of the bush. Cut off the

injured foliage of any of the evergreens that have suffered
by the severity of the winter, but leave every green part
which is essential to the support of these kind of plants. It
is expected that all pruning of the shrubbery is finished;
if not, get all expeditiously done according to directions
given in the preceding months. All work that can be
done in this month, should not be delayed, such as hoeing,
digging, raking and clearing away all leaves and litter of
every description that have been brought or blown into the
garden during autumn or winter.

OF FRAMING.

Where it is desired to have the more showy annuals
early in bloom, it is necessary to prepare a hot-bed frame,
for the purpose of bringing them forward. It is time,
about the first of the month, to collect and prepare manure for the desired hot-bed; and, as that operation, in
many instances, is very imperfectly performed, a few observations on the subject may be useful.

Take three parts of fresh hot stable manure, with one
part of fresh oak leaves. Have a sufficient quantity to make
the intended bed or beds from three to four feet high.
Shake and mix up both together in a compact conical heap
in order to encourage fermentation. If the weather is cold
and windy, cover it with straw or leaves and boards, which
is necessary to produce the desired effect. If fermentation
soon takes place, it will need to be thoroughly turned over
in eight or ten days. If any of it has become dry and musty
from excessive heat, as you proceed, water the affected
parts, pile all up neatly, and leave it protected in part as
before. In five or six days more, it will have to be turned
again, repeating it until the first extreme heat has been
over. In neglect of this, the heat, after making up the bed,
will be vehement for a week or two, frequently destroying
the vegetative purity of the soil, and proving destructive
to the seeds.

Allowing the manure to come to a lively heat, having
no unpleasant, rancid smell, proceed to mark off your intended bed, running it east and west as nearly as possible,
measure your frame, and allow the site of the bed eight

3

inches each way larger than the frame : at the corners, place a stick or rod perpendicularly. The ground ought to be higher than that around it, to prevent water from getting into the bed, which, if low, must be filled up ; or, if supposed that water may lodge there, a little brushwood might be put under the manure, which would keep it from being inundated. The manure must be built up square and level, shaking, mixing and beating it regularly with the back of the fork. When you have it to the desired height, (from two to three feet will be sufficient for annuals,) leave the centre of the bed a little higher than the sides, thus allowing it more to subside. When finished, put on the frame and sash or sashes, keep them close until the heat arises, covering them at night with mats or shutters. As soon as you feel the heat increased, give air by tilting the sashes a few inches to let off the steam and stagnated air, observing to close in the afternoon, and cover at night. If the heat is violent, about half an inch of air might be left during the night. In about three days, if all has been properly attended to, the bed will be what is termed sweet. Then put in about six inches of fine garden soil; if heavy, mix a little sand with it. Spread it level, and, when the soil is heated through, sow in small drills from one-eighth to an inch deep, according to the size of the seeds ; cover with very fine sifted soil. Some very small kinds do best when sown upon the surface. When sown, give gentle sprinklings of water until they come up, when it will be necessary to give air freely during the day to prevent them from being weak, or damping off, which many of them will do if they have not air regularly admitted.

LIST OF CHOICE FLOWERING ANNUALS
ADAPTED FOR SOWING ON A HOT-BED.

Argeratum Mexicanum, blue flowered Argeratum.
Asclepias curassavica, swallow wort, orange and red flow-
     ered.
Aster Chinensis, China Aster, or Queen Margarets, in great
     variety. The late imported German Asters are of
     extraordinary beauty.
Anagallis Phillipsii, blue Pimpernel.
Balsamina hortensis, Balsam, commonly called Ladies
     Slipper.
Browallia alata, upright blue and white Browallia.
Cacalia coccinea, scarlet Cacalia, or Venus' Paint Brush.
——— sonchifolia, orange Cacalia.
Calandrinia discolor, rosy purple, *very pretty.*
Celosia cristata, Coxcomb, two varieties, red and yellow.
Centaurea Americana, American Sultan.
——— suaveolens, yellow sweet Sultan.
Clarkia elegans, elegant rose-coloured Clarkia.
——— pulchella, showy purple Clarkia.
——————— alba, white flowered Clarkia.
Cleome grandiflora, large lilac flowering spider plant.
Clintonia elegans, elegant blue Clintonia.
Collinsia bicolor, two-coloured Collinsia.
———— heterophylla, lilac and white.
Commelina cœlestis, blue flowering Commelina.
Dianthus Chinensis, China pink, many fine double varie-
     ties.
Gomphrena globosa, red and white globe Amaranthus.
Hibiscus manihot, large yellow Hibiscus.
——— Africanus major, buff with black centre.
Helichrysum bracteatum } Yellow everlasting.
   Xeranthemum lucidum }
Lophospermum erubescens, ⎱ Rose-coloured flowers like
—————————— *scandens,* ⎰ the Digitalis, a fine climb-
                            ⎰ er for arbours.

Loasa lateritia, { Orange red, an interesting climbing plant blooming throughout the season.

Malope alba, white flowering Malope.

—— grandiflora, large red flowering Malope.

Mathiola annua, all the varieties of ten week stocks should be industriously cultivated, and seed sown also in April and May for autumn blooming.

Maurandia Barclayana, blue flowering, } Climbing plants for pillars, trel-

——semperflorens, pink flowering } lisses or ar- bours.

Mesembryanthemum glaciale, Frozen plant.

—————————— crystallinum, Ice plant.

Mimosa pudica, Sensitive plant,

Mimulus Wheelerii, Monkey flower, yellow and crimson,

—— Smithii, Smith's yellow and red, } Will grow best in wet places.

—— Variegatus, variegated pink and white,

—— cardinalis, scarlet,

—— roseus, rose-coloured,

Petunias of variety, a beautiful genus of plants of every variety of colour, from deep purple to pure white, blooming from June till frost; the seeds are small and require to be very lightly covered.

Portulaca splendens, splendid purple flowered Purslane.

—— Thellusonii, red flowered Purslane.

Salpiglossis picta, atropurpurea, &c., delight in a cool situation.

Schizanthus retusus, orange-coloured Schizanthus,

——————— pinnatus, calico Schizanthus,

And a few other varieties, } Like a rich soil, and a cool and partially shaded situation.

Shortia Californica, yellow Shortia, very profuse flowering.

Tagetes, Mary-gold, the new varieties of the French are very pretty—they like rich soil and plenty of moisture.

Tropæolum aduncum, Canary bird flower, a climber and a very scarce plant.

Tropæolum atrosanguineum, crimson Nastur- ⎫
  tium. ⎬ Climbing
Thunbergia alata, buff with black centre. ⎪ plants.
————— alba, white flowered. ⎭
————— aurantiaca, fine orange.
Verbena candidissima, pure white. ⎫ A lovely family
———— Mestonii, bright scarlet. ⎪ of pretty and
———— Algerii, pale rose. ⎪ profuse flower-
———— Blue Queen, blue with pale ⎬ ing plants gen-
  centre. ⎪ erally of a pro-
———— Wilsonii, very dark purple. ⎪ cumbent habit.
———— Julia, bright rose. ⎭
  Seeds may be obtained from the above, although they
cannot be relied upon to produce the same colours.
Vinca rosea, Madagascar Periwinkle, ⎫ Thrive best in a
———————— alba, white flowered Pe- ⎬ warm, dry, situa-
  riwinkle, ⎭ tion, with rich soil.
Zinnia elegans, splendid Zinnia. ⎫ Very showy plants,
————————— coccinea, scarlet. ⎪ and do best when
————————— alba, white. ⎬ they are well sup-
————————— pauciflora, yel- ⎪ plied with water.
  low. ⎭

Though the above will bloom much earlier by being
sown on a hot-bed, yet where that convenience cannot be
obtained, they will all succeed treated as hardy annuals.

After sowing, if the weather be clear, the sun acting on
the glass, will produce a too rapid evaporation of the moisture of the soil, and may otherwise affect seeds but thinly
covered, which must be guarded against by shading with
mats for a few hours during bright sunshine. In giving
water it ought always to be about milk warm, and passed
through a fine rose, to prevent the stems being broken or
bruised. Weeds must be drawn out as soon as they appear.

HARDY ANNUALS.

Many annual plants, though of short duration, are possessed of much beauty of hue and elegance of form: they
are farther valuable from their adaptation in filling up va-

cant spots through the flower garden or parterre. They
are, besides, of easy culture, many requiring nothing more
than to have the seeds sown in the spot where they are to
grow. The first sowing may take place about the end of
the month, when the ground is prepared and the weather
fine, but avoid it at all times when the ground will not pul-
verize properly. The neatest and most expeditious method
is to take a rod about one foot long and one inch in diameter, rounding at the end, with which draw a circle from
four to nine inches in diameter, and from one-eighth of an
inch to an inch deep, according to the size of the seeds.
Many very small seeds will grow best, if sown on the surface of fine mould. When sown, cover with fine mould,
placing a small twig or tally, with the name in the centre
of the circle to prevent mistakes, either in sowing, planting
or hoeing. When they have grown from one to two inches—the first moist day should be taken to remove such
as are too crowded, which can be generally transplanted
to some other situation, taking care to shade them a few
days, with flower pots, or some other substitute. A few
kinds do best with removing, such as Balsams, China
Asters, Mary-gold, 10 week stocks, Hibiscus, Zinnias, and
several others, of a free growing, and strong-wooded nature. Annuals are such plants as grow from seed, flower
and perfect their productions, and then die within one year.
The following sorts are well deserving of culture:

Adonis miniata, Flos Adonis or Pheasant's eye, red.
Amaranthus caudatus, Love lies Bleeding, red and yellow
      variety.
Amaranthus hypochondriacus, Prince's Feather, red.
———————— tricolor, three-coloured Amaranthus should
          be sown on rather poor soil—on rich soil it
          has little beauty.
Brachycome iberidifolia, fine dark blue.
Brugmansia Waymeria, double flowered, large and showy.
Centaurea moschata, purple sweet Sultan.
———————— cretica, white sweet Sultan.
———————— suaveolens, yellow sweet Sultan.
Collinsia grandiflora, blue Collins' flower.
Convolvulus, minor, dwarf blue Bindweed.

Calliopsis bicolor, formerly Coreopsis tinctoria or Fair
      Eye; a very gay plant, and flowers best when
      sown in October.
————— Drummondii, yellow calliopsis.
Collomia coccinea, scarlet flowered.
Delphinium ajacis, Rocket Larkspur, many varieties, all
      superb, and do best to be sown in rich ground in
      October.
————— consolida, branching Larkspur, various co-
      lours.
Euphorbia variegata, variegated Euphorbia.
Eschscholtzia crocea, Orange. (Now *chryseis*.)
————— Californica, yellow.
Erysimum Perowffskyanum, bright orange.
Gilia tricolor, three-coloured Gilia, ⎫
——— capitata, blue-coloured,   ⎬ Bloom all summer.
——— Achillæfolia, large blue,   ⎭
Heliophila Araboides, blue sun love, very pretty.
Hieracium meutabilis, changeable Hawkweed.
Helianthus Californicus, superb double dwarf sunflower.
Iberis amara, white Candytuft.
——— umbellata, purple Candytuft.
——— violacea, violet Candytuft.
——— odorata, white sweet-scented Candytuft.
——— splendens, large purple, sweet-scented Candytuft.
Ipomœa quamoclit, Cypress vine, the seed will grow freely,
      if soaked two or three hours in hot water.
Lathyrus odoratus, sweet Pea of many varieties.
Leptosiphon densiflorus, dense-flowered Leptosiphon.
Loasa lateritia, orange-coloured Loasa, a climbing plant.
Lupinus, many varieties; they require to be partially
      shaded from hot suns.
Malope grandiflora, scarlet Malope.
————— alba, white.
Mirabilis jalapa, marvel of Peru, many varieties. If the
      roots of this plant are lifted in October, and placed
      in a dry cellar, free from frost, and planted out next
      April, they will bloom much finer.
Nemophila insignis, or blue Grove Love, a pretty dwarf
      plant, requiring rich soil and a half shaded situa-
      tion.
————— atomaria, white with black spots.

Œnothera or tree Primrose; many varieties of the annual
    species produce their flowers in much greater
    perfection, if planted or sown in poor soil.   To
    this *ansiloba, sinuata, and tetraptera,* are excep-
    tions, as they flower the finest in a rich light
    loam.
Papaver Marseillii, double white poppy edged with red.
———— gigantea, large Dutch poppy.
Phlox Drummondii, many colours, a superb article, and
    blooms from May till October.   In dry situations it
    is apt to die off unless partially shaded.
Reseda odorata, Mignonette; to have it in perfection the
    whole season, there should be a sowing in May and
    July.   It delights in a rich loamy soil.
Tournefortia heliotropoides, summer Heliotrope.
Viola tricolor, Pansy or Heart's-ease, require very rich soil,
    and should be shaded from hot sun; if sown early
    in the season, they will flower profusely in the
    autumn.

    For other varieties of Annuals, see list adapted for hot-
bed sowing.   We have omitted many not agreeing with
our climate, or those very common for such, we refer our
readers to the lists published annually, by respectable
seedsmen.

BOX EDGINGS

    May be planted any time this month, or beginning of
next, which in most seasons will be preferable.   We will
give a few simple directions how to accomplish the work.
In the first place, dig over the ground deeply where the
edging is intended to be planted, breaking the soil fine, and
keeping it to a proper height, namely about one inch higher
than the side of the walk; but the taste of the operator
will best decide, according to the situation.   Rake the surface even, and tread it down with the feet, or beat it with
the spade.   Where it gives most, continue to add, keeping the surface at the desired height.   If the edging is to
be in a direct line, either on a level or inclined plane, you
may be correctly and simply regulated by making the de-

sired level at each end of the line.　Take three rods about
four feet long each, having a piece of one foot to cross at
one end, two of these pieces painted black, the other white.
Have a black one at each end of the line on the level, take
the white one for the centre, going along the line, and
about every twenty feet, level a spot to the exact height,
which will be seen by looking over the top of the rods
from one end.　Having found the level, drive in a peg to
it, so that no mistake may occur; beat and level between
them, leaving a smooth surface.　This being done, strain
the line, and with the spade proceed to cut out the trench
perpendicularly on the side next the walk, six, eight, ten,
or twelve inches deep, according to the length of the plants.
Afterwards take the plants, and cut the tops even, with the
knife or shears, at the same time shortening the roots.
Then with the left hand next the line, plant forward, keeping the tops of the plants level, and from one to two inches
above ground, keeping the plants close according to the
required thickness.　Put in the earth as you proceed, and
tread it firm, then rake the surface even, and with the
spade beat it smooth.　If the weather sets in very dry, the
box will be the better of a few waterings.　Sometimes box-
wood is planted without roots, but it seldom gives satisfaction; not growing equally.

GRASS AND OTHER EDGINGS.

Grass verges for walks and borders, although frequently
used, are by no means desirable, except where variety is
required; they are the most laborious to keep in order, and
at best are inelegant, and the only object in their favour is,
their being everywhere accessible.　Iris humilis, Viola
tricolor, thyme, Sea Pink, (Stattice Armeria,) Mignonette,
Phlox subulata, and Phlox procumbens, all make tolerable
edgings.　In the southern states, Verbena Tweediana—V.
alba, V. intermedia and other varieties, will make the most
lovely edging for walks and borders that can be imagined,
and will bloom profusely from May till November.

HARDY BIENNIALS.

Biennial plants are such as are of two years' duration.
Being sown this year they flower, seed, or fruit next year,
and soon after decay : the seeds should be sown about the
end of this month or beginning of next, either in the spot
where they are to remain or a compartment by themselves,
regularly marked, and to be transplanted in May or September. When they appear above ground thin them out
distinctly, that, when they are to be removed, a little earth
may adhere to them : and, if sown where they are to
stand, leave only three or four plants in each patch. The
following list are a few of the free-blooming and more elegant sorts :

Agrostemma coronaria, Rose Campion, blooms all summer.
Althea rosea, Hollyhock, and all its varieties, very showy
       in July and August. When any very desirable
       variety is procured, it can be multiplied by dividing
       the root.
Antirrhinum majus, Snap-dragon, and its varieties, require
       to be protected during winter with a few leaves or
       litter.
Cantua coronopifolia, flowers in August and September,
       beautiful scarlet, delights in dry gravelly soil.
    Ipomopsis elegans.
Campanula media, dark blue Canterbury
    bell,
Campanula media, semi-pleno, half dou-   Bloom in June
    ble Canterbury bell,   and July.
Campanula media, alba, white Canterbury
    bell,
Campanula thyrsoides.
Cheiranthus cheiri, Wall-flower, should be protected by
       leaves or boards during winter.
Digitalis purpurea, purple Fox glove.
——————————— alba, white Fox glove.
Dianthus barbatus, Sweet William pink.
——————————— coccineus crimson pink.
——————————— fl. pl. double-flowered ; the double sorts
               can be propagated by laying, same as
               carnations.

Gerardia purpurea, purple Gerardia,   ⎫ Natives
———— flava, yellow Gerardia,   ⎬ of   this
———— quercifolia, spotted flowered Gerardia, ⎭ country.
Hedysarum coronarium, red flowered French Honey-
    suckle.
Humea elegans, scarlet Humea, flowers in June and Sep-
    tember.
Lunaria biennis, Honesty, various colours, not beautiful, but
    curious in seed.
Œnothera corymbosa, dwarf Evening Primrose.
Papaver nudicaule, naked-stemmed yellow Poppy.
Scabiosa atropurpurea, musk-scented Scabious.
Silene multiflora, many-flowered Catch-fly.

There might be many other beautiful biennial plants
enumerated, which are justly considered worthy of attention; but most of them do not withstand the severity of
our winters, although very much prized in England.

PERENNIALS.

In every flower garden there ought to be a good selection of these plants. They are lasting ornaments; and,
when judiciously selected, will give yearly gratification.
In making a choice, a view should be to have those that
flower abundantly, are of free growth, beauty and continuation of bloom. It would go beyond our limits to give an
extensive description of any, but a few remarks on some
of the finest, with their names, are indispensable.

Adònis vernális, is a fine border flower, and will grow
in any common soil; flowers large, yellow rayed, having
in the rays about twelve petals; leaves much divided,
blooms in April and May.

Anemóne, Wind-flower. Several fine species, with
flowers from one to three inches in diameter, very celebrated in Europe, though succeeding poorly with us except
in cool latitudes. *A. alpina*, large white. *A. palmàta
flòre-plèno*, yellow; *A. stellàta versícolor*, various coloured; *A. pavonìna flòre-plèno*, scarlet; *A. narcissi-flòra*,
white. Any of these are very desirable.

Antirrhìnums, Snap-dragon. All the varieties of *A.*

mǎjus are esteemed in the flower borders; the pure white, bright red, rich crimson, and variegated, are very showy. A few of the species, *A. mólle* and *A. sículum*, where there is variety required, deserve a situation. The flowers are all large, and similar to the snout of an animal.

Anthèricum liliástrum, St. Burnos Lily, is an excellent liliacous plant, with orange-yellow flowers, blooming in June, July and August, and will grow in any common garden soil.

Asclèpias. The finest of this genus are native plants, and are highly esteemed in Europe, but frequently rejected with us, because " they are wild plants." *A. tuberòsa* has beautiful orange flowers, and delights in dry situations. *A. rùbra, A. nívea, A. purpuráscens;* and *A. incarnàta,* are the finest of the family. It is best to plant *A. tuberòsa* in October.

Aconìtums, Wolfs'-bane, one hundred and twenty-eight distinct species, with several varieties. Many of them are of consequence and beauty; the flower-stems rise from one and a half to six feet upright, and strong, furnished with many palmate and digitate leaves, terminated by spikes of blue, yellow, or white flowers, similar to a 'hood; hence the name of Monk's Hood is often applied to them. They are scarce in collections; but, in a few years, we have no doubt but many of them will be plentiful. The finest species are *A. speciòsum, A. Sieboldii,* large dark blue, *A. pyrenaiacum,* branching blue, *A. napéllus, A. venústum, A. pyramidàle, A. lycóctonum, A. versicolor,* or *variegatum, and A. grandiflorum.* They flower from May to September, and will grow in any common garden soil. The roots of *A. napéllus* are like small turneps, and are poisonous. They like a little shade and rich soil.

Cáltha palústris flòre-plèno is a good border plant, delights in moist situations, has large cordate, crenated leaves; flowers double yellow, blooming from April to June; and is a desirable plant.

Béllis perénnis horténsis, Daisy. We might almost say with another, " Every one knows the Daisy." It is named from being pretty, and is perfectly hardy, though generally kept under cover. They delight to have a shaded situation during summer, to protect them from the sun, which, ·as it were, scorches the roots. There are many double

varieties in the gardens, which flower early. The one
called *Crown*, or *Carnation* Daisy, is twice the size of the
common varieties, and has white and red petals alternately
and very double. Loamy soil, inclined to moisture, is best
adapted to their growth.

Campánula. This genus affords many very ornamental
plants for the Flower garden and Shrubbery, and they
flower superbly during the summer, agreeing better with
our climate than with that of Europe. Many have two
successions of flowers, *C. persicifòlia álba pléna; C. persicifòlia cœrùlea plèno; C. urticifòlia,* white. Of this last
there is also a double variety. *C. speciòsa; C. glomerata;
C. versicolor,* with several others, are worthy of a situation
in every garden. Their roots are strong, fleshy and
fibrous. They are easy of culture, and will retain their
situation in the severest of our winters. *C. grandiflòra* is
now *Wahlenbérgia grandiflòra.* It has superb large blue
flowers, stems are slender, and should be supported as soon
as they grow.

Cheiránthus Chéiri vulgàris is the common garden
Wall-flower. There are about ten varieties of it, all admired for their various colours and agreeable odour. The
common variety survives the mildest of our winters. The
most esteemed variety is *hœmánthus,* Double bloody.
They should all be protected by a frame. *C. mutábilis* is
a beautiful species; it has many shades of colour from lilac
to dark purple. The flowers are on extending racemose
spikes; blooming from April to June; it requires a light
rich soil; is a half shrubby evergreen plant.

Chélone. This genus belongs entirely to this continent, and possesses many fine species. It is a matter of
astonishment that they are not more cultivated and sought
for in our collections. *C. glábra; C. obliqua; C. barbáta;
C. atropurpùrea; C. pulchélla;* and *C. speciòsa;* are all
handsome, and flower from May to September; corolla
large, ringent, ventricose; flowers in spikes or panicles.

Chrysánthemums. There are few of this genus of any
consequence as herbaceous plants, except the varieties of
C. sinense, of which there are about ninety, all desirable;
but in small gardens, where there is a deficiency in room,
the following are select in colour and quality: *Admiration,*
yellow; *Celestial,* pale blush; *Coronet,* white; *Defiance,*

4

lemon yellow; *Etna*, dark-brown; *Hero*, rosy crimson; *King*, pale rose; *Perfection*, lilac; *Queen*, blush; *Triumphant*, buff and white; *Venus*, rose; *Wm. Penn*, large creamy white; *Marshal Messena*, yellow and red; *Indica rubra*, very dwarf early red; *Wheelerii*, large purple; *sanguinea*, a beautiful crimson. To grow these in perfection, they require rich light soil; and about the end of this month the roots should be lifted, divided and planted into fresh soil, either by giving them a new situation, or changing the earth they were in. Two or three stems together are quite sufficient. The flowers, by the above treatment, will be much larger, more double, and finer in colour: where they are wanted to grow low and bushy, top them in June, but not later than the first of July. Where the soil is rich, and the plant having only one stem, by topping it, makes a beautiful bush. They are in flower from the first of October until severe frost; thus beautifying our gardens at a season when they would be destitute of one single attraction. If the season be dry, to water them with liquid manure will add to their vigour. They are all natives of China, and greatly esteemed by the Chinese, who only allow a few blooms to come out on the top of each stem, thereby having the flowers much finer.

Within these three years, hundreds of varieties of this winter flower have been produced from seed in Europe; many of them very superb, and having more luxuriant foliage and greater diversity of colour.

Clématis, Virgin's-bower. A few species are good herbaceous plants, of upright growth, and blue flowers, *C. integrifòlia; C. angustifòlia;* and *C. erécta;* they grow best in light soil.

Coréopsis, chiefly native plants, and free-flowering; colour principally yellow; flowers rayed. *C. tenuifòlia, C. verticilláta, C. discolor, and C. tripteris,* are the finest of the genus, and will grow in any common garden soil.

Delphiniums. There are some showy border flowers of these, of strong growth. The leaves are much divided; the flowers in terminal spikes; colour blue, purple, pink, white and yellow, with various shades. *D. grandiflòrum,* and its varieties, are the best of the genus. *D. intermèdium,* and its varieties, *D. elátum,* Bee Larkspur, from the ringent part of the flower being very like a bee, and

D. montánum, are good varieties, and easily cultivated. When the plants become large, they ought to be divided, and planted in fresh soil. They are in bloom from May to September.

Diánthus. Some of the species of this genus are the most prominent of the flower garden, not only for their beauty, but also their fragrance, which is peculiarly grateful, especially in the well-known and celebrated Pink and Carnation, with the Sweet William, which was esteemed in the days of old " for its beauty to deck up the bosoms of the beautiful, and garlands and crowns for pleasure." The finest species are *D. barbàtus* and *D. barbàtus plèno*, Sweet William; *D. discolor; D. chinènsis; D. alpínus; D. supérbus; D. caryophyllus*, from which have originated the Picotee and the Carnation; *D. plumàrius*, from which originated the Double Pink. Several of these, although they will stand the severest cold, have to be protected in frames during winter, to have them in the perfection of beauty. For the character of a Pink and Carnation, see *May*.

Dictámnus. Two species of this genus, *D. fraxinélla* and *D. álbus*, have been cultivated and esteemed upwards of two hundred and forty years. A plant of the first of these species, when gently rubbed, emits an odour like that of lemon-peel; and when bruised emits a balsamic scent, which is strongest in the pedicles of the flowers. They have glands of a rusty colour, that exude a viscid juice, or resin, which exhales in vapour, and in a dark place may be seen to take fire. Its flowers are red, those of the other white, in loose terminal spikes; the flower has five petals, clawed and unequal, with glandular dots; in bloom from May to July; delights in sandy loam.

Dodecàtheon. This is a native genus, and commonly called American cowslip. The generic term, a name of the Romans, signifying twelve gods or divinities, is applied with great absurdity to a plant, a native of a world the Romans never saw nor had any idea of; neither resembling in any particular, the poetical fancy of their writers. The most admired species is *D. mèdia;* the flowers are in umbels, on a pedicle, from six to twelve inches high; the corolla is rotata reflexa, colour light purple, bottom of petals lake and yellow; blooming in May. The white variety is

very much esteemed, and surpasses the preceding. The
ground is pure white, the bottom of the petals the same
as the other. There is also a spotted variety found on the
banks of the Missouri. They delight in brown loam, a
half shady situation, inclining to moisture. The foliage
soon decays after flowering.

Digitàlis, Fox-glove, about forty species of annuals and
herbaceous plants. A few are cultivated in the flower borders, and are very showy. These are *D. leucophæa, D.
ferruginea, D. ochroleùca*, large yellow; and *D. purpuráscens;* and are good species. *D. purpúrea* and *D. álba*
are very conspicuous biennials; the flowers are solitary,
and in long spikes; the corolla of *D. purpúrea* is campanulate, ventricose and ringent; the interior is spotted, and
is considered the finest of the genus. Delights in poor
soil, with a little shade.

Dracocéphalum, Dragon's Head, about twenty species,
mostly ornamental. *D. virgínicum* is a profuse blooming
plant, with bluish pink flowers, and grows about four feet
high. *D. argunénse* is a superb dwarf, with large dark
blue flowers.

Eupatóriums. These generally are native plants, not
worthy of notice here, except for two species. *E. cœles-
tinum* has syngenesious flowers in flattened panicles, colour fine light blue, blooming from September to November,
desirable for its beauty at that season. *E. aromàticum*
may be cultivated for its spicy odour; flowers white, in
loose terminal panicles; blooming from August to October.
Either of them will grow in common soil.

Funkia, Japan Day Lily, three species, all beautiful. *F.
cœrùléa*, with blue flowers. *F. japónica*, pure white, and
F. variegata, with striped leaves and flowers. *F. lauri-
folia*, early blue. This genus has been separated from
Hemerocállis.

Gentiànas, a genus of very showy plants, and flower in
great abundance. The flowers are tubular and inflated;
colour generally blue. A few species are yellow, and some
white; flowers in whorls, terminal or solitary. They grow
best in a light rich soil. *G. lútea, G. purpúrea, G. sep-
témfida. G. acaúlis* is a pretty dwarf growing species,
the flower dark and light blue; interior of the corolla spotted; has a succession of flowers from April to June. These

are fine exotics, but may give place to our native species, such as *G. Catesbœi; G. ochroleûca; G. incarnàta;* with several others, and *G. crinàta,* which is a biennial, and finely fringed ; colour light blue.

Gèum. There are only four species that are worth cultivation, namely, *G. quéllyon,* once *G. coccíneum; G. splendens, G. Wiccea,* and *G. hybridum. G. urbànum* is sometimes cultivated for its roots, which, when chewed, sweeten the breath. They are all of easy culture. *G. quéllyon* and *splendens* flower from May to October, and are very desirable plants for the borders, and much esteemed in Europe.

Hemerocállis, Day Lily ; three species, *H. fúlva, H. gramínea,* and *H. Sieboldii,* flower well, and are remarkable among the border flowers for their large yellow or copper-coloured corollas, some of them about six inches in diameter; bloom from May to July, and will grow in almost any soil. There is a plant known in our gardens as *H. cærùlea,* which is *Fúnkia cærùlea,* and has a campanulate corolla, with a cylindrical tube ; flowers in spikes ; leaves· ovate, acuminate.

Hibíscus. There are several herbaceous species very showy and handsome, *H. palústris ; H. ròseus ; H. militàris ; H. speciòsus ; H. grandiflòrus ;* and *H. púngens.* They grow best in moist situations, and where there are not to be had, give them plenty of water, and plant in sandy soil enriched with decayed leaves. The flowers are about six inches in diameter, flowering up the stem, either solitary or in small bunches. *H. speciòsus* is the most splendid, and deserves a situation in every garden. The roots in winter ought to be covered by litter, tan, or saw-dust ; but a better method is to lift them, and put them in the cellar, covered with dry earth, and kept from the frost. All the above-mentioned species are improved by being protected during winter.

Iris, Flower-de-lis, has many fine species of various shades and colours, *I. subiflora, I. nepalénsis, I. Pallàsii, I. pállida, I. cristàta, I. arenària, I. furcàta, I. germánica, I. florentìna, I. vérna,* and *I. susiàna.* The last is the finest of the herbaceous species ; the flowers are very large and curiously spotted with brown ; it stands the severest of our winters unprotected. The roots of *I. flo-*

4*

rentìna is the orris root of the druggists. They are all of easy culture in any loamy soil inclining to moisture. The bulbous species will be treated of in *September* or *October.* Corolla six-petalled, three erect and three reclined alternately ; proceeding from spathes or sheaths with flowers in succession.

Lìatris is a genus of native plants, containing several fine species, *L. squarròsa,* large purple heads of beautiful flowers ; *L. élegans ; L. panìculàta. L. macróstachya,* now *L. spicàta,* is a fine large growing species. They have syngenesious purple flowers in long close spikes, differing from other spiked flowering genera by blooming first at the extremity. They grow best in strong heavy soil.

Lychnis. Three species are very desirable in the flower borders. *L. chalcedónica* has bright scarlet crowned flowers ; the double scarlet variety is splendid ; there is also a double white variety ; *L. fúlgens* and *L. flós-jòvis.* They ought to be frequently lifted, and planted afresh, or they will dwindle to nothing. The best time is when they begin to grow. There is a plant known in our collections as *Lychnis flós-cucùli,* ragged Robbin or French Pink, which is now *Agrostémma flós-cucùli ;* it is a fine and showy border plant with double red flowers, a double white variety of it has been recently introduced of the same character, with the additional quality of blooming the whole season. They delight in a light rich soil.

Lythrums. A few species flower well, and have small pink blossoms in great profusion, *L. alàtum, L. virgàtum, L. diffusum,* and *L. lanceolàtum.* They will grow in any common garden soil if not too much shaded ; and flower from June to September.

Mìmùlus, Monkey-flower. A few species may be cultivated. They will grow in any soil or situation. *M. lùteus* and *M. rivulàris* are the best. *M. moschátus* has a very strong musk scent, to many agreeable. The former two have large gaping flowers, of a golden yellow, and beautifully spotted with purple in the interior : they all grow in moist situations.

Monárdas, a fine native genus and showy. The foliage of several of the species is aromatic, and resembles mint. *M. dìdyma* has long scarlet ringlet flowers, in headed whorls; *M. kalmiana,* flowers very long, and a beautiful crimson, with fragrant leaves. *M. Russelliana* has red and white flowers; curious and handsome. *M. punctata* has yellow and red flowers; they grow in any common soil.

Mathíola is the generic of the Stock-gilly. None of them will survive severe winters in this latitude; yet many of them are indispensable in the flower garden. *M. simplicáulis,* Brompton-stock and its varieties; with *M. incána,* Queen-stock, and its varieties, require the protection of a good frame in winter, and about the end of this month, or beginning of next, plant them in good light rich soil to flower, which they will do all summer, if attended to with frequent supplies of water. *M. ánnua* has about forty varieties, valuable for flowering the first year from seed, and are all annuals. They ought to be sown on a gentle hot-bed about the first of this month, and carefully pricked out so as they may be ready to transplant about the end of April or the first of May. Plant them in light rich soil, and they will flower profusely through the season; if it is very dry, they must be watered to keep them growing. The scarlet, white and purple varieties are the finest; but there are many intermediate sorts, all handsome. *M. glábra* is the Wall-flower leaved stock, and requires the same treatment as the former two. There are about twenty varieties of this, all various in colour. In planting any of these into the open ground, choose cloudy weather, except they have been in pots; in such case, plant at any time in beds, or detached groups, through the borders, keeping each kind separate.

Œnothèras. The most of them are indigenous, and in Europe they afford a continual ornament to the flower garden from April to November, but in our gardens they are entirely neglected. By rejecting these and many others, our flower gardens are deprived both of much beauty and interest they might easily possess. The herbaceous sorts delight in light rich soil. *Œ. odoráta,* sweet-scented; *Œ. macrocárpa; Œ. mèdia; Œ. latiflòra; Œ. Frazèri; Œ. speciòsa; Œ. missouriensis,* and *Œ. pállida;* are all fine native herbaceous plants, mostly with large yellow four-petalled corollas; in bloom from May to September.

Phlóx, another American genus, and one of the most

handsome in cultivation. It consists of elegant border
flowers, valuable for flowering early, and during the whole
season, even till frost. While the majority of plants blooming late in the season are generally syngenesious, with yellow flowers, these delight us with their lively colours of
purple, red, white and striped. A collection of them properly attended to, would of themselves constitute a beautiful flower garden. It will be difficult to state which are
the finest, but the following are select varieties: *P. bicolor,
multiflora, Breckii, Carterii, Tournella, Van Houttii, Speciosa, Alcardii, longiflora, læta,* a superb white; *omniflora,*
beautiful dwarf white ; *P. odoràta; P. corymbosa; P.
suavèolens; P. refléxa; P. stolonifera; P. divaricàta;
P. nivàlis;* and *P. subulàta.* In the spring of 1831, an
eminent British collector* exclaimed, on seeing a patch of
P. subulàta in one of the pine barrens of New Jersey,
" The beauty of that alone is worth coming to America to
see, it is so splendid." Most of the species delight in a
rich light sandy loam. When the plants become large,
they ought to be divided, and planted in fresh ground.

Prímulas, Primrose. To this genus belong the celebrated *Cowslip, Oxslip, Primrose,* and the esteemed *Auricula.* The double varieties of Primrose have originated
from *P. vulgàris.* These are such as carry their flowers
on separate pedicles, rising from the root on a small stem.
The double varieties are desirable for their beauty, but require the protection of a frame during winter. They are
in colour red, white, yellow, lilac, purple, and crimson. *P.
elàtior* is the Oxslip, from which all the *Polyánthuses* have
been grown. They are in variety innumerable, and are
those whose flowers are in umbels, on a scape or flowerstalk, rising from three to nine inches. The rules for judging of their merits are wholly artificial, agreed on from
time to time by florists. The one that is the leading beauty
this year, would, in few years, be far in the rear. The
principal character is, that the corolla is not notched or
fringed ; the colours pure and distinct, not running into
one another; the tube small; the eye round, and a little
prominent. Being surrounded with white, and the ground
purple, is a fine character. *P. aurícula.* From this the

* Mr. Drummond.

highly esteemed varieties have originated. The cultivated
auricula has many admirers, both for its exquisite beauty
and fragrance. For the criterion of a fine flower, see
April. There are several other species worthy of a situation, such as *P. cortusoides, P. dentiflòra, P. suavèolens,
P. decòra,* with *P. scótica* and *P. farinòsa,* both small neat
species. A shady situation agrees best with them; and
they require loamy soil, free from any kind of manure, except it be fully decomposed. The leaves of *P. vèris* have
been recommended for feeding silk worms.

Potentíllas are similar to the strawberry in habit and
appearance. *P. nepalénsis* or *formòsa,* has rose-coloured
flowers; *P. atropurpúrea; P. Russelliàna,* scarlet; *P. Hop-
woodiàna,* buff and scarlet; and *P. spléndens,* yellow, with
superb leaves. These are the finest of the genus, and flower
from May to September. It will be well to protect them
with a few leaves or litter during the severity of winter;
they delight in light soil.

Saponària officinàlis, and *S. o. plèna,* are fine free flowering dwarf plants; the colour is pink in both double and
single varieties. The roots run under ground, and care
should be taken to keep them within bounds: they flower
from June to October. *S. cæspitòsa* is a neat growing species, of a rose colour. They will grow in any soil.

Silène. Several of this genus are popular annuals, but
the herbaceous species are very indifferent. *S. viscósu*
and *S. viscósa flòre plèna* are frequently cultivated for their
beauty ; they will grow well if not too much shaded.

Saxífraga, above one hundred species. Many of them
are beautiful plants for rock-work. They are regardless
of cold, but will not generally withstand much moisture. A
few of them are highly deserving a situation in any garden. *S. hirsùtum* and *S. crassifòlia* are used in some
countries for tanning. *S. granulàta multipléx* has fine
double white flowers, and is desirable. *S. umbròsa,* Lon-
don-pride, makes a beautiful edging for a flower border;
the flowers are small, but on close examination its colours
are unrivalled. It is sometimes called " none so pretty."
S. sarmentòsa is kept in the green-house, but is perfectly
hardy, and makes a fine plant in a shaded situation, and
will grow where grass and other plants generally die. We
have no doubt but it would make a good fancy edging. *S.*

pulchélla and *S. pyramidàlis* require protection; these are
easily cultivated, and flower in spikes from May to July.

Spiræas. A few species are showy plants, and continue
flowering from May to September. *S. ulmària múltiplex*,
Meadow-sweet, has sweet-scented white flowers, in long
dense spikes. *S. filipéndula múltiplex*, Drop-wort, double
white. *S. lobàta* is a native, and has fine rose-coloured
flowers, and blooms in June and July; *S. japonica*, beautiful dwarf white; these are the finest of the herbaceous
species, and will grow in any common garden soil.

Státice, Thrift. A genus containing many fine herbaceous plants; only a few of them are common in collections. The finest of them are scarce, and said to be "bad
to cultivate." *S. vulgàris*, once *Armèria vulgàris*, is a
valuable plant for an edging, and does well in our climate,
flowering in great profusion from May to July. When
done flowering, the stems should be cut off. The foliage
is an agreeable evergreen; the plant increases rapidly, and
in a few years may be planted to a great extent. *S. speciòsa* has red flowers, crowded in spreading panicles. *S.
tartàrica* has also very showy flowers, and is now given to
the genus *Taxànthema*. *S. latifòlia* and *S. maritima*
are the finest. *T. latifòlia* and *T. conspicua* deserve attention. They should be lifted every alternate year, and
sunk deeper into the soil, because they incline to grow out,
and are sometimes during summer killed by the drought.
Hence they are said to be "bad to cultivate."

Tróllius europæus and *T. asiàticus* are fine border
plants, with large yellow semi-double flowers; the petals
are much cupped, which causes the flowers to have a globular appearance. They are easily grown in any loamy
soil, and flower from May to July. Few flowers have the
curious globular character which these have.

Véronica, Speed-well. This genus consists of about
one hundred and twenty species of herbaceous plants, besides several varieties. The flowers are in long close
spikes, white, flesh-coloured, or blue; they are generally
of the latter colour. Above sixty species are equally fine,
and being generally of the same character, the catalogue
at the end of this work will contain the best selection that
we can make. Very few of them are in the collections of
the country, although they are very showy, and flower

from May to August. They will grow in any soil, but will not flourish where they are much shaded. *V. officinális* has been used in Germany and Sweden as a substitute for tea. Some prefer *V. chamædrys* for the same purpose.

Valerianas. Several species are showy border plants, with small flowers in large close flattened panicles. *V. dioíca* is remarkable for having the stamens and pistils in separate flowers, situated on different plants; the flowers are of a blush colour. *V. phù,* a large growing species with white flowers, and *V. rùbra,* with its varieties which bloom all the season, are the finest of the genus. They are now given to *Centrànthus.* They are all of easy culture in common garden earth, but preferring moist shady situations. In flower from May to September.

Vìola, a genus consisting of upwards of eighty species, of low pretty plants, of great diversity of colour and foliage. Many of them are natives, and well worth a situation in our gardens. They mostly delight in sandy loam, and a little shade. A few of the species grown in moist situations. The most esteemed varieties for fragrance are, *V. odoráta purpúrea plèna,* double purple, *V. odoráta álba plèna,* double white, and the double Neapolitan. They flower very early, and make good edgings where they are kept in order; flowering profusely from April to June, and again in autumn.

Yúcca, Adam's needle. This is a very showy and ornamental genus; their character forming a picturesque contrast in the flower garden; foliage long, narrow, lanceolate and stiff; with white campanulate flowers, about two inches in diameter, in conical spikes from two to four feet long, arising from the centre of the plant, containing frequently from two to four hundred florets. They are principally native plants. *Y. strícta; Y. supérba; Y. aloifòlia; Y. angustifòlia, Y. gloriosa, Y. recurvifolia,* and *Y. filamentòsa,* are all fine species, and will grow in any common soil. When in flower, if protected from the sun by an awning, they will be of considerable duration. There are variegated varieties of *strícta* and *aloifòlia,* which look very handsome in foliage, but are at present very rare, and it will be a number of years before they are plentiful.

There ought, at least, to be one specimen of each in every
garden.

Having given the names and characters of a few herbaceous plants, all or most of them easily obtained, many of
them extremely handsome, and such as agree best with
transplanting at this season of the year; for several others,
such as *Pæònias*, or any other strong tuberous or bulbous
sorts, see *October*. Where they are in pots, they can be
planted at any time, the weather permitting, provided the
ball of earth is not broken. But where they are only to
be removed, the best time is in October or November, or
just as vegetation commences in the spring. That herbaceous plants may look to the best advantage, and flower
well, they must not be allowed to get into large stools ; but
as soon as they are above one foot in diameter, they should
be divided.

Very frequently those who perform this operation, take
the spade, and cut a piece off all round, which, to a degree,
improves the look of the plant ; but this is only half justice.
It should be lifted entirely, fresh soil given, or removed a
few feet, and planted a little deeper than it was before, as
the plant tends apparently to grow out of the soil when
allowed to stand long. If the weather becomes dry shortly
after transplanting, give them a few waterings, until they
have taken fresh roots, which will be within two weeks.
Colour should be diversified through the garden as much
as practicable, and the highest growing sorts planted farthest from the walk, so as all may appear in view. At all
times avoid crowding plants together.

BULBOUS ROOTS.

About the middle of this month, let the covering of tan,
saw-dust, or decayed leaves, be cleared from the beds of such
as were directed to be covered in November ; afterwards
carefully stirring the surface among them with a kind of
wooden spatula, or wedge, breaking the surface fine ; then
dress all the alleys smooth and neat with the hoe and rake,
clearing away every particle of litter. When the leaves
of Tulips are expanding, they frequently become entangled so much, that the force of growth breaks the foliage :

if there are any appearances of this at any time, they should be set right with the hand. In early seasons these roots will be far advanced, and perhaps one night of frost, unexpectedly, might materially injure them. When there is any suspicion of cold weather, hoops should be spanned across the beds, so that the necessary mats or canvas could in a few minutes be placed over them, to ward off danger. Protect the finest sorts from heavy drenching rains, and give them small neat rods for support, as they grow up. If the rods and tyings are painted green, the effect will be improved. These directions equally apply to Narcissus, Jonquils, Iris and all Holland Bulbs.

CARNATIONS, PINKS, PRIMROSES, &c.,

Which have been protected by frames through the winter, must have at all favourable opportunities plenty of air admitted to them by lifting the sashes, and in fine mild days and nights, the sashes may be taken entirely off. Divest them of all decayed leaves, and stir up the earth on the surface of the pots; those that are intended to be planted in the garden may be set to one side, while those that are to be kept in pots must be more strictly attended to. Of these the Pinks and Carnations should be repotted about the first of the month. Those that have been kept in four inch pots, should be put into pots of seven inches, and those that are in five inch pots may be put into eight inch. Give a gentle watering after repotting. Pinks do not require the pots so large, but the same treatment in every other respect. Where the extremities of the leaves are decayed, cut them off, with any other decayed leaves: the pots must be well drained with shivers or fine gravel. Give them plenty of air, otherwise they will be weak in growth.

Primroses and *Daisies* may be planted out in shady situations; the sun destroys them during summer if exposed.

5

AURICULAS.

These beautiful and highly interesting plants are, to a great degree, neglected in our collections. .It cannot be from want of beauty or fragrance that they have not attracted our attention, for they are exquisite in both. We are rather inclined to think that those who have them do not give them the treatment they require yearly to perfect their bloom. They should now have the surface earth taken off about half an inch down, and fresh soil added, which will cause them to put on fresh fibres about the upper part of the roots, and greatly increase their growth. The frame in which they are placed should now face the east, as the sun will be too strong for them; and about the end of the month turn it to the north. The glass of the frame may be white-washed, which will partially shade them from the sun, that being their delight. Give them water sparingly until they begin to grow, and never water them over the foliage previous to flowering, as water injures that fine mealy-like substance found on many of the sorts, and which so greatly improves their beauty. Defend them, therefore, from rain and high winds. To have them flower strongly, only one flower stem should be allowed to grow. The first one that shows is generally the best. At all events leave the strongest, and cut off all the others, or only nip off the flower pips, which answers the same end. Never keep the sash off during night, in case it rain before morning.

RANUNCULUS AND ANEMONE.

The frames of Ranunculus and Anemone must have plenty of air, and give frequent sprinklings of water. The sashes or shutters should be taken entirely off every mild day, and in fine nights leave them exposed to the dew. Stir the earth among them, breaking it fine and making all neat and clean. They require liberal supplies of water after they begin to grow.

ROSES.

This is the most favourable month for planting all kinds
of garden roses, which must be done as soon as the weather opens, and the ground in a proper state.   The earlier
they are planted the more perfect they will flower.   Never
delay planting when there is an opportunity; for if delayed until the leaves are expanded, the bloom will be much
weakened, and the probability is, there will be no flowers,
and the plants meet with a premature death.   It has been
said, "there is a particular advantage in planting some every
ten days, even to the middle of May; for the flowering of
them may be retarded in this way: and the bloom of these
delightful shrubs continue for a much longer period."   One
moment's reflection will convince us, that nature, while in
her own element, will not be retarded, suppose there was
no danger of instantaneous death to the plants.   The artificial means that might be judiciously adopted, with which
we are acquainted, to keep back the blooming of hardy
plants, is to lift them as soon in spring as is practicable,
put them in boxes of earth, and then place them in the
driest part of an ice-house, until the desired time of planting, which may be delayed as long as the required time of
flowering.   This will be found a true method of retarding
the flowering of roses especially, and not going counter to
the rules and principles of nature.   There are many beautiful varieties of the garden rose in cultivation, the names
of the finest of which we will give in the following catalogue:

African black, very dark crimson, compact and very
    double.
Agreeable violet, large purplish red, expanded and double
    fine.
Aurora, bright pink, compact and double.
Belle amabile, fine dark red, large and double.
Belle Hebe, large purplish red, cupped, double and fine.
Belle rouennaise, a very superb rose, with red centre and
    blush edge.
Baron de Stael, bright cherry colour, globular, large and
    double.

Belle Africaine, same as *African black* or *African*.

Broomley rose, fine red with blush edge, very compact and
double.

Black Tuscany, dark crimson, changeable, expanded and
double.

Belgic or Dutch Provins, red with very large flowers, cupped and extra double.

Cabbage Provins, or ⎧ fine rose, very large, globular,
Centifolia of the French, ⎨ pendular, and extremely
⎩ double.

Cinder rose, large blush, with pink centre, expanded and
double.

Delicious, rosy colour, large compact and double.

Edinberger, violet purple, very compact and most perfectly
double.

Flanders, vermilion colour, compact and double.

Fanny parrissot, pale blush, very compact and double.

Grandis royal, deep pink, large, expanded and double.

Globe white hip, beautiful white, globular, and most perfectly double.

Helen, light pink, very large cupped and fine.

Harrisoni,* bright yellow, cupped, small and semi-double.

Isabella, blush pink, very profuse, cupped and double.

Imperial blush, delicate blush, expanded, large and double.

Juliana, delicate pink, compact and double.

King of Rome, deep red, very large, compact and exquisitely double.

King of the reds, red, expanded and double.

King of Mexico, reddish purple, imbricated and very double.

Leonore, purplish red, very compact, imbricated, and double.

La Belle Augusta, shaded blush and white, expanded and
double.

La folie de carse, red, robust habit, profuse flowering, imbricated and double.

Madam Hardy, pure white, large, globular and exquisitely
double.

Moss rose,† delicate rose, globular and perfectly double.

---

* This Rose with a "Florist's privilege," has been sold for the
yellow sweetbrier. It is also called Hogg's Yellow Rose.

† It has long been questioned, whether the Moss Rose was a distinct species, or merely a seminal variety of the Provins Rose. I

Moss blush, pale blush, globular and very double.
—— white, old white pale flesh colour, expanded and
     double.
—— white bath, or Clifton, white moss, fine white cupped
     and double.
—— crimson or Damask, very bright rose, expanded and
     double, and very mossy.

—— crested moss or crested Provins, ⎰ This is not properly a moss rose, but has a curiously mossy calyx that envelops the bud—pink, globular and double.

—— Luxemburg, bright red, compact and double.
—— Marbree, red, very faintly mottled.
—— panache, frequently striped.
—— poncteau, semi-double, spotted.
—— perpetual white, blooming in clusters.
—— unique de Provence, white.
Nonpareil, rosy red, compact and perfectly double.
Negritina, pink, very compact, imbricated and double.
Ombre superb, dark crimson, cupped and double.
Provins cabbage, see *Cabbage Provins.*
—— red, see *red Provins.*
—— white, see *white Provins.*
Prince de Joinville, bright rose, large, expanded and finely
     double.
Proserpine negro, dark red, globular, fine and double.
Prolific blush, changeable blush, expanded and double.
Queen of violets, violet colour, compact, cupped and very
     double.
Queen of Roses, beautiful rosy purple, imbricated and
     double.
Queen Caroline, fine changeable red, cupped and double.
Royal Portugal, fine pink, very compact, and exquisitely
     double.
Royal virgin, blush, expanded, large, and double.

perfectly agree with the latter opinion—for in June, 1836, I saw in
my nursery a plant of the Moss rose with a large shoot that had
sported back to the Provins Rose, and entirely destitute of moss
on either shoots or buds. We have no faith in black and yellow
Moss Roses; all we have seen for such, have proven false to their
character.

5*

Sweet Brier, single pink.
————————— celestial, blush, *fine* double flowered.
Swiss Rose, large pink, expanded, and profusely double.
Tuscany, see *Black Tuscany.*
Unique or white Provins, pure white, very large globular,
    and double, superb.
Unique striped, often is perfectly white, and merely a sport
    from the former.
Violatum, violet purple, expanded and double.   ·
Vandal carmine, compact, imbricated, and double.

We mention these as fine; but among several thousand
cultivated varieties of the garden rose, there must be many
of equal, if not surpassing beauty; of *Rosa spinosíssima,*
there are about five hundred varieties; *Rosa gallica,* two
hundred; *R. centifòlia,* one hundred and fifty; *R. damas-
cène,* above one hundred; *R. álba,* fifty; *R. rubiginòsa,*
thirty; and of various sorts above eleven hundred. In
several individual collections of Europe, there are cultivated above fifteen hundred species, sub-species, and varieties.
    When planted, they are too frequently crowded indiscri-
minately among other shrubs, which prevents them having
the effect they would have if planted singly or grouped.
They vary in size in different sorts from one to ten feet.
When planted in the latter method, they should be assimilated in size of leaves and manner of growth, with the
greatest variation of flower; or if planted in small patches,
each distinct in colour, will have a very picturesque effect.
Another desirable and fanciful method, is to plant them in
figures, with edgings of wire, willow, or any other substitute, in imitation of basket work, which is called " bas-
kets of roses;" the ground enclosed in the basket margin
to be made convex, which will present a greater surface to
the eye; the strong shoots to be layered, or kept down by
pegs in the ground, having the points of the shoots only to
appear above the soil, which should be covered with moss.
With this treatment, in a few years the whole surface of
the basket will be covered with rose buds and leaves, of
one or various sorts. If two or three of the larger growing
sorts are taken, such as *Moss* or *Provins,* they may be
trained so as to cover a surface of several square yards.

A modern invention in the cultivation of the rose is, to grow them in shape of trees, by budding on strong growing kinds at different heights from the ground, according to taste, and the purposes intended. If budded on *Rosa Cánina*, or Dog Rose, they are much more valuable: it is a lasting and strong growing stock, and the worst of all stocks is the Boursalt rose, and it is too frequently resorted to, being easy of propagation. They will form in a few years handsome round heads, which will flower more freely than by layers, or trained on their own stalk. They are particularly desirable among low shrubs. When planted, they should be well supported by strong rods, to prevent the wind from destroying them. If any of the roots have been bruised in lifting, cut off the bruised part with the knife, and likewise shorten the young shoots; breaking the earth well about their roots when planting. The rose has been an esteemed shrub among all civilized nations. The flowers are double, semi-double, and single; the colours are pink, red, purple, white, yellow, and striped, with almost every shade and mixture ; the odour universally grateful. This plant is cultivated in every garden, from the humblest cottager to the loftiest prince, and by commercial gardeners in Europe extensively, for distilling rose water, and making the essential oil of roses. They delight in a rich loamy soil, and require plenty of moisture while in a growing state. Those sorts which throw up numerous suckers should be lifted every three or four years, reduced, and then transplanted. When thus removing them, avoid as much as possible exposing their roots; and when newly planted, mulching is of considerable advantage ; that is, putting half rotten stable-manure on the surface of the ground round their roots, which prevents evaporation, and keeps up a constant moisture. If this were done in general to our roses in dry seasons, it would greatly improve their flowering. For Chinese and other roses, see next month.

CLIMBING ROSES.

This is the best time to prune ever-blooming climbing roses, such as *Champney, Noisette,* &c. Many of these, when allowed to grow year after year without pruning, become unsightly : they never bear flowers on the old wood, that is, wood of three or four years. Having a tendency to throw out young shoots from the bottom of the stem, the old wood should be cut out, thus encouraging the young wood, which the second year bears the most and finest flowers. In severe winters, the extremities of the shoots are frequently killed, and we have often seen all the wood black or brown, and apparently dead. When that is the case, it is best to leave it until they begin to grow, which will show what is dead or alive, when they can be pruned to better advantage.

DECIDUOUS ORNAMENTAL FLOWERING SHRUBS.

The earlier the planting of these shrubs is attended to in this month, the more will their growth and flowering be promoted, having all finished before the buds begin to expand. (For kinds recommended, see list, end of the volume.) They should never be planted too thick, but leave space for them to grow as they respectively require, and according as they are designed for open or close shrubberies, clumps, or thickets. Have all in readiness, that it may be done with as much expedition as possible, to prevent their roots from being dried by the sun and wind in time of planting. Make the holes intended for their reception round, capacious, and deep enough to hold their roots, without confining them in the least, and loosen well the bottom, putting new and fresh soil under their roots, breaking and pulverizing it during the operation, and frequently shaking the plant as you progress in filling up. When done, make all firm with the foot, leaving a circular cavity to hold the water they will require during dry weather. Give rods, and tie with bands all that need that support before they are left, lest they should be neglected. Cut off any of the bruised roots or irregular growths of the branches.

GRASS PLATS AND WALKS.

A most wonderful renovator of grass plats may be found in Guano—take at the rate of one pound to twelve square

yards, mix it with double the quantity of sand, and before
rain in April or May, sow the mixture over the grass—in
a few days its effects will be seen. Where grass lawns
are poor, and of a pale yellow colour, about four hundred
weight to the acre, mixed with sand or dry earth, will
effectually restore them to a luxuriant verdure.

Rake and sweep off from these all litter, and worm-cast
earth, and give an occasional rolling to settle the ground,
and render the surface smooth, where the sythe is to be
used. The grass will likewise grow better by rolling it
where the frost has partially thrown it out, and add greatly
to its beauty. Cut the edgings with an edging iron or
spade, so that the whole will have a finished appearance.
If any new turf is required to be laid down, this is a very
good time to do it, before vegetation is strong; as the turf
that is now laid will have taken root before the dry season
commences. Where a great extent is to be done, sowing
might be adopted; but it will not have the effect of turf
under three years, and during that time must be carefully
cut, after the first season, every three weeks, while growing, nor must it be too frequently walked upon. White
clover and true perennial rye-grass are the seeds most
proper for sowing. The ground must, in the first place,
be all equally made up, and leveled with the spade and
rake; not "cart loads of soil laid down and leveled," which
would finally become very uneven, and would need to be
lifted and relaid next year. The best turf is that of a close
growing pasture or common, free from all kinds of weeds
or strong roots, and the grass short. To cut it expeditiously,
be provided with a turfing-iron; but if that cannot be conveniently had, a spade may do very well. Strain a line
tight, cutting the turf lengthwise, at equal distances, from
twelve to eighteen inches. Next draw the line across, cutting from one and a half to two feet; then cut them up with
the spade, about one and a half inch thick. In laying, join
them close and alternately; when done, beat them firm with
a level wooden beater, and roll with a heavy roller.

Grass walks, in the last century, were very popular; but
time having put them to the test, they are found unfit for
walking upon or using in any manner, almost for one-half
of the year; therefore, not answering the purposes intended. They require great attention to keep them in order;

and if not always neat and clean, they are a disagreeable
object in a garden; but when they are well dressed, their
effect is very enlivening. Where they are desired, prepare the ground as above directed; making the walk a
little higher than the adjoining borders, to prevent the earth
from being washed on it by the rain. Allowing the walks
to be six feet wide, make the centre five inches higher than
the sides, or about seven-eighths of an inch to the foot
whatever the breadth may be, which will form a gentle declivity to throw off the rain. When laid, beat and roll it
well; cutting the edge neat and even. Water frequently
if the weather sets in dry. To keep grass walks or plats
in order, they should be mown once every three or four
weeks from May to September, and the grass each time
swept clean off. When the grass is allowed to get long
before being cut, the roots become tender; and die when
exposed to the sun; at last the grass is all in spots, and in
another year requires to be relaid.

GRAVEL WALKS.

A practice once existed of turning these into heaps, or
ridges during winter, to destroy weeds, &c. But this has
almost been given up as unnecessary, unsightly, inconvenient, and not doing any material service.

Where the surface of these has become foul, irregular,
or mossy, they had better be turned over four or five inches
deep where the gravel will admit of it; but if not, hoe and
rake them perfectly clean, give a new coat of gravel, and
pick up any stones that you think too large; then give
them a good rolling, applying it frequently after showers
of rain. When they are well attended to just now, they
will look well all the season; but if neglected, they take
more labour, and are never in such good condition.

Fancy-edgings of *Thyme, Thrift, Gentiana, Lavender,*
and *Violets*—(*Daisies* may be used if the situation is
shaded.) The whole of these may be planted by the line
with the dibber except *Thyme,* which lay as directed for
Box. See this month, under that head. Any time in this
or beginning of next month will answer to make edgings
of these; and if dry weather occurs before they begin to

grow after planting, they must have frequent waterings until they have taken fresh root. Thyme requires to be dressed twice during the season to keep it in order.

OF GRAFTING.

There are four methods of grafting. It can be applied to all kinds of shrubbery, choosing a common species from the same genus that the sort belongs to, which is intended to be multiplied. The one we will describe is *whip* or *tongue grafting*, which is the preferable and most expeditious plan with all deciduous shrubs or trees. The stock upon which it is performed must be slender, from two-thirds of an inch to any diameter suitable to the thickness of the graft. Having headed the stock at a clear smooth part, slope it on one side with a sharp knife at a very acute angle, make a slit on the lower side of the slope about an inch downward, to receive the tongue or wedge of the graft or scion. Secondly, having the prepared scions cut into lengths of 3, 4 or 5 eyes, take one which matches the stock in size, and slope the bottom of it so as to fit the stock, that the rinds of both may correspond exactly, especially on one side and at bottom ; make also a slit upward in the graft, like that in the slope of the stock, so as the one may be inserted in the other as evenly and completely as possible. Let the graft be carefully held in its due position, while a bandage is applied. Take strands of Russian mat, and bind them in a neat manner several times round the stock and graft. Lastly, cover the joint with well-worked clay, coat from half an inch below the bottom of the graft to an inch above the top of the stock, and to the thickness of half an inch all round, finish it in an oblong globular form, taking care to work it close, that no air may penetrate. If the clay is covered with moss, it will partially prevent it from cracking.

The grafts will have taken when they begin to grow freely : then the clay may be broken off, and the bandage loosened, and put on again, but not so tight as formerly ; give the drafts a stake for support, tying them thereto to prevent accidents from the wind. Allow no shoots to arise from the stock.

APRIL.

The ambition of every amateur and gardener during this month is, to be at the head of every department and over every spot. The operator's activity, in this month, almost regulates the whole season. Every weed ought to be cut down as soon as it appears, and the proverbial saying will be realized, " A garden that is well kept is easily kept;" one hour of laborious industry now will save two in the heat of summer. A wet day need cause no loss of time: prepare rods, bands and tallies, to be in readiness when required. Many, in the height of bustle, never finish properly as they proceed, which is the worst of practices. Every operation ought to be completely and properly finished before another is taken in hand, which will ultimately prove the quickest and best method to work upon.

Let digging, hoeing and raking be done as expeditiously as strength will allow, that the time may be devoted, for a few weeks, to the beautifying of the garden and parterre, by sowing and planting.

ANNUALS.

Those that are tender and were sown last month, according to directions, will be ready to prick out into another glass frame. Keep them a few inches apart to let the air circulate. Give them frequent sprinklings with water, and shade them with a mat for a few days until they have taken fresh root; then give them plenty of air, and by the first of next month, expose them night and day, to harden the plants for the open ground. A few of the annual seeds of every description, and of every country and climate, may be sown any time after the middle of the month. If the season prove favourable, they will do well; but reserving a part to sow about the 15th of May, will guard against every extreme.

BIENNIALS AND PERENNIALS.

Any biennials that are intended to be removed, and not done last month, must not be delayed longer. The roots of many of them will be very strong, and, if possible, a cloudy day should be chosen for the operation. Give one or two copious waterings, and, if necessary, shade them from the sun till they begin to grow.

Perennials.—For a limited description of several genera and species, see last month. Where dividing the root or replanting is required, let it be done forthwith. If the weather is dry, they must be carefully watered and shaded for a few days.

ROSES.

The subject of garden roses was touched upon last month, as far as our limits would admit. We will now give short descriptions of the other varieties of Roses that are of more delicate character—and, for distinction and perspicuity, we will give them under the various divisions to which they belong.

HYBRID CHINESE ROSES.

All the varieties of this fine division of Roses owe their origin to the Chinese tea-scented, Noisette and Bourbon Roses impregnated with the French Provins, and other garden Roses. The seeds of such fertilized flowers produce hybrid Chinese Roses. These have, in many instances, resulted from accident; but latterly, from the regular impregnating process. The superb varieties of this fine division give a combination of all that is grand and beautiful in roses. Their flowers are of the most elegant forms and richest colours; their foliage of great luxuriance, and their branches flexile and vigorous. They are of first rate importance for covering pillars and trellises, their shoots frequently growing from six to ten feet in one season : these

6

shoots may be thinned out year after year, but *never short-ened*. They require very rich soil, and do best on their own bottom, except *elegans*, *Bizzare de le Chine*, *Wellington*, and other dwarf growing sorts, which do well as standards. If they only possessed the property of *ever-blooming*, they would be decidedly the finest division of the tribe; however, their general beauty and richness of colour greatly make up for the deficiency. Many of them are also delightfully fragrant. The following are select sorts:

Blanchefleur, white, a free grower.
Belle parabère, shaded crimson, a strong grower.
Bon Ginneure, bright red, *very early*.
Belle Marie, bright pink, a fine dwarf.
Bizzare de la Chine, brilliant crimson, superb form, profuse in flower, and perfectly double.
Bouquet blanc, white expanded, large and very double.
Brennus or *Brutus*, of some French collections, vivid red or nearly scarlet, and as a pillar rose is one of the finest objects I have ever witnessed; flowers extremely large, and of the most exquisite form, cupped, and perfectly double.
Catel, dark crimson, globular shape and very double.
Duke of Devonshire, rosy lilac faintly striped with white, imbricated and perfect in its shape.
Duc de Choiseul, pink, blush and rose, perfect form, and makes a fine standard rose.
Egerie, brilliant red, a free grower.
Fabvier, very large changeable pink and red.
Fulgens or *Malton*, unique in brilliancy, approaching bright scarlet, with large globular flowers, and of vigorous growth, and foliage finely tinted with red.
General Lamarque, very dark crimson, of luxuriant growth, and very distinct.
George the Fourth (Rivers's) most beautiful crimson, very large and exquisitely double, and of globular form. If in good rich soil, the shoots will grow eight feet in one season; foliage of a shining dark reddish green, and is unquestionably one of the finest of the family.
Georgiana, deep pink, cupped, large and finely double.

L'ingenue, shaded violet crimson.

Louis Philippe, very splendid dark rose, a strong grower, *superb*.

Lady Stuart, flesh colour, the form of the flowers before expansion is perfectly spherical, and of exceeding beauty.

Parny or *La tourterelle*, lilac or dove colour, cupped and very double, requires to grow to a large bush before its beauty of form and profusion of bloom can be seen.

Princess, delicate rose, globular and perfectly double, and makes an excellent standard of itself, not being very subject to make shoots from the root.

Pallagi, *Ne plus ultra*, or *Gloire des hybrids*, brilliant red, globular, showy, and perfectly double.

Prolifere, dark rosy crimson, changing to violet, very perfect form, *a dwarf*.

Triomphe de Laffay, rosy white, large and very beautiful.

Victor Hugo, changeable rosy violet.

Violet de Belgique, dark violet crimson, very profuse and perfect.

Watts' Celestial, *Celestial Wells' Cabbage China, Flora perfecta*, &c., (it is known under all these names,) delicate rose, petals finely cupped, flower rather flat, is a free grower, and very profuse of bloom.

Wellington, (Lee's,) rich purple crimson, flower beautifully formed; globular and very double. The first view of it is similar to *Bizzare de la Chine ;* but it is very distinct in growth, and the colour fades much sooner than in the latter rose, and, indeed, is never so bright.

William the Fourth, blush red, extremely large, very perfect form, and is unquestionably a hybrid from the Cabbage Provins, and makes an excellent standard or tea rose.

HYBRID ROSES THAT ARE STRIPED, SPOTTED OR MARBLED.

Abbe Berlèse, beautiful crimson, spotted with violet, and of the most perfect form.

Camaïeu, delicate rose, with lilac stripes, large and double.

Prince de Chimay, *entirely new*, crimson purple, beautifully marbled with rose, large and very perfect.

Sandeur, *Sandeur Panachée, of the French, and King of Hybrids* of the English, bright rose-colour, beautifully spotted and striped with white, very double, and of perfect form—luxuriant in growth, and the shoots must never be shortened—we have seen it several years in perfect bloom.

Village Maid, rose, striped with white, very compact and double, and makes a fine standard. *This rose is a French hybrid of their Cent-feuilles ; but has been brought to notice under an English name, a system too much practised by the English growers, to keep from their brother-craft the original and genuine French name of the article ; and we find that this system is occasionally attempted by our American brethren. Shame!*

PERPETUAL ROSES.

This division of Roses has been brought to notice but very recently in this country, and even in Europe was not known till about 1817, except in the red and white four season's roses, which have, no doubt, contributed a large portion of their " Sweet assistance ;" for in many of them the powerful and agreeable fragrance of these two old roses is very evident. Unfortunately, there are two-thirds of these roses received both from France and England under the head of Perpetuals, which only bloom once in our arid and hot climate ; of course they will not make a second or third blooming, unless they, at the same time, grow freely and make strong shoots; consequently, they require very rich and deep soil strongly manured, and repeated manurings given every year, also, very frequent waterings during the summer season with liquid manure: without such nourishment, the best of perpetual roses will only flower but once a year. It is a peculiar feature in this tribe of roses, that they are nearly all reluctant in rooting from layers, therefore, it will be difficult to procure them on their own bottoms. However, they grow admirably, grafted on, or budded into, any of our strong-growing native roses; although the French Eglantine is most generally preferred. When grown in a luxuriant and well cultivated state, they require twice pruning. First, in November, when the beds are dressed, cut off every shoot of the preceding summer's growth about two-thirds, and if they are crowded, displace some of them entirely. If this autumnal pruning be properly attended to, they will, early in the following June, throw out a great number of luxuriant shoots, each having one or more flowers. When a little sacrifice must be made to have a fine autumnal bloom, therefore, leave only about half the number of shoots to bring forth flowers, the remainder shorten to less than half their lengths. Each shortened branch will soon put forth buds, and in July and August the plants will again be covered with flowers. Our fine growing fall months will greatly assist the plants without farther aid in bringing forth their third blooming, which will be in September and October; and Rose du Roi will even continue in mild seasons to bloom till November. It is necessary, at all times, as soon as the flower begins to fade, to cut it off, which greatly assists the vigour of the plants. Although in colour many of them approximate each other, yet the following sorts will prove sufficiently distinct:

Antinous, light crimson, beautifully formed, and perfectly double.

Belle Fabvier, dark rose, very large and double.

Billiard, rose-colour, very neat form, exceedingly sweet, and perfectly double.

D'Angers, delicate rose, large size, compact and double.

D'Esquermes, bright rose, globular shape and double.

Du Roi, or *Lee's crimson perpetual*, bright red, cupped shape, perfectly double, and exquisitely scented : in warm dry weather, this rose is apt to become much lighter in colour. It is still admitted by cultivators that this rose is yet the king of perpetuals.

Grande et Belle, *or Monstreuse* rose, very large, cupped and perfectly double.

Jean Hachette, (of the English,) delicate pink, extremely large, cupped and extra double.

Pulcherie, dark purple, compact and double—*pretty*.

6*

Palmyra, rosy pink.

Queen of Perpetuals, or *Palotte picotée*, pale blush, cupped and perfectly double.

Scotch Perpetual, pale blush, a profuse and constant
bloomer.

Stanwell, perpetual blush, expanded and very double; it
has much the habit of a Scotch Rose: when budded it is a constant and free bloomer.

Four season's pale rose, cupped and double.

White four seasons, nearly white, expanded and double;
but rarely blooms oftener than once in the season.

Perpetual white moss, white, blooms in large clusters, and
when in bud, is very handsome; but the flower of
itself is miserably indifferent, and, moreover, it is
not a true perpetual. It is one of those floricultu-
ral *misnomers* expressing what the public would
wish it to be, and not what it actually is.

GRAFTING ROSES.

The operation of grafting, from the pithy nature of the
stems of the rose, is more troublesome and seldom succeeds
so well as budding, though when the buds inserted the previous summer fail, it is worth while to have recourse to
grafting, which may succeed, and thus make up for the
failure. The cleft grafting is much practised, especially
on the continent of Europe, and is the most successful
method. It is necessary that the scion, (or young shoot
that is intended to be multiplied,) should be cut from the
bush before vegetation commences, and placed in some
shaded situation till the time of operation, which will be
after the buds begin to swell on the stock, when the head
of the stock may be cut horizontally to its desired height,
and a slit made in its crown downward one and a half or
two inches. The scion should be cut into lengths of two
and a half or three inches, and then cutting its lower end
into a wedge-like shape, inserting it into the slit of the
stock, keeping the back of the stock and scion in contact,
which must be held firmly and bound with ligatures of
soft bast-mat or worsted, and, in order to render it water-
proof, cover it with a paste made of pitch and bees-wax,

or clay mixed with old slacked lime; if the latter is used,
it will sometimes crack, which must be carefully filled up.
In August ·or September the ligatures may be cut on one
side, allowing the clay or wax to be displaced with the
natural growth of the plant. Should the graft fail, you
have still the resource of budding in August on the young
shoots that will grow from the stock. It must be observed
that grafting leaves a worse wound to heal over than budding, unless the stock and scion be nearly of the same
size. Every bud which appears below the graft should
be carefully rubbed off, except one or two nearest the
crown, to encourage the sap upward to the grafts, and as
soon as the latter begin to throw out leaves, the shoots from
the stock should be shortened, and in one or two weeks
more entirely taken off, if the scion has fairly grown. For
whip grafting, see page 59.

L'ISLE DE BOURBON ROSES.

This group of Roses is one of the finest in the whole
family of the " Queen of Flowers." They are generally
perfectly hardy, of luxuriant growth, and will grow almost
in any soil. They are profuse in blooming, and many of
them delightful in fragrance, from June to October. They
are flowering ornaments of the garden either as standards,
climbers, or bushes; their foliage is large, exuberant and
agreeable, and when the plants are established and well
nurtured, they produce their flowers in immense clusters.
There are now many varieties; the talent and ingenuity
of the French in rose culture and reproduction, will soon
give the floral world a farther supply of some fine varieties, and many *finer* names. I can cheerfully recommend
the following sorts, which require pruning similar to hybrid
Roses :

Acidalie, rose white, large and perfect.
Bouquet de Flore, bright rose, large flower and a profuse
    bloomer.
Augustine Lelieur, ·bright rose, beautifully globular, and
    perfectly double.

General Dubourg, pale rose, globular, large and very
    double.
Hermosa, bright rose, most perfect cupped form, a profuse
    bloomer, and highly esteemed.   During the summer
    mer months it loses much of its colour; but in au-
    tumn it is truly charming.
Le Phœnix, bright red, very perfect and fragrant.
Madame Desprez, dark rose, globular, and perfectly double,
    blooms in large clusters, and approaches more the
    Noisette tribe than any other of the Bourbon Roses.
Marechal De Villars, bright purple, compact and perfectly
    double : it is a most beautiful variety.
Paul Joseph, brilliant crimson, very double and perfect,
    though not so large a flower as many others.
Proserpine, purplish crimson, perfectly double.
Philippar, bright rose, compact and perfectly double, of
    very luxuriant habit, and, when well established, a
    great bloomer.
Queen of the Bourbons, beautiful waxy blush, perfect in
    form, profuse of flower—*exquisite.*
    There might be several others added to the above, though
we consider these the best and most distinct in colour and
character.

ROSA INDICA OR (BENGAL OF THE FRENCH) CHINESE EVER-BLOOMING ROSES.

    Perhaps no Rose has been so universally distributed and
industriously cultivated as Rosa indica, (common Chinese
or daily Rose,) and Rosa Semperflorens, (crimson or sanguinea Rose.)   It has been a favourite from the cottage to
the mansion, and is truly a floral pioneer.   They will
almost withstand every vicissitude of treatment; but will
not well survive the winters in the open air, north of this
latitude, and even here they require some simple protection with straw, mats, litter, or other dry material during
winter.
    The extensive demand for roses has induced many large
importations, and some superb additions within these few
years ; and many of those thought fine in the first edition
of this work, are now entirely discarded, giving place to

others of surpassing beauty. They require a very rich loamy soil, well pulverized, and from fifteen to twenty inches in depth.

The best season of the year for pruning them is about the first of this month. In doing so it is not advisable to shorten any of the young shoots, except in cutting off the injured parts, that being the wood most productive of bloom; but where there is old stinted wood, it should be cut out as close to the surface of the ground as the other parts of the bush will permit, with any other of the oldest wood that is too crowded. Dig every season in among their roots a good supply of well decomposed manure, and stir and hoe them frequently during the summer.

If I were to describe all I have seen of the China or Bengal Rose, half of this volume would not contain them, and three-fourths of them would not be worth a sight or even a name; nevertheless, some of them are beautifully distinct and worthy of the utmost care. Such are

Agrippina, or Cramoisi Superieur, brilliant crimson, cup form, large and finely double.

Arsenie delicate rose, of large size, perfectly double, a strong grower, and profuse bloomer.

Boisnard, sulphury white, very perfect form.

Bengal Triomphant, *La Superbe, Grande et Belle.* This, like many fine roses, has its several names, but the former is the name under which I first knew it. It is a strong grower, with very large well-formed flowers of a rich purple crimson, which are extremely double, and always open well.

Beau carmine, dark crimson of a very distinct habit and colour, is an excellent bloomer and finely formed.

Belle de Monza, changeable from pink to crimson, a very compact and large flower, a rapid grower, and a general favourite of long standing.

Belle Isidore is also a changeable rose; it will open a light pink colour, and before evening will be a rich crimson, is a regular and very double large rose, of strong growth and easy culture, and when known will be generally cultivated.

Cels, or *Bengal Cels,* flesh colour, of the most perfect form, extremely double and always opens perfect, is a very profuse bloomer, and of a strong growing habit; it has much the appearance of a superb tea rose.

Comble de Gloir, rich reddish crimson, a free bloomer, and possesses considerable fragrance.

Duchess of Kent, delicate pink, a perfect flower of a globular form, and free bloom.

Gros Charles, shaded rose, extremely large and fine.

Hortensia, flesh colour, very double, and an excellent rose.

Indica or *common daily*, dark blush or rose colour—it is the prototype of the family, and is a free growing and profuse blooming plant, and can withstand every variety of treatment. The flower is about three inches in diameter; and in our descriptions, where the word *large* is used, it signifies that the flower is larger than the present variety, and *very large* means still larger, say four inches; extremely large, between four and five inches. We have even seen roses in favourable soils and cloudy weather six inches in diameter, and would not be alarmed to see a HYBRID Rose twenty-one inches in circumference.

Icterose, creamy white, large and perfectly double.

Indica alba, *white daily* or *sarmeteuse* of some, pure white, perfectly double, free growing, and profuse in flowering; it is much more tender than the former, but does tolerably well when protected during winter. In the southern states it is a great and growing favourite. Thousands of this rose have been grown and sold in Philadelphia within these five years.

Indica minor var, Lawrencia flore pleno, delicate rose, a perfect rose in perfect miniature.

Jacksonia,* *hundred leaved daily*, or *crimson daily*, bright red, large and most perfectly double, of luxuriant growth, and more prickly (spines) than any other rose of the sort we have seen.

L' Etna, bright light crimson, very double, globular, and very distinct, is of a strong growing habit.

Lady Warrender, pure white, large cup form, very double and a great bloomer.

* In compliment to Ex-President Jackson.

La Cæmens, rosy shaded crimson, very perfect form.

Louis Philippe, dark crimson, very compact, globular, and extremely double.

Madam Hersant, bright rose, very large, showy and double.

Marjolin, large, dark crimson, a very strong grower—*fine*.

Mrs. Bosanquet, beautiful creamy blush, very large, perfectly formed—*quite distinct*.

Prince Eugène, very bright red, perfectly double cup form, and a profuse bloomer.

Queen of France, shaded red, very large and perfectly double.

Roi de Cramoisis or Eugene Beauharnais, bright crimson, fine cup form—*fragrant*.

Vesuvius, very dark crimson, perfectly double and quite sweet scented—a rare variety.

Queen of Lombardy, *Reine de Lombardie*, brilliant cherry red, cupped, perfectly double, a strong grower, and will be a great favourite—*superb*.

Semperflorens, *Crimson Chinese* or *Sanguinea*, the type of all the scarlet and crimson varieties of this division; it is perfectly double, of a rich crimson colour, and is everywhere cultivated, and will not be easily displaced from the window of the cottage, or the veranda of the palace.

Websteria,* rich blush with pink centre, very compact and perfectly double, plant of free growth and profuse in bloom.

ROSA ODORATA OR TEA ROSE.

The original Rosa odorata or tea rose, has been and will be a lasting favourite. It is supposed to have been imported from China so late as 1810, and is the leading parent of all the fine varieties we now possess. As this very popular and interesting group of Roses require more care in their culture than any yet described, I will endeavour to give the most explicit directions I am able, so as to ensure, at least, a great chance of success. They delight to grow in a rich soil with a dry bottom, and in rather an

---

* Named in compliment to the Hon. D. Webster.

elevated situation, and a southern aspect. Select a spot of
the dimensions requisite for a quantity of plants to be
planted, and dig therefrom soil to the depth of at least
eighteen inches; six inches of the bottom may be filled
with pieces of bricks, stone, or lime—rubbish of any sort;
on this, place a layer of compost, (at least fifteen inches
thick, to allow for its settling,) half turf, or good garden
mould, and half well rotted manure, with about an eighth
of sand, all completely mixed together. A few weeks after
the bed is thus prepared—say about the first of May, the
roses may be planted about two feet apart. In this latitude,
during the severity of winter, they should be protected by
a temporary frame: if covered with glass, so much the
better; but boards will serve where glass frames are not at
hand. With this treatment they will never receive the
least injury from our severest winters, and they will bloom
in the greatest perfection the whole season. The only
pruning they require is, merely to remove any old shoots
to give room for those of younger growth, and to occasionally shorten any of extra length. However, where there
are only solitary plants, they will do very well covered
with branches of cedar, or a box or barrel perforated in
several places to allow the moisture to evaporate. Those
that are grafted or budded, will not generally stand the
winters of our eastern or middle states, and should be lifted
and put in a back shed, or tied close to the ground and
covered with earth. About the first of the month they can
be raised up and pruned of any dead or superfluous wood,
when they will bloom nearly as perfect as those that have
received finer treatment. In the southern states they enjoy
the great luxury of this rose in its utmost perfection; there
they grow in "wild luxuriance," displaying their varied
beau ies, and perfuming the air with their delightful fragrance. Every flower garden in mild latitudes, should
have a full and perfect collection of such " pleasing flowers." Among.the many distinct varieties known to be
worth culture, are

Antherose, pale pinkish white, large and compact.
Aikinton, flesh colour, very double, large and perfect.
Barbot, deep pink inclining to creamy blush, very large.
Boutrand, large double pink.

Bougere, rosy lilac, extremely large, a strong grower, cup shaped.

Belle Marguerite, *Countess of Albemarle, of the English,* (and even a spurious rose of the latter name has been introduced to our collections)—pale rose, changing to dark pink in the centre, large and extremely double.

Bon Silene, cherry red, shaded with blush, very large, beautifully cupped petals, and perfectly double ; is of strong growth and finely scented ; is a new and very scarce rose ; even in France it is but in a few collections.

Bourbon, white with greenish white centre, a very double rose, free in growing and profuse in flowering, and is generally known.

Caroline, bright rosy pink, very large, beautifully formed— pendulous and highly esteemed.

Clara Sylvain, pure white, most perfectly double, a strong grower, and abundant in bloom, very sweet and highly esteemed.

Devoniensis, yellowish white, with pink centre, very large, always perfect, finely cupped—delightfully fragrant —If I were confined to cultivate *only* twelve roses, this magnificent variety would be one of the number.

Duc de Orleans, bright rose, large, globular, and finely double.

Elisa Sauvage, canary yellow, fading to creamy white, very large and double.

Flavescens, *lutea* or *yellow tea,* pale straw colour, cupped petals, very large, and though only semi-double, has not a rival of its colour; it was introduced to England from China by Mr. Parkes in 1824; is a strong grower, but more tender than any other tea rose of its habit.

Floralie, beautiful blush, bloomy in clusters, very fragrant, and as yet quite rare.

Goubault, rosy blush with yellow centre, very large.

Hippolyte, yellowish white, large and double, a strong grower and profuse bloomer.

Hyménée, white, with cream centre, globular, large, and very double.

Jaune panache, pale straw, with rose shades.

La Sylphide, rosy buff changing to creamy white, very
    perfect and always beautiful.
Lilicine, lilac, very distinct, compact, and perfectly double.
Lyonnais, very large, pale pink inclining to deep blush.
Madame Desprez, or *Bengal* Madame Desprez, pure
    white, cupped, large and finely double, is a beauti-
    ful rose, and is rarely excelled in delicacy of fra-
    grance.
Mansais, buff, very large, finely double, and highly fra-
    grant.
Mirabile, changeable, white, yellow or pink, fully double,
    and very distinct.
Moire, rose and blush, beautifully cup formed, very per-
    fect, and proves to be a fine grower.
Odorata, or common tea Rose, fine blush, very large cupped
    petals, delightfully scented, and everywhere ad-
    mired, and is the foundation of this *sweet-scented*
    family.
Princess Marie, flesh colour, a most superb rose of first
    rate merit, perfectly double, and finely scented;
    when well grown, will have flowers about five
    inches in diameter.
Safrano, when the bud first opens it is of a fine saffron co-
    lour, very pretty.
Strombio, creamy white, perfectly double, large and glo-
    bular.
Triomphe du Luxembourg, yellow flesh or copper colour,
    extremely large and perfectly double; is a rampant
    grower, has a most splendid bud.
Victorie modesta, blush, cupped, very large and double.

NOISETTE ROSES.

It is a remarkable fact, that the original of this famous
group of Roses originated in Charleston, South Carolina,
with Mr. Noisette, about 1815, who sent it to his brother,
the well-known nurseryman, at Paris (France). It was
supposed to be produced between the *white musk*, cluster
and the common China rose, and created a very great excitement among the Parisian florists and amateurs; but
since its introduction to France, thousands of seedlings

have been raised from it, and so many of these are evidently hybrids, of the tea-scented and other roses, that some of the roses called " Noisettes," have almost lost every character of the division. They are generally hardy plants, requiring rich soil and a routine of treatment similar to the "Isle de Bourbon Roses." They will amply repay for *extra* attention to their culture. The great profusion and perpetual succession of flowers from June till November, of immense clusters, frequently from fifty to one hundred in each, make them truly ornamental objects, and are well calculated for covering fences, pillars, or trellis-work. Although they are hardy, they will be benefited by a light covering of mats or litter : south of this, nothing of the kind is required. It must be kept in mind, that pillar roses can scarcely have too much manure when planting, and they also require a regular annual dressing of some enriching material. We consider the annexed list indispensable to a flower garden. The flower of a Noisette Rose varies from one to three inches in diameter in the following descriptions; we take two inches as our standard :

Alba, white, a beautiful dwarf with small flowers ; but in the greatest profusion, and the whole bush is frequently like one Bouquet.

Aimée vibert, *unique* or *Rosa nevia*, snowy white, very compact and perfectly double, and, if well treated, is one of the finest white dwarf Noisette Roses, and is a profuse autumnal bloomer.

Belle de Esquermes, dark rose, very compact and double ; a strong grower and fine pillar rose.

Bengal Lee, *Noisette Lee, Blush perpetual China,* cœlestis, *grandiflora, monstrosa,* and *Triomphe des Noisettes,* are all one and the same rose, blush or creamy white, very double, of strong growth, and flowers in large clusters ; it is a good old rose and fortunate in *new* names.

Conque de Venus, creamy white, with darker centre, very compact and double; blooms in large clusters, and is delightfully scented, a regular good article.

Champneyana or Champney's pink cluster, light pink—a

rampant grower, profuse bloomer, and universally cultivated,

Charles the Tenth, rosy purple, very double, and in dry weather blooms well, but in moist weather, its buds do not open ; is an excellent rose in a southern latitude.

Cœurjaune and *Cœur suffre* are alike yellowish white, a hardy rose of strong growth, and profusion of flowers.

Cloth of Gold, or chromatella—deep sulphur yellow, very large flower, cupped and fine—fragrant.

Cora L. Barton, fine rosy pink, very large flower, a profuse bloomer, fragrant.

Euphrosine, rosy buff, inclining to yellow, very fragrant—a very profuse blooming variety of medium growth.

Fellenberg, bright crimson, double, a strong grower, profuse in bloom, and a decided, distinct, and excellent rose.

Jaune Desprez, or French yellow Noisette, rosy buff, large and perfectly double, flowers in large clusters ; is a strong grower and delightfully fragrant, very hardy and well calculated for a pillar rose.

Julia, rosy lilac, of strong growth, profuse in bloom—very perfect and double.

Julienne le Sourd, dark rose, a most profuse bloomer, perfectly double, and a fine dwarf.

Lamarque, greenish white, extremely large, profuse in bloom, perfectly double—and agreeably scented—closely approaches the tea rose in its size and fragrance; it makes a splendid pillar rose, frequently growing ten feet in one season.

La Biche, pale flesh, large and double, a fine pillar rose, and very distinct and fragrant.

Lady Byron, pink, very compact, and perfectly double, and is a good pillar rose.

Lutea or Smithii, pale yellow, large double flowers, but does not open well in moist weather ; it is a superb article when perfect, and is quite a dwarf, having very little of the Noisette character, but delightfully scented.

Luxembourg, fine rosy purple, very perfect, a free grower and fragrant.

Orloff, bright pink, large and showy, though not very double—a profuse bloomer when well established—is a very strong grower, and excellent for covering arbours or trellises.

Pompone, rosy pink, a very strong grower, with dense foliage, sweet scented.

Solfatare, sulphur yellow, large and perfectly double, a strong grower, very fragrant, when well established blooming profusely.

Superb, delicate pink, an old rose, perfectly double, blooms in large clusters; is of strong habit, and flowers profusely. This, with Noisette Lee, are our two best old Noisette Roses.

MUSK-SCENTED ROSES, (ROSA MOSCHATA.)

The white musk-scented cluster rose is one of the oldest inhabitants of the rose garden, and is known all over the earth, where the rose has been cultivated, or its name been heard. It is supposed that it is the famed rose of the Persian poets. Although there are several varieties under this head, very few of them, indeed, have that peculiar fragrance which the genuine old species possesses. They require similar treatment to the Bourbon and Noisette Roses, and, in fact, fanciers have been, if possible, too minute, to separate this group from the Noisette Roses, merely because they are, in some degree, musk-scented.

Old musk cluster, yellowish white, expanded and semi-double, blooms in immense clusters and finely scented.

Frazerii, *Blush musk and Pink musk,* all the same rose, blush pink, semi-double, much puffed in Europe, being the only one of colour in the group.

Herbemonte, pure white, very large flower in fine clusters.

Princesse de Nassau, creamy white, perfectly double, very fragrant, and blooms in large clusters.

Ranunculus, musk cluster, pure white, very double; flowers in very large clusters.

Susanna, small yellowish white, very fragrant.

CLIMBING ROSES THAT BLOOM *ONLY* ONCE IN THE SEASON.

Under this head we will have to place several roses from very different countries, but all agreeing in habit and flowering disposition. Our readers will now be fully impressed with the knowledge that all roses of luxuriant growth require copious nourishment. Such is the case with many of those we are now about to describe; but others of them will grow and bloom most beautifully perfect even on the poorest of soil, and are very capable of covering rock-work, a sterile bank, or naked wall, or any disagreeable object, where it is not convenient to excavate for the purpose of introducing nutritious soils; and several of them are of such a hardy nature, that they will withstand the utmost severity of our northern states; others are more delicate, and can only bear the mild winters of a southern climate, where they richly display both flowers and foliage, and even retain their foliage during winter, and are evergreens for screening disagreeable objects or covering arbours. The best of the united groups are

(*r*) * Ayrshire tea scented, or *Rosa Ruga*, delicate blush, flowers very compact and perfectly double; it is a free grower and an excellent pillar rose, with a delightful fragrance. There are several others of the Ayrshire Rose, under very tempting names, such as *Double Crimson, Mottled, Eclipse, Ayrshire Queen, Elegans*, &c. These may do for those who wish a multiplicity of names; but will not take with our floral public, who wish every plant to have some merit as well as a name to recommend it.

Boursalt, pink or reddish pink, semi-double, profuse flowering, and is our earliest rose—is a free grower, and of the most hardy nature; in fact, all the Boursalts are equally hardy, and withstand the severest cold.

Boursalt, white, *Rose de Lisle, Boursalt Florida, Calypso, Pompone Florida*, and *Bengal Florida*, &c., for it

* Those marked thus (*r*) will do admirably for rock-work.

is known by all these names, and I have imported
it four times, under different names; it is a blush
white, and frequently exceedingly large and handsome, and is a pillar rose; its very double delicate
flowers have a fine effect.

Boursalt elegans, *Purple Boursalt, Purple Noisette,* &c.,
flowers of a vivid purple crimson, with an occasional stripe of white, nearly double, and an early
and profuse bloomer; is an excellent rose for an
arbour.

Boursalt Inermis, very large, bright pink, a little fragrant,
grows and blooms freely.

Banksia alba, white, with pink centre, very small, but perfectly double, has an agreeable violet perfume, and
is a profuse bloomer, but is entirely too delicate to
withstand our winters. This and the following are
natives of China:

Banksia lutea, yellow inclining to buff, in every other character similar to the former. They are elegant
evergreens in the gardens of our southern states,
and are very highly esteemed; frequently known
under the name of *White Evergreen Multiflora,*
and *Yellow Evergreen Multiflora.*

Bourbon, bright rosy red, nearly double, and flowers profusely, and is a good pillar rose; and although the
parent of the celebrated L'Isle de Bourbon Roses,
it only blooms in May or June.

Bengalensis scandens, or *Reuse de blanc,* rose white, large
double flower, and of free growth.

(*r*) Felicite de perpetua, *Noisette florabunda, Abelard sempervirens, Noisette compacta, Mademoiselle Eu-
phrasie,* and perhaps many other high-sounding
names; it is a beautiful cream white, with perfect
shaped flowers, and makes a lovely rock-work or
pillar rose; but is rather delicate for our severe
winters.

Grevillia, or *seven sisters,* is a very curious rose, flowered
the first time with us in June, 1830. It is of the
Multiflora variety, and is a native of China; growth
free and luxuriant; leaves large and deeply nerved;
flowers in large clusters, almost every eye of the
wood of last year producing one cluster, having on

it from eight to twenty roses, according to the state of the plant, each rose expanding differently in colour or shade. Many suppose that they expand all of the same colour, and change afterward. This is not the case. We have seen them white, pink, red, purple, and various other shades when the bloom expanded; and on two clusters we have observed twenty-two distinct shades of colour. In fact, it is a complete nondescript, having roses single, semi-double, and double, large and small, and every colour between white and purple, forming, in every garden where it is planted, a wonder of the vegetable world.

(*r*) Lepoldine de Orleans, beautiful blush, very compact and profuse in bloom, and is a very celebrated rose.

Multiflora, beautiful pink, very compact and double; it is rather tender for this latitude. Celebrated as being the first climbing rose that was planted in or about Philadelphia, and was so much admired, that twenty dollars were frequently given for a single plant.

Multiflora alba, similar to the former, but lighter in colour, though not a pure white.

Graulhie, pure white, cup form in large clusters, very double, a strong grower and free bloomer.

Multiflora Laure de Voust, changeable pale blush, pink or white, very compact, of the most perfect form, and a profuse bloomer, of rampant growth, and more hardy than the two preceding; it is one of the most beautiful and elegant of climbing roses, with rather large flowers and luxuriant foliage.

(*r*) Princess Maria and Princess Louise are unquestionably the same, a beautiful pale rose of exquisite form and beautifully cupped petals.

Prairie Rose, a few elegant sorts have been grown from this single flowered native rose; all are of rapid growth and partaking of the parent in blooming later than roses generally that flower only once in the season; they are admirably adapted for covering arbours, rock-work, or out-buildings of any kind, being of the most hardy nature and standing the severest of our winters even in the most northern states.

Beauty of Prairies, or Queen of Prairies, dark rose, cup
form, very large, and frequently striped with white;
it is highly esteemed and a strong grower.

Prairie Baltimore Belle, nearly white, very perfect form,
quite double, blooming in clusters.

Prairie Superba, blush, a very profuse bloomer in rich
clusters, perfectly double.

Prairie Purpurea, rosy purple, imbricated, very double,
said to bloom again in the autumn.

Russelliana, *Cottage Rose, and Scarlet Grevillia:* this is
a distinct article in growth from any other of this
group; it is perfectly hardy, and does not climb so
freely; still it makes a lovely pillar rose with large
clusters of bright crimson shaded flowers.

(*r*) Sempervirens pleno alba, pure white, flowers perfectly
double and profuse; the strong shoots of last year
will produce a large cluster of flowers almost from
every eye; this Rose is termed evergreen in Europe, but with us is perfectly deciduous; although
in our southern states it retains its foliage during
winter.

Triomphe de Bollwiller, is certainly a most superb blush
white rose, globular and double, and blooms in fine
clusters, having an agreeable and rather delightful
fragrance, and is a magnificent pillar plant.

ROSA MICROPHYLLA, (OR SMALL-LEAVED ROSE.)

This pretty little Rose was originally from China, and
since it has been introduced, several additions have been
made by cultivation; although we have not yet seen any
to excel the original Rosa microphylla. They delight in
light rich dry soils, and form very fine bushes for grass
plats or small lawns, and generally flower the whole summer, producing their blooms from short young shoots produced from the wood of two or three years' growth. The
plants should all have a little protection the first winter
after planting, and in pruning the shoots should only be
thinned out, or any dead piece cut off: we have had several roses under very enticing names added to this group,
such as *striped microphylla, crimson microphylla, scarlet*

microphylla, all deceptive; and even the first plant that came out as double white, proved to be entirely single; but there is now a genuine double white, though not properly a microphylla. The following few are all we have seen worth cultivating:

Microphylla. This rose is unique in every character. The foliage is very small and neat, and the calyx thick and bristly. The flowers are produced at the extremity of the young shoots in twos or threes, according to the strength of the plant; they are large and double; the exterior petals large and full; those of the interior are very short and thick-set; the colour in the centre is dark, shading lighter toward the exterior; the spines are in pairs on each side of the compound leaves. It is perfectly hardy, and greatly esteemed, and not so subject to be attacked by insects as other roses.

Microphylla rubra, dark red, having every character of the preceding. They are frequently called "The Burr Rose," from the appearance of the bud.

Microphylla violacé, reddish violet; in habit very similar to the former, but much darker in colour, and is a true microphylla.

Maria Leonida, white, centre tinged with pink; is very sweet scented—blooms all the season—but has more the habit of a Macartney than Microphylla Rose.

Microphylla odorata alba, yellowish white, perfectly double, and finely scented; is a strong grower and a good deal of the Macartney Rose habit.

We have now concluded our few descriptions of the beautiful family of Roses; informing our readers, if they should think it brief, we can assure them it is candid, and, as far as we know, in every respect impartial. No doubt we could have given many beautiful details of "things" we never saw and probably never will; and we also promise that a few of our descriptions will, in some situations and peculiar seasons, "come short," or perhaps "overshoot the mark;" for it is well known to the cultivator, that double roses will occasionally come single, and red roses become blush, and blush roses frequently bloom entirely white, and *vice versa.* We have also seen a moss bush have roses and shoots entirely without their "mossy coat." We have also avoided a few of high standing in character; but not being entirely known to us in their intrinsic worth, a description of them would have been too hazardous, knowing that much exaggeration exists.

The Roses and all their allies, described in this month, should be planted from the first to the middle of the month; and we would again enforce upon our rose amateurs the actual necessity of giving soil of enriching qualities to all their roses; they will be amply repaid for their trouble: nearly all the failures of roses giving a grateful and even universal satisfaction, can be traced to bad and shallow soils, more especially in our city gardens, where cheapness of workmanship is the best recommendation; consequently, there are a few inches of *tolerable-looking clay* thrown over brick-bats and lime rubbish, and, when finished, is considered a "fine job," because it is done cheap; the result is, that often the very next season the whole has to be gone over and done in a permanent manner; not less than sixteen or eighteen inches of the best dark loam should be in every garden, and that well incorporated with manure at least one year old, and also have a portion of sand or fine rotten rock thoroughly mixed with it; and then, and not till then, the proprietor may expect satisfaction.

CLIMBING PLANTS.

As shade is much required in this country, and plants suitable for covering arbours, &c., eagerly sought for, we will make a few remarks on those which are preferred for their beauty, growth, hardiness, &c.

Aristolóchia sipho Birthwort or Dutchman's pipe, is a very curious blooming plant, with extraordinary large foliage, and makes an excellent arbour twiner, affording a dense and cooling shade.

Clématis viticélla pulchélla, or double virgin's bower, is an esteemed climbing plant, of rapid growth, with large flowers in great profusion from June to September. There are several varieties of the above, two of

them single, and it is said that there is likewise a
double red.

Clématis cærùlea, C. cærulea grandiflora, and *C. azurca
grandiflora.* This beautiful and entirely new
climber is already distinguished by three distinct
names, and has been several times figured, each
time with more or less flattery. I must confess the
first representation I saw of it truly enchanted me;
the brilliancy of its blue surpassing every flower I
had ever beheld; and named *C. azurea grandiflora.*
The flowers are frequently four or five inches in
diameter, of a fine bluish violet colour, blooming
freely and perfectly hardy, the most magnificent of
the family.

Clématis Siebóldii, or bicolor. This is another of Dr. Van
Siebold's Japan additions, and is nearly related to
C. florida. The leaves and branches, however,
are rather more downy, and the petals suffused
with violet spots; the anthers are also of a violet
colour, which has given it the name of bicolor; it
is of graceful habit, and the size and beauty of its
blossoms render it an attractive inhabitant of the
flower garden.

C. flámmula, sweet-scented virgin's bower, is of very rapid
growth. Established plants will grow from twenty
to forty feet in one season, producing at the axils
of the young shoots, large panicles of small white
flowers of exquisite fragrance; the leaves are compound pinnate; in bloom from July to November,
but in August, September and October, the flowers
are in great profusion, perfuming the whole garden. This is one of the best climbing hardy
plants, and ought to have a situation in every
garden.

C. Virginiàna is of rapid growth, and well adapted for
arbours; flowers small white in axillary panicles,
diœcious, leaves ternate, segments cordate, acute,
coarsely toothed and lobed, in bloom from June to
August. A native, and a little fragrant.

C. crispa, or Bell Clematis, is a native plant of free growth
—flowers of a pink colour, in clusters, bell-shaped,
the points of the petals folding backwards—a little

grant. There is also a variety having purple flowers.

C. flòrida plenò is a fine free flowering plant; though generally considered a shrub, is more herbaceous than shrubby; the flowers are large double white; in growth will not exceed ten feet in one season.

Glycine frutéscens, a beautiful native climbing shrub, known in our gardens under that name, but is properly *Wistèria frutéscens.* It has large pendulous branches of blue leguminose (pea-like) flowers, blooming from May to August; pinnated leaves with nine ovate downy leaflets; grows freely.

Glycine chinénsis is given to *Wistèria,* and is the finest climbing shrub of the phaseolius tribe. The flowers are light blue, in long nodding many-flowered racemose spikes, blooming from May to August, profusely; leaves pinnated, with eleven ovate lanceolate silky leaflets, and is of a very rapid growth. It is perfectly hardy, withstanding the severity of our winters without protection.

Bignònia crucigera is an evergreen which is very desirable in many situations, being likewise of luxuriant growth. It will cover in a few years an area of fifty feet; flowers of an orange scarlet colour, blooming from May to August.

B. grandiflòra, now given to *Tecòma,* has large orange-coloured flowers, blooming from June to August, and grows very fast. It is perfectly hardy, and a most magnificent plant.

B. ràdicans is likewise given to *Tecòma,* and is a native plant. When in flower it is highly ornamental, but it requires great attention to keep it in regular order, being of a strong rough nature; in bloom from June to August.

Periplàca græca, silk vine, is a climber of extraordinary growth. Well established plants grow thirty or forty feet in one season; flowers in clusters from May to July, of a brownish-yellow colour, and hairy inside; leaves smooth, ovate, lanceolate, wood slender, twining and elastic.

Hedéra Hélix, Irish Ivy, is a valuable evergreen for covering naked walls, or any other unsightly object. The

8

foliage is of a lively green, leaves from three to five angled. There are several varieties of it, all valuable for growing in confined shady situations where no other plant will thrive.

Ampelòpsis hederàcea. This plant is commonly employed for covering walls, for which the rapidity of its growth and the largeness of the leaves render it extremely appropriate. There are several species of the genus, all resembling the *Vine* in habit and in flower.

Jasminum officinále, garden Jasmine. This delightful climbing shrub has been in common use all over Europe for covering arbours from time immemorial; its white, delicate, and lovely fragrant flowers render it a great acquisition: unfortunately, with us, it is rather delicate for our winters, unless well protected by a south wall or other building, and even then, when in a young state, must be protected: but, in the south, this plant and also the yellow *Jasminum revolùtum* grow luxuriantly and bloom profusely, and even *J. grandiflórum* is a hardy shrub in South Carolina and Georgia.

Lonicera, or more properly Caprifolium. *The Honeysuckle.* This genus of flowering odoriferous climbing shrubs are principally natives of this country: they are all equally beautiful; but where there is not space in our city gardens to cultivate the whole family, it is indispensable to have *C. flexuósum,* the Chinese sweet scented or evergreen; it blooms in May and September, and is a very rapid grower; *C. Belgica* is also a charming species; it blooms the whole summer, and is very odorous. Our native *C. sempervìrens,* or Coral Honeysuckle, is not easily surpassed; its profuse and brilliant scarlet flowers render it the most attractive object in all our country gardens. *C. Japònicum* is also an excellent Chinese species, with delicate orange-coloured flowers of agreeable sweetness; but will not bear our winters north of the southern part of Virginia.

Passiflòra, or Passion vine. There are several hardy species for this latitude; but the only very beautiful one is *P. incarnàta,* which, although it dies to the ground every winter, yet will, during the summer, put forth shoots from twenty to forty feet long, all covered with a profusion of beautiful purple flowers.

There are several other climbing plants, both curious and ornamental; but our limits will not admit of farther detail.

DECIDUOUS SHRUBS.

Finish planting all deciduous shrubs in the early part of the month. These plants are generally delayed too long ; the leaves in many instances are beginning to expand, thereby giving a check to the ascending sap, which we may safely assert causes the death of one-third of the plants, when perhaps the operator or some individual more distantly concerned is blamed.

These shrubs, if properly removed and planted at the exact starting of vegetation, pressing the earth close to their roots when planting, (previously taking care that the small fibres have not become dry, by exposure,) there will not one out of fifty fail by these simple attentions. Those that are late planted should have frequent waterings, and, if large, firmly supported, that the wind may have no effect in disturbing the young and tender fibrous roots.

OF PLANTING EVERGREEN SHRUBS.

Now is the season to plant all kinds of evergreen trees and shrubs. In most seasons, the middle of the month is the most proper time, the weather then being mild and moist; or if a late season, defer it to the end of the month. When planted earlier, they will remain dormant until this time, and their tender fibrous roots in that case frequently perish from their liability to injury from frost or frosty winds, being more susceptible of such injury than fibres of deciduous plants. They now begin to vegetate, which is the *grand criterion* for transplanting any plant. The buds begin to swell, the roots to push, and if they can be

quickly lifted and replanted, they will hardly receive a
check. At all events, care must be taken that they are not
long out of the ground and exposed to the air, which
greatly assists the success in planting. It may be observed
that evergreens in general succeed the better the smaller
they are, although we have seen plants, trees and evergreens successfully lifted upward of thirteen feet high,
and fifteen in diameter, and carried several miles.* By the
second year there was no appearance that such operation
had taken place. In preparing a hole for the reception of
these plants, make it larger than the roots, breaking the
bottom thereof fine, and putting in some fresh soil. Place
the plant upright in the centre, putting in the earth and
breaking it fine, and give the plant a few gentle shakes.
When the roots are more than half covered, put in a pot
or pailful of water, allowing it to subside, then cover all the
roots, give a second or third pailful, and when subsided,
the earth will be close to all the roots. Cover with more
earth, pressing all firm with the foot. Put more soil loosely
on, which will give it a finished appearance, and prevent
it from becoming dry, and not require mulching, which has
an unsightly appearance. All that the wind will have
any hurtful effect upon must be firmly supported, especially
large plants. If the weather sets in dry and hot, they
should be watered as often as necessity shall direct.

Those that are established, it will be necessary to go
over them (if not already done) to cut off all wood killed
in winter, and also to thin them if too thick and crowded.

When the above is done, let every part of the shrubbery be dressed off as directed in *March.* Shrubs of all
kinds will now begin to look gay and lively, which may
be very much heightened or depreciated, according to the
state in which the ground and contiguous walks are kept.
Always keep in view that weeds are no objects of beauty.

CARE OF CHOICE BULBS.

Hyacinths of the earliest sorts will begin to expand and
show their colours; of which we can boast of a few as fine

* See Mr. M'Nab's rich pamphlet treatise on removing evergreens, &c.

sorts in the vicinity of Philadelphia, as in any garden of
Europe; but even these very superior sorts, when in bloom,
are too frequently neglected, being allowed to stand without
rods, stakes, or any means of support, likewise equally exposed to drenching rains and scorching suns; and the finest
collections may be seen after heavy rains prostrate on the
ground, whereas a few hours' trouble would give them the
requisite support, thereby preserving their beauty much
longer, and giving more gratification. As soon as the
stems advance to any height, they should be supported by
wires, rods, &c., and tied slightly thereto with threads of
matting, or any other substitute; repeat the tying as they
advance, avoid tying among the florets, because they grow
by extension, and are liable to be broken off by so doing.
The sun deteriorates the colours very much, especially the
red, blue, and yellow sorts; whereas, if they were simply
protected from the sun by an awning of thin canvas, the
colours would be preserved and the beauty protracted. If
there are stakes drove into the ground on each side of the
beds, about three feet high, with others in the centre about
eight feet, having laths or hoops from the side to the centre,
formed similar to the roof of a house, so that people may
walk or sit under it, the canvas or awning being thin to
admit of the light freely, the effect in the time of sunshine,
from the brilliancy of the colours, is peculiarly gratifying.
Where an awning is thus erected, it requires to be kept on
only from nine to three o'clock in sunshine days, and during
nights or time of rain, allowing the awning on the most
northern side to come close to the ground, when necessary,
to shelter them from cold cutting winds.

The properties of a good Hyacinth are, namely—the
stem strong and erect, the florets or bells occupying one-
half of the stem, each floret suspended by a short strong
footstalk, longest at the bottom; the uppermost floret quite
erect, so that the whole may form a pyramid. Each floret
well filled with petals rising toward the centre, that it may
appear to the eye a little convex. Regarding colour, fancy
does not agree, and the most scrupulous cultivators differ
materially. However, the more pure and bright the finer,
or a white with a pink centre, or the centre of the petals
with a paler or deeper colour appearing striped, which is
considered to have a good effect.

8*

Tulips in every respect should have the same care and protection, never neglecting to have the beds with a smooth clean surface, and the stems neatly tied up, although they are not in so much danger as Hyacinths.

The characters of a good *Tulip* are—the stem strong, elastic, and erect, about two feet high, the flower large and composed of six petals, proceeding a little horizontally at first, and then turning upward, forming a flat-bottomed cup, rather widest at the top; the three exterior petals should be larger than the three interior ones, and broader at their base; the edges of the petals entire, free from notch or ruggedness; the top of each well rounded; the colour of the flower at the bottom of the cup ought to be pure, white, or yellow, and the rich-coloured stripes, which are the principal ornament, should be pure, bold, regular, and distinct on the margin, and terminate in fine points elegantly penciled. The centre of each petal should have one bold stripe, or blotch, of rich colouring. The ground colours that are most esteemed are white, the purer the finer; or, on the other hand, the dark grounds, and of course the darker the better; but these vary in estimation according to the prevailing taste of amateurs.

ANEMONES AND RANUNCULUS.

Moist weather and frequent showers are highly essential to the perfecting of these flowers, and if these should fail at this season of the year, artificial means must be used to supply the deficiency. Take a watering-pot without the rose, and run the water (river or rain water is best) gently between the rows, taking care not to make holes in the ground. When they have got a good watering at root, take the syringe and give them a gentle sprinkling in fine evenings, observing not to use force for fear of breaking the flower stems. In dry weather the result of a deficiency of water would be, that the stems and flowers of the strongest roots will be weak and make no progress, and many of them will not bloom; the foliage of a sickly, yellow appearance, from which they would not recover; and the roots, when taken up, are of little use for farther transplanting.

A good plan in dry seasons is to cover the ground be-

tween the rows with cow manure, which will prevent the
moisture from evaporating, and the rain or water passing
through it greatly enriches the soil and strengthens the
roots.

CHARACTER OF A FINE RANUNCULUS.

" It is indispensable for a good ranunculus to have a stem
about eight or twelve inches high, strong enough to support the flower, and quite upright.　The form of the flower
should be hemispherical, not less than two inches in diameter, consisting of numerous petals, gradually diminishing
in size to the centre, lying over each other, so as neither
to be too close nor too much separated, but having more of
a perpendicular than a horizontal direction, in order to display the colours with better effect.　The petals should be
broad, with entire well-rounded edges, their colours dark,
clear, rich, or brilliant, either of one colour or variously
diversified, on a ground of cinerous white, primrose, yellow,
or flame colour, or diversified with elegant stripes, spots,
or mottlings."

AURICULAS.

Having under this head last month given ample directions for the treatment of these plants previous to flowering,
we refer to that head to avoid repetition.

CHARACTER OF A FINE AURICULA.

The pips should be large, flat, and round, with ground
colour equal on every side of the eye, which should be
quite circular, *as well as the edge.*　The tube a bright
lemon yellow perfectly *round*, well filled with the anthers
or thrum, the eye round and large, the body colour black
or violet, the meal fine, the colour, in green-edged flowers,
should be a whole one, not a shaded green.　The stem
strong, and sufficiently long to bear the truss above the
foliage—the truss to consist of not less than five full-blown
pips; only one stem allowed.

CARNATIONS, PINKS, &c.

If any of these were omitted to be shifted last month, or planted out according to directions therein given, let it be done forthwith. Where they are still protected with frames, give them plenty of air, keeping the sashes entirely off during the day, keep the pots perfectly free from weeds, and give the foliage frequent sprinklings with water.

Polyanthus and *Primroses* will be exhibiting their beautiful flowers. They require the same treatment, and delight in moisture and a shaded situation. Do not sprinkle them while in flower, and keep them clear of weeds or decayed leaves, never exposing them to the sun. They are very hardy, and, where required, may be planted in very shady situations, for they will suffer more from the influence of the sun's rays than from frost. Those plants in pots in general that have been protected in frames, and are destined for the borders, should now as soon as possible be planted in their destined situations, having nothing to fear from chilling winds or frosts after the middle of this month, except in uncommon seasons. Those that are to be kept in pots, if not repotted, do it immediately, and give regular supplies of water.

CHARACTER OF A POLYANTHUS.

The pips large, flat, and round, with small indentures between each division of the limb, dividing the pip into heart-like segments edged with bright yellow; the edge and the eye ought to be of the same colour, the truss to consist of not less than five full-blown pips, supported on a strong stem, standing well above the foliage.

POLIANTHUS TUBEROSA FLORE PLENO.

This very popular bulb, generally known as *Tuberose*, has been cultivated in England upwards of two centuries, whence we no doubt have received it, and now can return those of our production to supply their demand. The flowers are many and highly odoriferous, and of the purest white, and on a flower stem from three to five feet high. .To have them in the greatest perfection, they should be planted in a lively hot-bed, about the first of this month, in six inch pots filled with light rich earth, giving very little water until they begin to grow, when they ought to be liberally supplied with plenty of air, and about the end of next month they may be planted in the borders, providing a spot for them that is or has been well worked, and enriched with well decomposed manure.   Secure their flower stems to proper rods.   Previous to planting the roots, all the off-sets should be taken off and planted separately; keep the crown of the bulb level with the surface of the pot, and when they are replanted in the open ground, put them two inches deeper.

But when the convenience of a hot-bed cannot be obtained, they will succeed very well if planted about the end of this month or first of next in the garden, in a bed of earth prepared for their reception.   Let it be dug deep, and make the soil light and rich, by giving it a good supply of manure two years old, well broken and incorporated with the earth, adding a little sand where the soil is heavy.   The black earth from the woods produced from decayed leaves is equally as good without sand.   Having the ground in proper order, draw drills about four inches deep and eighteen inches apart; plant the bulbs (after divesting them of their off-sets) nine inches apart in the row, covering the crown of the bulb about an inch and a half.   When done, carefully rake and finish off the beds.   When they shoot up their flower stems, give them neat rods for their support.   Plant the off-sets in closer rows to produce flowering roots for next year, because they seldom flower the second time.

ON THE CULTURE OF THE HEARTSEASE OR PANSY, (VIOLA TRICOLOUR.)

The simplicity and striking beauty of this lovely little flower have attracted notice from the earliest floral times, but it is only within these few years that it has come into high estimation as a florist's flower.   Indeed, when the figures

and descriptive characters of these " little gems" came first
from England to this country, we were almost induced to
believe they were exaggerated "pictures of fancy," till we
actually cultivated within these last two years in our own
parterre upwards of two inches in diameter.

They delight in a situation partially shaded from the hot
rays of the sun, either fully exposed to the morning rays
till ten o'clock, or the afternoon sun from three o'clock ; a
soil composed of four parts good loam and one part thoroughly rotted manure, or three parts loam and one part
decayed leaves, not less than one foot deep : the soil must
not be more elevated than the surrounding surface, as they
like a good supply of moisture. If they are to be cultivated
from seeds they should be thinly sown about the first of the
month, or about the end of August or first of September,
and very lightly covered with fine soil, giving them very
frequent waterings in dry weather. Those sown now will
bloom in July, and very profusely in the autumn ; but those
sown in the latter period will not bloom till early the following spring. When any very esteemed variety is raised, it
should be propagated, which is very easily done, either by
layers or cuttings, and sometimes by division of the root,
but the two former methods are preferable. The best time
for laying is about the first of September : an inch or two
of the soil may be removed all round the plant, the shoots
laid down in the hollow, and covered over with light rich
compost. The shoots will root more freely if they get a
gentle twist when laying them down. The best period for
propagating by cuttings is about the middle of this month
or September. Cuttings should be chosen from young
shoots about two or three inches long ; for when shoots are
woody or hollow they will either not strike at all or produce
unhealthy plants. A shaded but airy situation is preferable, and if the soil is of a light sandy nature, the better
success will attend the operation : the cuttings should be
firmly inserted from one to two inches deep in the ground,
and covered with a glass, or where that convenience is not
at hand, they may be shaded during the day with oiled
paper, or any similar substitutes. In preparing the cuttings, care ought to be taken to cut close to a joint, a rule
which should be strictly attended to in making cuttings of
every description. When they have fairly rooted and

taken a growth, they can be removed in cloudy, moist weather, to their proper allotments. Seeds ought to be carefully collected from the finer sorts, and sown as soon thereafter as convenience will allow, as they deteriorate by long keeping. Many hundreds of named varieties are carefully cultivated in England. A *select* list sent contains *only* three hundred and seventy-four names. To attempt a general or even brief description of them in this work would be considered by many of our friends prolix and unnecessary; but the following criteria of a fine Pansy has just passed a select committee of the Pennsylvania Horticultural Society:

"The chief object to be desired is symmetry of the flower. The petals should be large, broad and flat, lying upon each other so as to form a circle, and prevent any thing like angles or intersections of this circular outline. The petals should be as nearly of a size as possible, the two top ones being the largest, but so covered with the two side ones as not to appear disproportioned. The top petals should not wave or bend back. The bottom petal should be broad and two-lobed, flat, and not curving inward; above an inch in breadth is a good size; the colours should be clear, brilliant, and not changing. The eye should not be too large, and it is accounted finest when the penciling is so arranged as to form a dark angular spot.

"The flower stalk should be long and stiff, rather than slender."

GLADIOLUS OR SWORD LILY.

It is now a well ascertained fact that the whole of this beautiful family will succeed well with a treatment similar to the tube rose, requiring to be two or three weeks earlier planted: indeed, *G. communis* and its varieties are perfectly hardy; but the splendid *G. psittacinus*, with large yellow, red, and green flowers; *G. cardinalis*, scarlet and white; *G. blandus*, rose and white; *G. florabundus*, shaded rose, *G. formosissimus*, magnificent scarlet, and several others are worthy of the greatest care and attention; their large spikes of showy flowers will well compensate for an extra degree of care in preparation of soil, &c.

AMARYLLIS FORMOSISSIMA, OR JACOBEA LILY.

About the end of this or beginning of next month is the most proper time for planting out these bulbs. This flower is of the most beautiful and rich crimson velvet colour. The bulb generally produces two stems, the one after the other, about the end of May or first of June. The stem is from nine inches to one foot high, surmounted by a single flower, composed of six petals, three hanging down, three erect and recurved; the stamens droop on the .centre of the under petals. The flower thus appears nodding on one side of the stem, and has a most graceful and charming appearance. If planted in a bed, prepare the ground as before directed for *Tuberoses.* Keep the rows one foot asunder, and the bulbs six inches apart in the rows, covering them two inches over their crowns. This plant is now called *Spreikèlia formosíssima,* and we think properly, too, for its character and habit differ from *Amaryllis.*

We have not the smallest doubt, that in a few years, not only this superb South American bulb will adorn our flower gardens, but many of the rich bulbs of Brazil and South America generally will yearly exhibit to us the beauty of their colours, and the beautiful construction of their flowers and foliage, of which we are now generally deprived, perhaps because we have not the conveniency of a proper hot-house for their protection during winter. But it will be found, in many instances, that these bulbs will do perfectly well to be kept dry in a warm room from October to May, when the heat of our summer is sufficient for the perfection of their flowers, and many species will ripen their seeds. The bulb that is known as *Amaryllis Belladónna,* now called *Belladónna purpuráscens,* is hardy.

TIGER FLOWER.

Tigrídia, a genus of Mexican bulbs belonging to *Monadelphia Triándria,* producing the most beautiful flowers of the natural order of *Irideæ. T. pavònia* is of the brightest scarlet, tinged and spotted with pure yellow. *T. conchiflòra,* colour rich yellow, tinged and spotted with bright crimson; flower larger than the former. The colours are very rich, and purely contrasted. The corolla is about four inches in diameter, composed of six petals; the outer are reflexed, the flower, though splendid in beauty, exists only one day; but, to compensate for that, a plant will produce flowers for several weeks; and where a bed of them can be collected, they will bloom in profusion from July to September. They like a light, rich, free soil, from twelve to eighteen inches deep. Lift the bulbs in October, and preserve them as directed in that month for *Tuberoses.* Be sure that they be kept dry and secure from frost. A bed of these should be in every garden. A writer says, " it is the most beautiful flower that is cultivated." Plant them about the end of this or first of next month; if in beds, keep them six inches apart in the row, and one foot apart from row to row.

WALKS.

The walks in general should be put in the neatest order during this month. Little requires to be added to the observations of last month, but if these have not been executed, fail not to have it done the first opportunity, choosing dry weather for the operation of *turning* the old, or adding new gravel to them, leveling, raking, and rolling neatly as you proceed. Always after rain give the whole of the gravel walks a good rolling. This being frequently done during the early part of the season, will be a saving of much labour and time through the summer. The walks having a firm surface, the growth of weeds will be retarded, and the heavy rains will not be so apt to injure them. Where there are any pretensions to keeping these in order, they ought to be picked of weeds and litter once a week, and gone over with the roller at least once every two weeks during the season.

Sweep and divest the grass walks or plats of all worm-casts, litter, &c., cutting the edgings neatly. Mow the grass every two or three weeks from this time to October, sweeping off the grass clean each time, and give frequent rollings to keep the surface smooth. If any require to be laid with turf, delay it no longer. For direction, see last month. The above observations on walks in general, will apply through the season; therefore, we will not repeat this subject until October.

EVERGREEN HEDGES.

We have previously observed, under the head Evergreens, that this is the best season for their replanting. We cannot pass over the observations of this month, without having reference to evergreen hedges, so much neglected among us, and yet so important to the diversity of aspect, and especially to soften a little the gloomy appearance of our winters. There are three indigenous shrubs, and at least one exotic, that are well adapted for the purpose, viz., *Pinus canadénsis*, Hemlock-spruce; *Thùja occidentàlis*, American arborvitæ; *Thùja orientàlis*, Chinese arborvitæ; and *Juníperis virginiàna*, Red-cedar. Where there is to be a hedge of any of these planted, select plants about two feet high; lift them carefully, preserving the roots as much as possible. Dig a trench from one and a half to two feet wide, and from one to one foot and a half deep. This will admit the soil to be well broken about the roots, which must be done in planting. Keep the plants in the centre of the trench, mixing the shortest and the tallest, that it may be of one height, putting the earth close about their roots as you proceed, and make it firm with the foot; fill up, and water as directed for evergreens in this month. If the season is very dry, give it frequent copious waterings.

None of them should be topped for a few seasons, except such as are much above the others in height, keeping the sides regular and even by clipping or shearing once a year, either in this month or at the end of August. It is better to keep the top (when they have got to the desired height) pointed, than broad. The latter method retains a heavy weight of snow, which frequently breaks down, or otherwise deforms, that which has cost much labour to put into shape.

BOX EDGINGS.

Where these have not been laid, this month is the proper time. Do not delay the planting of such any later. For ample directions, see *March*, under this head. Clipping of these should be done about the middle of this month. There will then be no danger of frosts to brown the leaves, and the young foliage will not be expanded. To keep these edgings in order, they must be cut once a year, and never be allowed to get above four inches high and two inches wide. What we consider the neatest edging is three inches high, two inches wide at the bottom, tapering to a thin edge at the top. It is very unsightly to see large bushy edgings, especially to narrow walks.

The use of edgings is to keep the soil from the gravel, and the larger they are allowed to grow, the more ineffectual they become; growing more open below as they advance in height. The operation may be done very expeditiously by clipping the tops level, going longitudinally along with shears for the purpose, called "box shears." Strain a line along the centre of the edgings, cutting perpendicularly from the line to the bottom on each side, leaving only the breadth of the line at top. Edgings cut in this manner, every spring, will always look well, and the trouble, comparatively, is a mere trifle.

GENERAL CARE OF PLANTS COMING INTO FLOWER.

Every part of the flower ground should be put into neat order, giving such plants about the borders as are shooting up their flower stems, and are tender, and in danger of being hurt or broken by the wind, proper sticks or rods for their support. In doing this, endeavour to conceal the rods, &c., as much as possible, by dressing the stems and leaves in a natural-looking manner over them. Let the stakes be in proportion to the height and growth of the plants. It looks very unsightly to see strong stakes to short and weak growing plants. The tyings likewise should be proportionate.

Examine all the beds and patches of seedling flowers

now coming up, and let them be refreshed with water as
it may be necessary, and pick out the weeds as they appear.

We cannot leave this department at this season of the
year, without enforcing the benefit and beauty that will
result from keeping the weeds down during this and the
next month. Therefore strictly observe that there are
none running to seed in any part of the garden; in fact,
they ought not to be allowed to rear their heads one day in
sight.

MAY.

As the season for planting out the Dahlia is now approaching, we will endeavour to give our readers the whole
subject of their management, so as to ensure a good bloom
of this the most fashionable and popular ornamental plant
of the present day. As very many are entirely unac-
quainted with the nature and even the habits of the plant,
a brief synopsis of its history will assist in giving a key to
its culture. The plant was first discovered by Humboldt,
in Mexico, growing in sandy plains, three thousand feet
above the level of the sea. The date is not precisely
known, but supposed to be about 1785-6. Indisputable
authority, however, speaks of its being introduced into
England in 1789; but was lost and again introduced in
1803, from Madrid, by Lady Holland; from which period
till 1830, it had but little notice in cultivation. Indeed it
seems to have been reserved for the intelligent growers of
the last few years to bring it into general notice; and if we
take a retrospective view of the rapid progress of Dahlia
culture within these last five years, we will be led to ex-
claim, " Where will all this terminate?" but time alone can
solve the question; at present it is impossible to come to
any satisfactory conclusions. Only a few years ago, and
who would have conceived the idea of having tipped,
striped, and spotted Dahlias of almost every hue and colour;
and although historical writers on the genus alluded to the
improbability of a blue flower ever being produced, yet it
is not unreasonable to imagine that ere long we will have

flowers beautifully and distinctly striped with black and white, and even combining the gaudy colours of the tulip, or the choicest hues of the carnation; perhaps the criteria of character may change to those of huge globular forms or balls—nay, even the odour of the Rose or the Jasmine may be imparted, and what then? Only let amateurs and cultivators persevere with the spirit they have done during the last few years, and we think all we have advanced will be realized.

Propagation. This operation may be performed in various ways, either by division of the root, by cutting of the young shoots, or by grafting. For general planting, division of the root will be sufficient; about the first of the month the old root, entire, should be planted in some warm and sheltered spot of the garden, covering it with sand, vegetable mould, or any light soil; in about two weeks the eyes or young shoots will have sprouted: then it will be properly seen how they can be most carefully divided; the root should be carefully cut into as many pieces as there are eyes or sprouts, leaving only one tuber to each, when they can be planted into the situation appropriated for their blooming.

Propagation by Cuttings. Prepare a hot-bed in March, as therein described, and place a frame and lights of the required size upon it, scatter over the surface of the bed four or five inches of sand, old bark, or any light soil; after four or five days, the fresh steam will have subsided, when the roots may be laid thereon, covering them (but not over the crowns) with light sandy soil; but where large pots can be obtained, I prefer planting them in the pots; by this means the plants are kept distinct, and can be taken out at any time and examined. They should be frequently sprinkled with water that is partially warm; and if, after they are thus placed in the bed, a rank and dense steam should arise, the lights should be slightly raised both night and day, till it subsides; and if the nights are cold, cover the lights with mats or shutters. This gentle bottom heat will speedily induce the eyes to grow, and when the shoots have attained the height of three or four inches, they should be cut off close to the base, which makes the best plant. After the cuttings are taken off, pot them singly into very small pots filled with light sandy loam, containing

9*

a good portion of black earth from the woods, and placed
in another moderate hot-bed and give a gentle supply of
water. Particular care must be paid to shading them from
the violent rays of the sun, for if they are once exposed,
they seldom recover: in this state they should continue till
they have formed their roots, which, in a temperature of
from sixty to seventy degrees, will be in from two to three
weeks. Where a great stock of any particular sort is
wanted, the cuttings should be taken off just below a joint,
leaving two or three eyes at the base of the shoot, which
will again speedily produce new shoots, that can be again
removed in a similar manner.

When the plants are rooted, they may then be considered established, and all that is necessary is, to shift them
into larger pots as they require ; and gradually inure them
to a lower temperature, till they can endure the open air,
which will not be before the middle of May.

Propagation by Grafting. Where only a few plants
are wanted, this is a very successful method, as an operation can be conducted in the office or parlour window. The
cutting intended for the graft should have about three joints ;
when obtained, select a good tuber without eyes from any
common sort, and with a sharp knife cut a slice from the
upper part of the root downward about two inches in length,
and about half an inch in depth, and then cut it off horizontally, leaving a ledge whereon to rest the graft; next cut
the graft sloping to fit, and cut it so that an eye or joint may
be at the bottom of it to rest on the aforesaid ledge. After
the graft has been firmly tied, a piece of clay should be
put round it, pot the root in fine soil, in a pot that will bury
the graft half way in the mould, and cover it with a glass,
(a large tumbler will do,) and in two weeks it will have
taken root, the glass may then be removed, and the plant
gradually inured to the open air.

Soil. As far as my observations enable me to judge,
the soil best adapted for the Dahlia is a sandy loam, not
retentive of moisture, and not too rich, as they will grow to
leaves and branches, producing few flowers, and even then
imperfect : not too poor, as in such they will be very indifferent, meagre in size and general appearance. Where
soils are rich and heavy, a portion of sand or gravel should
be mixed in the soil where they are planted : but if poor,

incorporate with the sand well decomposed manure; and when the plants are planted, a stick in proportion to the plant should be put with it, and at least eighteen inches in the ground, and not less than two inches in diameter, to which they must be carefully tied as they grow, never allowing more than one stem to each plant; and the side branches should be cut off from one to three feet from the ground, according to the height of the plant. *Oakley's Surprise,* the most favourite crimson Dahlia, tipped with white, comes invariably true to its character in sandy soil, whereas, in rich heavy soil, it is frequently only crimson. The worst of all soils for the Dahlia, is a rich loam retentive of moisture; in such they grow to wood and foliage, producing few and very imperfect flowers.

The best disposition or arrangement in planting the Dahlia, I think, is in groups; each group should be composed of a different section of colour: this affords a close comparison, and gives greater diversity of landscape, than combining the colours; the tallest growing sorts should be carefully planted in the centre or at the back of each group. The roots should be planted from three to four feet from each other every way. But where they are planted in rows along walks or avenues, two or three feet will be a sufficient distance from plant to plant. Individual plants look extremely well if they are of a dwarf habit. To have a continued succession of bloom, there should be two plantings; the first about the fifteenth of the month, and the latest about the end of June; it is the June planting that generally produces the finest flowers; this fact (though lately discovered) is now well understood by some cultivators, and is easily accounted for. When plants are forced and planted early, they are in a flowering state much earlier, to be sure, but they are overtaken with, perhaps, a hot, dry summer, which "blights" the buds, and are more subject to the disease called "curl;" the young leaves, as they expand, are perforated with numerous holes; the margins become brownish, as if burnt; they then become curled, placid, and the whole plant unhealthy and dwarfish. The principal stem ceases to grow, and numerous suckers and stems arise from below, forming a dense bush. The flowers of such plant, as might be expected, are small and irregular; and however excellent the variety may be, they

yield nothing but disappointment to the anxiously expect-
ant cultivator. This disease is caused by an insect, *Cymix
Chloroterus*, or green bug. It inhabits the extremities of
the Dahlia, and grows and feeds on the under surface of
the young leaves, and in its destruction is aided by our
frequently hot and arid months of July and August.
Hence, the reason that the late planting gives most satisfaction, they are in these months in a rapid growing state,
and if attacked outgrow the effects, and push at once into
bloom in the more moist and cooling month of September.
The only remedy that is known for the above evil is, to
look over the plants cautiously in the morning when the
first attacks are perceptible, and pick off the insect; it has
to be approached with caution, as it instinctively throws
itself down among the leaves if disturbed; and if it escapes,
it again climbs up, and commences its depredations. It is
admitted that there are exceeding one thousand distinct
named varieties now in cultivation, and it may be desirable
to some that a select list of the choicest named sorts now in
cultivation should be given: but such is the almost endless
multiplicity of kinds, and such the numerous additions
every year made, that in a few years those I may mention
now as being fine, will then most probably be considered
wholly useless. However, for immediate profit and benefit, I recommend the following:

PURE WHITE.

Antagonist,	Lewisham Rival,
Cheltenham Queen,	Miss Percival,
Lady Langston,	Pride of Sussex,
White Defiance,	Virgin Queen.

WHITE OR BLUSH, SHADED OR EDGED WITH PINK OR RED.

Beauty of Sussex,	Countess of Pembroke,
Exquisite,	Beauty of Wakefield,
Emma Noke,	Favourite,
Lady Antrobus,	Lady St. Maur,
Mrs. Rushton,	Diana,
Phenomenon,	Queen of the Isles.

LILAC.

Formosa,　　　　　　　Hon. Miss Abbot,
Lady Harland,　　　　　Lady Middleton,
Mrs. Jones,　　　　　　 Mrs. Shelley,
Princess Royal,　　　　 Queen of Beauties.

ROSE OR PINK.

Hero of Tippecanoe,　　 Hope,
Kingscote Rival,　　　　 Queen, (Widnall's,)
Rose Unique,　　　　　　Beauty of Kent.

PURE YELLOW.

Apollo,　　　　　　　　 Argo,
Ophir,　　　　　　　　　Prince of Wales,
Yellow Victory,　　　　　Winterton Rival.

YELLOW OR BUFF, STRIPED OR TIPPED WITH RED.

Bloomsbury, buff,　　　　Unique,
Desdemona,　　　　　　　Harlequin,
Princess Royal, (Hudson,)　Pontiac.

ORANGE.

Aurantia,　　　　　　　 Orange Superb.

RED OR ROSY RED.

Perfection, (McKenzie's,)　Prince Albert,
Sir W. Middleton,　　　　Duchess of Richmond.

SCARLET.

Bloomsbury, (Lee's),   Fire King,
Eclipse,   Tournament,
Vivid.

ROSY CRIMSON.

Caleb Cope,   Hero of the West,
Marechal Soult,   Sir Fred. Johnson,
Thomas Clarkson,   Henry Clay, (Schmitz.)

CRIMSON.

Bedford Surprise,   Ne plus ultra,
Roderick,   Thomas C. Percival,
Springfield Rival,   Rival Sussex.

PURPLE.

General Houston,   Sultan,
Pickwick,   Violet Perfection.

DARK MAROON AND VERY DARK.

Admiral Stopford,   Competitor,
Conqueror,   . Essex Triumph,
Hero of Stonehenge,   Horace Binney,
Standard of Perfection,   Washington Irving.

CRIMSON PERMANENTLY TIPPED WITH WHITE.

Oakley's Surprise,   Evêque de Tournay.

STRIPED.

Striata formosissima,   Formosa.

The above are the choicest in cultivation at the present time, and for farther description in regard to colour, height and price, we beg to refer our readers to the periodical catalogues of our respectable nurserymen that are issued every spring, and contain many other sorts of eminence; and not a few equally desirable with the above, though the descriptions of some that are annually received from England are more tempting than the article: whether there are some sorts that do produce more perfect and beautiful flowers in their humid climate than they do when transferred to ours, we cannot practically decide, but presume that it is the fact, for we are confident, and every season does more fully confirm it, that the seedlings grown in this country from seed sowed here do grow better, and flower finer, than the generality of those imported; and, to prevent us adopting inferior sorts, and giving them *dashing* names, we subjoin the following rules for judging:

CHARACTER OF A FINE DAHLIA.

" The best judges distinguish Dahlias by the three criteria of form, colour and size.

" 1. *Form.*—The front view of the blossom should be perfectly circular, without notches or inequalities, caused by the petals being pointed, and not as they should be, rounded, smooth at the edges, and slightly concave, but not so much as to show any of the back. One of the most perfect flowers, in this respect, is the Springfield Rival. When the petals are pointed, notched, fringed, piped, quilled, concave, convex, or flat, the perfectness of the circle is broken, and one indispensable beauty in the eye of the florist is deficient.

" When the eye or disc is shown in the full-blown flower, it is also a striking defect.

" The side view of a first rate flower should be that of a perfect hemisphere.

" There is, perhaps, no example of this perfection of form without some slight deficiency. The Countess of Liverpool is one of the nearest to a perfect flower in this respect.

" 2. *Colour.*—This is looked upon by florists as an infe-

rior consideration to form, though it is usually the first to
attract the notice of common observers.

" In flowers of one colour, or selfs, the colour ought to be
bright and distinct, without any breaking or blotching.
When there are stripes, mottlings, shadings, or edgings,
these should be clear and uniformly marked, the colours
distinct without clouding or running.

" 3. *Size.*—Although large flowers with superior form
and clear distinct colours are esteemed superior to small
flowers with the same properties, yet size alone is looked
upon by florists as *nothing* when form and colour are defective."

Particular care should be taken with seeds, especially
such as are saved from fine sorts. If they are sown about
the first of April, on a gentle hot-bed, or in a green-house
in plots, filled with light rich earth, covering the seeds
about three-eighths of an inch, and when they have made
leaves, pot them off singly into small pots, till time for
planting out, or where a quantity is grown, three plants
may be put into one pot, and thus planted, and when they
bloom the bad can be pulled up, leaving those of good character to stand for farther trial: none should be kept but
such as come up to the above rules; and if they do not do
so the first year, there is little hope of their being more
perfect the second.

ANNUALS, HARDY AND TENDER.

By the first of the month finish sowing all hardy Annuals and Biennials ; and about the middle of the month
all those that are tropical. The weather being now warm,
they will vegetate in a few days or weeks. Attend to thinning of those that are too thick, giving gentle waterings to
such as are weak in dry weather. Those that have been
protected in frames should be fully exposed therein night
and day; take the first opportunity of damp cloudy days
to have them transplanted into the borders or beds, lifting
them out of the frame with as much earth as will adhere
to their roots.

CARE OF HYACINTHS, TULIPS, &c.

For the treatment of these, while in bloom, see last month. The best time to take them out of the ground, is about five weeks after they are done flowering, or when the stem appears what may be termed half decayed. The best method to dry them is to place the roots in rows, with bulb to bulb, the stems lying north and south, or east and west. Give the bulbs a very thin covering of earth, merely to exclude the sun, so that they may not dry too rapidly, being thereby liable to become soft. When they have thoroughly dried in this situation, which will be in eight or ten days in dry weather, (and if it rains cover them with boards,) take them to an airy dry loft or shade, clearing off the fibres or stems, and in a few weeks put them in close drawers, or cover them with sand perfectly dry, until the time of planting, for which see October.

It is not advisable to allow any of the bulbs of either Hyacinths or Tulips to seed, as it retards their ripening and weakens the root, except where there are a few desired for new varieties. The small off-sets must be carefully kept in dry sand, or immediately planted.

ANEMONES AND RANUNCULUS.

These, while in bloom, should be carefully shaded from the sun by hoops and thin canvas, or an erect temporary awning; and as soon as they are done flowering, they must be fully exposed and the waterings given up.

TUBEROSES AND AMARYLLIS,

That are not planted, should now be done. For full directions, see last month. In many seasons, any time before the twelfth is quite soon enough; but nothing ought to be delayed when the season will permit it to be done. It is necessary to have them properly labeled.

10

AURICULAS, POLYANTHUS, AND PRIMROSES,

Will now be done flowering, but still must be carefully kept in a cool, shady situation, and all decayed leaves cut off as soon as they appear. Examine them carefully and frequently, in case slugs of any description be preying upon them. A dusting of hot lime will kill them, or they may be otherwise destroyed. Some have recommended to repot and slip those plants when done flowering, "or they will contract a destructive disease;" which disease is a loss of verdure, and is induced by too much heat and drought, and a few other causes from inattention; but if attended to as above, until September, when they should be fresh-potted, they will have time to be sufficiently established before winter, which is the most judicious time to take off slips, for two reasons, namely, they do not want so much nursing through the most precarious season of the year (summer) for these plants, and they begin to grow, and will root afresh sooner.

DOUBLE WALL-FLOWERS.

As these are very seldom grown from seed, and are semi-biennials, art has to be used to preserve or renew them. About the end of this month, take shoots of this year about three inches long, cutting them carefully off, and smoothing the cut end with a sharp knife: from this cut the lower leaves off about one inch and a half, and then put it in the ground; choose a very shady spot, mixing the soil with a little sand and earth, or decayed leaves. Sprinkle them three times a day until they have taken root, which will be in a few weeks. Keep the cuttings about four inches apart.

GENERAL OBSERVATIONS.

We do not consider that it is essential every month to repeat the necessity of tying up plants, cutting down weeds, raking, &c., with many other similar observations.

We have already been full on these subjects, and expect these to be remembered through the season. Particular care, however, is required to *carnations*, *pinks*, or any plants that have heavy heads and slender stems. If carnations are desired to flower strongly, cut off all the buds except three, leaving the uppermost and any other two of the largest. All climbing plants should have timely support, and tied securely every week while they are growing.

JUNE AND JULY.

HOLLAND BULBS.

THE lifting of these will be general in June. For directions, see *May*. It is not advisable to take up *Jonquils*, *Fritillària*, *Crocus*, and *Iris*, oftener than every alternate year. *Jonquils* may stand three years. *Anemones* and *Ranunculus* should be carefully lifted after their leaves begin to fade. Do not expose them to the sun, but cover slightly with earth or sand until they are perfectly dry, when they may be sifted out of the earth, and put into drawers carefully labeled. Some recommend to soak these roots in soap-suds, to destroy a worm with which they are frequently attacked. We know not how far this may be carried, nor the good or bad effects, never having practised it.

AUTUMN FLOWERING BULBS.

These are *Amaryllis lùtea*, now called *Sternbérgia lùtea; A. Belladónna*, now *Belladónna purpuráscens; Cròcus sativus, C. Pallàsii, C. serotìnus,* and *C. nudiflorus,* and all the species of *Cólchicum,* with species of several other genera not introduced into the country. They should all be lifted as soon as the foliage is decayed, and kept only a few weeks out of the ground, and then again replanted

in fresh soil. The economy of the genus *Cólchicum* in
regard to its bulbs, flowers, and seeds, is altogether singular, and may be termed an anomaly of nature. In producing the new bulbs or off-sets, in a very curious manner
the old one perishes. The flowers, which arise with long
slender tubes from the root, die off in October, without
leaving any external appearance of seeds. These lie
buried all the winter within the bulb; in spring they throw
up a fruit stalk, and are ripe about the first of June. How
beautiful and admirable is this provision! The plant
blooming so late in the year, would not have time to mature its seeds before winter; and is, therefore, so contrived
that it may be performed out of the reach of the usual
effects of frost, and they are brought above the surface
when perfected, and at a proper season for sowing.

CARNATIONS AND PINKS.

In order to make the former flower well, if the weather
is dry, give them frequent waterings at the root, and tie
them up neatly to their rods. *The criterion of a fine Carnation is*—The stem strong and straight, from thirty to
forty inches high, the corolla three inches in diameter, consisting of large, round, well formed petals, but not so many
as to crowd it, nor so few as to make it appear thin or
empty; the outside petals should rise above the calyx about
half an inch, and then turn off in a horizontal direction, to
support the interior petals, they forming nearly a hemispherical corolla. The interior petals should decrease in
size toward the centre, all regularly disposed on every
side; they should have a small degree of concavity at the
lamina or broad end, the edges perfectly entire. The calyx
above one inch in length, with strong broad points in a
close and circular body. The colours must be perfectly
distinct, disposed in regular long stripes, broadest at the
edge of the lamina, and gradually becoming narrower as
they approach the unguis or base of the petal, there termi-
nating in a fine point. Those that contain two colours
upon a white ground are esteemed the finest.

The criterion of a double pink.—The stem about twelve
inches, the calyx smaller, but similar to a carnation; the

flower two inches and a half in diameter; petals rose edges; colour white and pure purple, or rich crimson; the nearer it approaches to black the more is it esteemed; proportions equal as in carnation. Those that are very tasteful with these flowers are attentive to the manner of their opening. Where the calyx is deficient in regular expansion, to display the petals; that is, where there is a tendency to burst open on one side more than on the other, the opposite side in two or three different indentations should be slit a little at several times with the point of a small sharp knife, taking care not to cut the petals, and about the centre of the calyx tie a thread three or four times round to prevent any further irregularity. Some florists and connoisseurs place cards on them. This is done when the calyx is small. Take a piece of thin pasteboard, about the size of a dollar, cut a small aperture in its centre to admit the bud to pass through. When on, tie it tight to the rod, to prevent the wind from blowing it about; and when the flower is expanded, draw up the card to about the middle of the calyx, and spread the petals one over the other regularly upon it. When these plants are in flower, their beauty may be prolonged by giving them a little shade from the mid-day sun by an awning of any simple description. Where they are in pots, they can be removed to a cool shady situation (but not directly under trees).

OF LAYING CARNATIONS AND PINKS.

This is a necessary and yearly operation to keep a supply of plants, and likewise to have them always in perfection. As the process of laying, though simple, may not be known to all who are desirous of cultivating these plants, we will give an outline of the mode of operation. Provide first a quantity of small hooked twigs, (pieces of *Asparagus* stems are very suitable,) about three inches long, for pegging the layers down in the earth. Select the outward, strongest and lowest shoots that are round the plant; trim off a few of the under leaves, and shorten the top ones even with the knife, and then applying it at a joint about the middle of the under side of the shoot, cut about half through in a slanting direction, making an up-

10*

ward slit toward the next joint, near an inch in extent; and
loosening the earth, make a small oblong cavity one or two
inches deep, putting a little fresh light earth therein. Lay
the stem part where the slit is made into the earth, keeping the cut part open, and the head of the layer upright
one or two inches out of the earth; and in that position
peg down the layer with one of the hooked twigs, and
cover the inserted part to the depth of one inch with some
of the fresh earth, pressing it gently down. In this manner proceed to lay all the proper shoots of each plant.
Keep the earth a little full around the plant, to retain
longer the water that may be applied. Give immediately
a moderate watering, with a rose watering-pot, and in dry
weather give light waterings every evening. Choose a
cloudy day for the above operation. In about two months
they will be well rooted.

OF BUDDING OR INOCULATION OF ROSES.

According to what we have previously hinted in regard
to having roses as standards, where such are desired, the
month of July or August is a proper time for the operation of budding. The kinds to be taken for stocks should
be of a strong free growth: such as *Maiden's blush*, *Dutch
tree*, *R. villòsa*, *R. canina*, and frequently the *French Eglantine* are taken. Be provided with a proper budding
knife, which has a sharp, thin blade, adapted to prepare
the bud, with a tapering ivory haft, made thin at the end,
for raising the bark of the stock. For tyings, use bass
strings from Russia mats, which should be soaked in water
to make them more pliable. The height of the stock or
stem at which the bud is to be inserted, is to be determined
by the intended destination of the tree (as it may be properly called). Choose a smooth part of the stem, from one
to three years old. Having marked the place, prune away
all the lateral shoots about and underneath it. With the
knife directed horizontally, make an incision about half an
inch long in the bark of the stock, cutting to the wood, but
not deeper; then applying the point of the knife to the
middle of this line, make a perpendicular incision under
the first, extending from it between one and two inches.

Having a healthy shoot of the growth of this year provided of the kind that is desired, begin at the lower end of this shoot, cut away all the leaves, leaving the footstalk of each. Being fixed on a promising bud, insert the knife about half an inch above the eye, slanting it downward, and about half through the shoot. Draw it out about an inch below the eye, so as to bring away the bud unimpaired with the bark, and part of the wood adhering to it; the wood now must be carefully detached from the bark. To do this, insert the point of the knife between the bark and wood at one end, and, holding the bark tenderly, strip off the woody part, which will readily part from the bark, if the shoot from which the piece is taken has been properly imbued with sap.* Look at the inner rind of the separated bark, to see if that be entire: if there be a hole in it, the eye of the bud has been pulled away with the wood, rendering the bud useless, which throw away; if there be no hole, return to the stock, and with the haft of the knife gently raise the bark on each side of the perpendicular incision, opening the lips wide enough to admit the prepared slip with the eye. If the slip is longer than the upright incision in the stock, reduce the largest end. Stock and bud being ready, keep the latter in its natural position; introduce it between the bark and wood of the stock, pushing it gently downward until it reaches the bottom of the perpendicular incision. Let the eye of the bud project through the centre of the lips; lay the slip with the bud as smooth as possible, and press down the raised bark of the stock. The bud being deposited, bind that part of the stock moderately tight with bass, beginning a little below the incision, proceeding upward so as to keep the eye uncovered, finishing above the incision. In a month after the operation, examine whether the bud has united with the stock. If it has succeeded, the bud will be full and fresh; if not, it will be brown and contracted. When it has taken, untie the bandage, that the bud may swell, and in a few days afterwards cut the head of the stock off about

* We once budded three eyes of the white moss rose, after they had, by mistake, been carried in the pocket of a coat three days. The shoot was soaked six hours in water, and two of the buds grew. From this we infer that shoots, if properly wrapped up, may be carried very great distances, and grow successfully.

six inches above the inoculation, and prevent all shoots from growing by pinching them off. This will forward the bud, which will push and ripen wood this season; but it must be carefully tied as it grows to the remaining head of the stock. Some do not head down the stock until the following spring, thereby not encouraging the bud to grow, which, if winter sets in early, is the safest method.

OF WATERING.

If the season be dry, look over the lately planted shrubs, and give them frequent copious waterings; and a few of the finest annuals that are wanted to flower perfectly should be attended to. We do confess that we used to be advocates for giving plenty of water to the Dahlia, but the severe drought of 1838 put our science to the test, and the result was, that of about one hundred plants of our most choice kinds, which we regularly watered three times a week, for nine weeks, during which period we had not a drop of rain, the plants grew luxuriantly, but many of them never produced a perfect bloom; and those that had no attention whatever paid to them, except a little manure or litter laid on the surface over the roots, flowered almost as well as in our more moist seasons. Hence we infer that an occasional watering may be of service, but continued and repeated artificial waterings are injurious.

AUGUST.

EVERGREEN HEDGES.

These always make two growths in the season, and the best time to perform the operation of clipping or dressing them is before the plants begin their second growth. Choose, if possible, dull and cloudy days, as in such weather they will not be so liable to get brown or bruised by shearing. The general practice in forming these is to have the sides even and the top level, forming a right angle on each side. However neat in appearance this may be considered, it certainly is stiff and formal. We never approve of clipping where it can be avoided, and, when adopted, nature ought to be imitated. Therefore, have all hedges and edgings tapering toward the top.

CARNATIONS AND PINKS,

If laid about the end of June, and have been properly attended, will, by the end of this month, be well rotted and fit for transplanting. Clear away the earth lightly, and cut them clean off from the parent plant, nearer the stool than the original slit. Raise them neatly out of the earth, with as many of the root-fibres as possible; cut off the naked part of the stem close to the fibrous roots, and trim away the strangling leaves. Plant the finest sorts in four-inch pots, and those more common, three plants in five-inch pots, in the form of a triangle, which can be separated in spring to plant in the garden. Any of the principal stools should be (if in the ground) lifted and put into seven-inch pots to be preserved: the others may be allowed to stand through the winter, covering them with a few dry leaves. Keep them in the shade a few weeks, when they may be fully exposed. Give gentle and frequent sprinklings of water until they have taken fresh root; or, if in want of pots, mark out a bed that can be covered with a frame, preparing the soil therein properly. Plant them from four to six inches apart. Shade them from the sun until they begin to grow, giving sprinklings of water over the foliage every evening.

BULBOUS ROOTS.

Look over the bulbs that are out of the ground, and examine those that require planting. Of *Fritillària* there are about twenty species, but few of them generally cultivated, except *F. imperiàlis*, Crown Imperial, and *F. pérsica*. Of the former there are many very splendid varieties, such as

Crown upon crown, *Lutea Maxima*, *Striped leaved*, *Double flowered*, &c. These will require planting, and ought not to be lifted oftener than every third year. They require a deep, rich, loamy soil, and, if in beds, plant them from five to seven inches deep, and one foot apart. They will grow under the shade of trees, or in any situation where the soil is adapted for them. No imbricated or scaly bulb ought to be retained long out of the ground. When any of these are lifted, and the young bulbs taken off, they should be planted at once. See particularly, on bulbous roots in general, next month.

SOWING SEEDS OF BULBOUS ROOTS.

Where any seeds of these are saved, with the intention of sowing, let it be done this month. Procure boxes about seven inches deep, and, in size, proportioned to the quantity to be sown. Put five inches of light sandy soil in the box, level it smoothly, and sow the seeds separately and thickly; cover with half an inch of light sandy loam, with a portion of earth from the woods. Keep the box or boxes in a sheltered situation, giving frequent sprinklings of water, to keep the earth damp, which must be protected with a frame, or covered with leaves during winter. The plants will appear in the spring, and must be watered and kept in the shade: when the leaves decay in June, put one inch more soil upon them, and the second year they can be planted with the small off-sets in the garden, and treated as other bulbs. They must be carefully marked every year. Tulips require several years of trial before their qualities are known; and a poor soil is best suited to produce their characters after the first bloom.

SEPTEMBER,

OF DAHLIAS.

SEE that all these plants are supported with proper
stakes, rods, &c., that the wind may have no effect in
breaking down or otherwise destroying the flower stems.
Strictly observe their respective heights and colours, that
they may be duly disposed and interspersed next year, if
not done so this.   Attend particularly to the merits of those
grown from seed.

GENERAL CARE OF PLANTS IN POTS.

All the flowers that are in pots, and intended to be kept
in frames during winter should have a top-dressing and a
general preparation for their winter quarters, by tying up,
&c.   The carnation and pink layers that were lifted and
potted last month, must be brought from the shade as soon
as they begin to grow, and those that are not lifted, have
them done forthwith, that they may be rooted afresh before
the frost sets in.   All Wall-flowers and Stocks should be
lifted about the end of this month, and planted in five to
seven inch pots, and treated as directed for carnation layers
last month, until they begin to grow, when they must be
fully exposed.

PREPARE BEDS AND BORDERS FOR BULBOUS ROOTS.

Bulbous roots of every character delight in deep free
soil; consequently, wherever they are desired to be planted,
due attention must be paid to put the soil in proper order,
to have them in perfection.   Where there is a quantity
intended to be planted, to have them in beds is the general
and preferable method.   These ought to be dug from
eighteen inches to two feet deep, at the bottom of which
place three or four inches of decayed manure.   Where

the soil is poor it should be enriched with well decomposed
manure, and earth from the woods, incorporating both well
with the soil, breaking it all fine. This being done, allow
it to stand until the middle of next month, which see for
farther directions.

GENERAL OBSERVATIONS.

Tie up carefully all the *Chrysánthemums, Tuberoses,*
&c. Clear away the stems or haulm of any decayed
annuals or herbaceous plants, that nothing unsightly may
appear. Propagate the *Pansy* by layers, &c. See page
94.

SOWING AND SAVING SEEDS.

About the end of this month or beginning of next is an
advisable period to sow seed of *Delphinium Ajácis flòre
plèno,* or Double Rocket Larkspur. This plant does not
flower in perfection unless sown in autumn, and grown a
little above ground before winter; when a few leaves can
be lightly thrown among them, but not to cover them entirely, or a few branches thickly laid on will answer as
well. There are several other annuals that bloom more
early and much finer by being sown about this period:
such as *Gília, Coreópsis, Centaurèa, Clárkia, Collínsia,*
&c. Be attentive in collecting and saving all kinds of
seeds, and have them correctly named, with the year in
which they were grown.

The finer kinds of Pansy seeds that may have been collected during the season, should now be sown in a rich,
free, loamy soil, and in a situation where they can be
covered during winter with a temporary frame of boards:
although they are perfectly hardy, yet they will bloom earlier and more superb in the spring by having a slight protection.

OCTOBER.

OF PLANTING VARIOUS BULBOUS AND TUBEROUS ROOTS.

FROM the first of October to the middle of November is the best period for a general planting of bulbs, corns, and tubers, which, if the ground has been prepared, as formerly directed, will now be in readiness. We will give the names and descriptions of a few of the leading sorts.

Anemòne hortènsis. The cultivation of this tuber has been attended with less satisfaction than any other floral plant that has been introduced into this country. The general failure may, in part, be attributed to the very inferior roots annually sent from Holland, which rarely arrive in good order, and those that do grow, are very discouraging, never making a tuber sufficient for another year's planting. Several hundred varieties are cultivated in England with great care and complete success. They are planted in a deep rich soil, using a considerable portion of cow manure and decomposed leaves, covering the crowns of the roots about two inches. The tubes are flat, but the eye from whence the flower-stem arises is apparent on one of the sides, which must be laid uppermost. During the severity of winter, they should be protected by a frame, and have a sprinkling of very dry leaves strewn among them.

Cròcus. There are upwards of one hundred varieties of this vernal flower in cultivation, attended with universal success. They delight in rich soils, and may either be planted in beds or rows, at least two inches deep, and six inches from row to row—they seldom require removal; every three or four years will be sufficient. They can be purchased at from seventy-five cents to two dollars per hundred, according to quality. When they are done blooming, the foliage should not be removed till perfectly decayed.

Fritillària, or Crown Imperial. See last month.

11

Hyacinths. The ground that was prepared for these last month, should all be divided into beds four feet wide, leaving between each alleys of twenty inches. Skim off four or five inches of the surface of the former into the latter, level the bed smoothly with the rake, and mark it off in rows eight inches apart. Plant the roots in the row eight inches asunder. Thus they will be in squares, and by planting the different colours, alternately, the bed will be beautifully diversified. Cover each bulb with sand, when it can be procured. Put about four inches of earth over the crowns, which will make the beds from two to three inches higher than the alleys. The beds, before and after planting, should be gently rounded from the middle to each side, to let the rain pass off. Finish all by raking evenly, straighten the edgings with the line, and clear out the alleys or pathways.

We have grown Hyacinths in great perfection—when, in addition to the above, we covered them with two to three inches of cow manure. The Dutch florists name nearly two thousand varieties of this flower, and have large fields devoted to their culture. When the double varieties were first brought into notice, they sold at from one to two thousand guilders a root, (about from four to eight hundred dollars.) The finer kinds can be purchased at from two to four dollars per dozen.

Iris, or Fleur de luce. The English and Parisian irises are coming into repute as showy garden flowers. They will grow in any well prepared soil, and require to be planted in the same manner as the tulip.

Jonquils. Double and single. Plant these in the same soil as *Tulips,* six inches apart, and cover three inches deep. They do not flower so well the first year as in the second and third, therefore should only be lifted every third year.

Lilium. The family of Lilies are all splendid, very interesting, and easy of culture, requiring merely a good deep loamy soil—no wise inclined to moisture. They are all hardy, except *L. japònicum* and *L. longiflòrum,* which we lift in November, and again plant them about the first of March, keeping them through the winter in dry sand, in a cellar free from frost. The hardy kinds, deserving most attention, are *L. Cándidum,* (the double variety of it is not worth growing,) *L. Chalcedónicum*, and its varieties, *L. Tigrìnum. L. Cóncolor* and *L. Mártagon;* these, with the species indigenous to this country, are all very beautiful. They should be planted from three to five inches deep, according to the size of the bulb, and need not be taken up oftener than once in every three or four years. None of the species can be transplanted after they have grown, without injuring their flowering.

Narcìssus require treatment similar to the Lily, except the soil, which must be richer, and even then they do not bloom so finely in a few years as they do when first imported; but they are cheap, and can annually be procured.

Pæònias are all magnificent in flower, and, for display, are not surpassed by any spring blooming plant; and we do cheerfully urge our readers to cultivate the choice sorts, which can scarcely be said to have a rival. Such are—

P. Moután Bánksii, common double blush tree Pæonia.

P. Moután papaverácea, single white tree Pæonia, with purple centre.

P. Moután ròsea, large rose, semi-double tree Pæonia.

P. Moután odoráta, sweet-scented, rose-coloured tree Pæonia.

P. Moután albida pleno, double white tree Pæonia.

P. èdulis albiflòra, single white herbaceous Pæonia.

P. èdulis whitlèji, superb double white herbaceous Pæonia.

P. èdulis Hùmei, very large double rose herbaceous Pæonia.

P. èdulis frágrans, double red, sweet-scented herbaceous Pæonia.

P. èdulis Réevesiana, Chinese double crimson herbaceous Pæonia.

P. officinàlis rùbra, common double herbaceous Pæonia.

P. officinàlis atropurpùrea, very dark crimson herbaceous Pæonia.

P. officinàlis álbicans, changeable white rose, or blush herbaceous Pæonia.

There are several other splendid double varieties in some rare collections of Europe, which have not yet made their appearance in general culture. There are also a few very choice single kinds that are desirable for growing to raise new sorts from; for it is from the single species that the Chinese have been so successful in procuring the magnificent double varieties, which are so anxiously and perseveringly sought for. The seeds mature well in this country, and should be sown as soon as ripe; they will vegetate the following spring, and in three years may be expected to bloom. The Pæony will grow in any rich loamy soil, which should be at least fifteen inches deep. An eastern situation or aspect is best adapted for them in this latitude; but in the more southern states, they will display their flowers better on a northern aspect, or where they will be shaded from the sun, but not under the dripping of trees. The most suitable time for planting them is in September, October, or November. Spring-planted roots never succeed well the first year. Pæony moutan and its varieties are all of a shrubby nature, and will grow into large bushes, producing from fifty to one hundred blooms of not less than fifteen inches in circumference; they can be propagated by division of the root, or by layers.

Tulips. As this flower will soon be a decided favourite over this mighty country, we will give a minute description of the soil most genial to it, at the same time remarking that it will grow in almost any soil or situation, though less perfect. Many of the kinds are of the most splendid colours and strong in growth, frequently growing over three feet in height, with *cups* sufficiently large to satisfy the greatest *Bacchus*. All writers agree that Tulip beds should be "four feet wide;" though I think three and a half will be found more convenient, and, in length, according to the number of roots to be planted. The soil should consist of good fresh loam, mixed with a small portion of well rotted stable manure, at least two years old. The whole should be incorporated together four months previous to using. The common soil should be taken out sixteen inches deep, and filled with the above compost. Raise the beds not less than three inches above the paths at the outside, and about six or eight inches in the middle; this convexity will assist in throwing off the water in times of heavy and continued rains. The bed thus formed, plant the bulbs in rows, lengthwise on the bed, about six inches from bulb to bulb, and seven inches from row to row. The bed may be marked out by straining a line very tight, lengthwise on the bed, and beating it with the back of the spade, leaving a lined groove along the ground. Then, with a lath four feet long, let the bed be marked across at six inches distance, so as to leave distinct impressions at each crossing of the ground lines; for these will form the spots where the bulbs are to be planted, by means of a dibber, made larger than the largest bulb, and flattened at the end. The holes are to be made four inches deep, and about half an inch of sharp sand ought to be dropped in each. The centre line ought to be planted with the tallest kinds, and the outside of the bed with the lowest. In severe frosts they should be protected by boards or branches. Tulips have ever been held in the highest estimation. As early as 1637 history records one hundred and twenty Tulips being sold at public auction for no less a sum than nine thousand guilders, equal to thirty-six hundred dollars; and, in England, at the present day, a good collection is valued at five thousand dollars. Florists generally divide them into three classes, viz.: first, *Bybloemens*, such as have a white ground, variegated with purple, as *Bienfait* or *Washington*, &c.; secondly, *Bizarres*, having a yellow ground, variegated with scarlet, purple, rose, or velvet, as *Trafalgar, Duc de Savoie*, &c.; and, thirdly, Roses with white ground, variegated with rose, scarlet, or crimson, as *La Tendresse, Rose mignonne*, &c.

The superb kinds are often very expensive; even fifty pounds sterling is frequently given for a single bulb; and we doubt much if these high-priced kinds are finer than *Washington, Milo*, or *Trafalgar*, which, with many others, can be procured for less than one dollar each.

PLANTING AND TRANSPLANTING.

This is a very proper period to plant the beautiful and early flowering *Pyrus japónica*, now called *Cydónia japónica*. The blossoms are of a rich scarlet colour. It is the earliest flowering shrub of the garden, and deciduous, though said by some to be " an evergreen." The plant is bushy, and well adapted for single plants in grass plats, or forming low ornamental hedges.   There is likewise *C. j. álba*, a fine blush variety of the same habit, and both are of the hardiest nature.

Double Primroses, Polyanthus, Daisies, &c.   Any of these that were planted in shaded situations in spring, and have been preserved through the summer, should have for their farther protection a bed well sheltered from the north-west, in which they should be planted four inches apart. Give them a few sprinklings of water in the morning, and have a temporary frame of rough boards put together to place over them during the severity of winter.   The frame may be covered with the same in place of glass, which must be kept over them while they are in a frozen state.

Any other plants that are in the ground, which are in-tended to be protected with frames through the winter, ought to be immediately lifted and potted, and treated as directed for all new-potted plants.

GRASS AND GRAVEL WALKS.

The former should be trimly cut and well rolled this month, that they may appear neat all winter.   Never allow decayed leaves to lie any time upon them, as they are apt to rot out the grass.   The latter should be divested of every weed, and receive a firm rolling.   Clear them at all times of leaves and other litter.   These, if on a declivity, and have not a firm substantial bottom, will be subject to be cut up with every heavy rain.   A break should be put in every twenty, forty, or eighty feet to throw off the water. A strong plank will answer perfectly well, but in such situations we would prefer grass walks.

PLANTING EVERGREENS.

This month is the best period in autumn to plant these shrubs; and where there is a great extent to be planted, it would be advisable to do a part of it now; but we give the preference to April, which see for directions.

GENERAL OBSERVATIONS.

When the plantings of bulbs, &c., are finished, every part of the garden should have a thorough cleaning. All annual flowers will have passed the season of their beauty; therefore, remove the decayed flower stems or haulm, and trim off the borders. Dig all vacant ground, especially that intended to be planted with shrubs in the ensuing spring, which ought to be dug from one to two feet deep.

NOVEMBER.

DAHLIAS.

IT is not advisable to delay lifting the roots of the Dahlia after the first of the month, as frequently severe frosts set in about this period, and would totally destroy them. Choose a dry day for the purpose, and with a spade carefully lift every root, divesting it of any earth that may adhere thereto, but not to shake it off, as thereby the neck of the tubers would be bruised, and probably entirely destroy the vitality of the plant for the coming season. With us, the frost generally destroys the foliage and stems of the plants from about the middle of October to the beginning of the present month. The stems should then be cut to within a few inches of the ground: when the roots should be lifted directly thereafter, and the labels properly secured to them with metallic wire. Many opinions are given for the best method of securing them during winter from the effects of frost, which is their certain destruction. In this country, a dry close cellar, that will retain a temperature of not less than thirty-five degrees, and not over forty-five, will be the most proper place: if the tubers are small, they should be covered with dry sand or earth. The method we have adopted with our finest kinds, which has resulted in complete success, is to lay dry boards on the cellar-floor, and place the roots closely thereon, covering them to the stem with dry sand, laying mats over all: in this manner they preserve till spring in the most perfect order. They can also be kept in a cool green-house; but must be protected from drippings of water falling upon them.

TUBEROSES, TIGRIDIAS AND AMARYLLIS.

These tubers and bulbs, as soon as the frost has partly injured the foliage, should be taken up, and dried thoroughly in the sun, taking care, at all times, to keep them clear from frost. When they are dry, divest them of their foliage and fibres, and pack them in boxes with dry sand or moss. Store these away for the winter, either in a room or a dry cellar, where they will, at all times, be exempt from frost, the least touch of which would destroy them. We have kept them completely secure in the cellar.

ERYTHRINAS.

Where there any plants of *E. herbàcea, E. laurifòlia*, and *E. crista-gálla*, which are intended to be lifted, they should be carefully done and preserved in half dry earth, and kept beside the *Dáhlias*. They are magnificent ornaments in the flower garden.

PRIMROSES, POLYANTHUS AND DAISIES,

That were planted in a sheltered spot, as directed last month, should have a frame placed over them, and their covering in readiness for the approach of winter; giving the plants a light covering of leaves, which will preserve their foliage from the effects of frost.

CHOICE CARNATIONS, PINKS, PANSIES AND AURI-
CULAS,

That are in pots, should be placed in the frame intended for their abode during winter. If the pots are plunged to the rims in dry leaves or saw-dust, it will greatly protect their roots from the severe effects of frost. Where glass is used for these frames, they should have besides a covering of boards or straw mats ; those that are in beds may be covered as above directed for Primroses, &c.

They ought not to be uncovered while in a frozen state. It is not altogether the intensity of cold that destroys these plants so much as the alternate thawing and freezing.

All half hardy plants, such as *Wall-flower German stocks, Sweet-bay,* tender roses, with several others, should be protected as above directed for Carnations. Earth or tan should be put round the outside of these frames, which will be a partial shelter from the changing state of the atmosphere. Oak leaves answer the purpose very well, but they are a harbour for all kinds of vermin, especially rats and mice, which would destroy every thing. It may be useful to say a few words on the nature of tan or tanner's bark. Many suppose that the smallest quantity will produce heat. If three or four cart loads of it are put into one heap, and protected from the rain, it will ferment; and when the first fermentation is abated, by mixing it with leaves, a substantial hot-bed may be made, or put it by itself into a pit; and, when there is no pit, boards may be substituted to keep it together : either of these methods will produce a lasting heat. But in small quantities, and exposed to rain, &c., no heat will be produced, but rather the contrary. It is excellent, when dry, in keeping out frost from any plants ; being a body not easily penetrated, similar to dry sand, saw-dust, or dry leaves. Frequently the same opinion is held in regard to stable manure, small portions of which will never produce heat.

OF PROTECTING PLANTS IN THE GARDEN.

During this or next month, according to the state of the season, protect all the plants that are in the ground, which are not completely hardy. The coverings may be straw, Russia mats, canvas, boxes or barrels. The two latter must be perforated in the top, to let the damp air pass off, or the plant would become musty and decay. Those covered with straw or mats should have small stakes placed round the plants, and covering tied thereto, and remain so until the month of March or first of April. Herbaceous plants that are tender, may be covered with three or four inches of tan, saw-dust, or half decayed leaves, which will tend greatly to preserve their roots. These coverings must be carefully removed on the first opening of spring. The shrubs that are otherwise covered would be greatly benefited by having their roots protected in a similar manner, as directed for herbaceous plants.

PROTECTION OF SEEDLING BULBS.

If any seeds of *Hyacinths, Tulips,* or *Fritillàra,* were sown in pots or boxes, let them be removed to a dry, sheltered situation, and plunged level with the ground; or fill the spaces between them with dry leaves or tanner's bark, and cover the whole with new-fallen leaves, laying over all a few boards to prevent the wind blowing them off. These form better coverings than straw or haulm, which is liable to become musty, and communicate the effect to the roots. The above covering is not required until the approach of severe frost.

OF PLANTING DECIDUOUS TREES AND SHRUBS.

It is not recommendable to make a general planting of these at this period of the year; the success entirely depending on the nature of the season and the state of the soil. If any are planted, let them be those of the hardiest nature, and in light and absorbent soil, not subject to be stagnated or over-flooded during winter. When this and next month are mild, autumn plantings are very frequently as sure as those of the spring. But the precarious state of the season is not to be depended upon, therefore avoid large plantings of any kind, and more especially of delicate roses, the roots of which are apt to rot off, except they have been previously grown in pots. Nothing can be more injurious to a plant, at this season particularly, than to bed its roots in mortar, by which the tender fibres either perish or are cramped ever afterward. The soil at the time of planting should be so friable as not to adhere to the spade, which is a good rule in planting at any season, or in any soil.

GENERAL OBSERVATIONS.

Carry out of the garden all decayed leaves and litter of every description, cutting down any weeds that remain. Collect all the stakes and rods that have been supporting plants, tie them up in bundles for the use of next year, and put them under cover. Look over every part of the garden, and see that nothing has been omitted in the way of covering or other protection. The sashes that are to be used on the frames should be perfectly whole, every interstice in the glass puttied, and all ready for use when occasion may require. Attend to all plants in pots, and give them gentle waterings as they stand in need; but never during the time the soil is frozen about the roots.

DECEMBER.

GENERAL OBSERVATIONS.

HAVING in the preceding months under this head given details for the protection of plants of a delicate nature, and the forwarding of necessary work, only a few remarks remain to be added. If there is any part therein described omitted, have it done forthwith: every day increases the danger of severe weather. If there are doubts of any plants or shrubs not standing without some light covering, it is best to err on the side of safety. Valuable plants on walls, and in danger of being destroyed, it is advisable to be at the expense of having a frame made to surround them, and cover the same with oil-cloth. The frame thus covered, should be taken off in mild weather, and replaced again when necessary, causing very little trouble; and, if properly taken care of, will last many years. Coverings of any construction, and of the same material, would answer for any part of the garden, and are the best in our opinion that could be adopted.

THE

AMERICAN FLOWER GARDEN

DIRECTORY.

HOT-HOUSE.

ON THE CONSTRUCTION OF A HOT-HOUSE.

THERE have been many plans devised and visionary
projects offered to the public as the best for a well-regulated hot-house. As we intend forming one for practical
purposes, we shall adopt a convenient size, have flues for
the conveyance of heat, and coal or wood for fuel.

Site and Aspect.—The house should stand on a situation
naturally dry, and, if possible, sheltered from the north-
west, and clear from all shade on the south, east, and west,
so that the sun may at all times act effectually upon the
house. The standard principle, as to aspect, is to set the
front directly to the south. Any deviation from that point
should incline to the east.

Dimensions.—The length may be from ten feet upward; but, if beyond forty feet, the number of fires and
flues are multiplied. The medium width is from twelve
to sixteen feet. Our directions will apply to the two extreme points, viz.: forty feet by sixteen, and in height, at
back, from twelve to eighteen feet; the height in front six
feet, including about three feet in brick basement, to support the front glass, which will be two and a half feet,
allowing six inches for frame-work.

Furnace and Flues.—It is of great importance to have
these erected in such a manner as will effectually heat the

12

house. The greatest difficulty is to have the furnace to
draw well. As workmen are not generally conversant on
the subject, nor yet understand the effect or distribution of
heat in these departments, we will give minute details on
their construction. The furnace should be outside of the
house, either at back or end ; the former is preferable, circumstances not always allowing it on the other plan. Dig
out the furnace-hole, or what is termed stock-hole, about
five feet deep. Let the door of the furnace be in the back
wall of the house, thereby having all the heated building
inside, that no heat may be lost. The brick-work round
the furnace should be nine inches thick, laying the inside
with fire-brick. Around the outside leave a vacuum two
or three inches wide, to allow the heat to arise from around
the furnace into the interior of the house, thereby saving
the whole heat of the fuel. The furnace will require to be
two and a half feet long, ten inches wide, and one foot
high, before the spring of the arch and clear of the bars ;
leave one foot for an ash-pit, then lay the bars. They
should be sixteen inches long, one inch broad on the upper
side, two inches deep, and two-eights broad on the lower
side, and, with the door and frame, should be cast iron.
Half an inch between each bar will be sufficient. The
flue should rise from the furnace by a steep declivity of
from twenty inches to two feet, and pass the door of the
house, (without a dip,) when it must be elevated above the
level of the floor of the house along the front, and at the
opposite end of the house must dip to pass the door. The
dip must not be lower than the bottom of the flue at the
neck of the furnace, and should be of a concave form,
(avoiding acute angles.) Lead it along the back to enter
the wall over the furnace. When thus taken round the
house, the heat will be expanded before it enters the chimney. The inside of the flues should be from six to ten
inches wide, and eight inches deep; plaster the bottom of
it, but no other part, as plaster is partially a non-conductor.
The above description is for burning anthracite coal; but
where wood is to be the fuel, the furnace must be one-half
larger. We have been particular in the description of
furnace bars, as those generally used are miserable substitutes. Circumstances may cause the furnace to be placed
at the end or front of the house. In either case the stock

hole will not require to be so deep; or where there is only one door in the house, a stock-hole three and a half feet deep will be enough, which should be built like a cellar, to keep out any under water. In all instances pass the first flue to the front of the house, over which have a close table, covered with two inches of sand, and, by keeping it moist, will afford a very congenial heat to young and valuable plants. Likewise over the furnace have a frame in the same manner, which will be found useful for propagating. Any part of the furnace or flue that is under the floor of the house, should have a vacuity on both sides to let the heat pass upward.

Furnaces and flues on the above construction are the most simple in arrangement, and the easiest to manage at all times. But where capital, taste, and practical science can be united, a more elegant disposition of heating convenience can be adopted: an excavation should be made for the flue to pass along under the pathway, which pathway may be a casting of iron, or wooden slats, fancifully put together, and at least six inches above the flue. In building the furnace, place thereon a boiler of cast-iron or copper, about two feet deep, two feet long, and four inches wide, with a zinc or copper lid: having it prepared to receive two pipes, one near the bottom and the other about four inches from the top: these pipes may be from four to six inches in diameter, and are to be taken along under the table in front of the house, in a level position, and, at the end of the house, joined together by a perpendicular pipe, or joint which should have an end about one foot higher than the highest part of the upper pipe. When all is properly fixed, fill the boiler with rain or river water, if possible: the air in the pipes will pass out at the perpendicular end, and, when all are full, put a perforated cover on the end of the pipe. As soon as the water becomes heated, it will arise from the bottom of the boiler, and pass along the upper pipe, and return cool by the under one. Or, in place of the pipe returning again by the front, it can pass all round the house, only there must be a piece of perpendicular pipe to allow the air to get out—the consumption of water will not be over half a gallon in twenty-four hours. If the pipes require to be higher than the boiler, the boiler cover must be hermetically sealed, and the filling operation conducted by the upright tube or pipe, which must always be full of water. This we consider the most economical method of heating by hot water, and it is by far the most simple—simple indeed in every part, though volumes have been written on the subject.

Park Pit.—We consider such an erection in the centre of a hot-house a nuisance, and prefer a stage, which may be constructed according to taste. It should be made of the best Carolina pine, leaving a passage all round, to cause a free circulation of air. The back and end paths may be about two feet wide, and the front three feet. The angle of the stage should be parallel with the glass, having the steps from six inches to one foot apart.

Where there are some large plants, they may stand on the floor behind the stage, or on tressels, according to their height.

Angle of the glazed Roof.—The pitch of the roof is usually varied to agree with the design of the house, and the size of the plants to be grown therein. Where pleasure and ornament are the principal objects, the angle should be about 33° from the level line; but a few degrees of inclination either way is of minor importance.

Materials for glazing Sashes.—Caroline pine is the best material for the wood-work, as it is not so subject to decay from moisture and heat as the other kinds of pine wood. The frames or sashes can be of any convenient length, not exceeding ten feet, and about three and a half or four feet wide, and made from plank two inches thick, divided so as they can be glazed with glass six inches wide.

Of Glazing.—The pieces of glass should not exceed six inches by eight, though six by six is preferable; the lappings about one quarter of an inch. The frames ought to have two coats of paint previous to glazing, and the glass bedded in putty. Some prefer the lappings to be puttied also. It is our opinion that in a hot-house these should not be puttied, but, in the green-house, the closer they can be made the better.

Of Shutters.—These should be made of three-quarters of an inch white pine, and bound on both ends and sides, having a cross piece in the middle of the same. They ought to be painted at least once in three years.

HOT-HOUSE.

JANUARY.

At all times be very careful of the temperature of this department, and more especially at this season of the year, as a few minutes' neglect might materially injure many of the delicate plants. The thermometer ought to range between 55° and 65°. In fine sunshine days admit a little air by having some of the top sashes let down one, two, or three inches, according to the weather, and let it always be done from eleven to one o'clock; but by no means in such a manner as to cause a draught in the interior of the house, which would be very prejudicial. Therefore, be always cautious during cold weather, in administering that necessary element to vegetation, which is so conducive to health.

OF FIRING AND FUEL.

The hot-house ought never to be left entirely to inexperienced persons, because they are not aware of what might be the result of inattention even for an hour. Attention to the following observations will obviate every difficulty: About this season of the year frost generally sets in very severe in the middle states. Suppose the day may have all the clemency of spring, the night may be directly the reverse. Every precaution is necessary to guard against extremes. The shutters are put on every night at sundown, and, in severe weather, as soon as the sun goes off the glass. If the shutters are omitted till late in severe frost, it will so reduce the heat of the house, that you cannot overcome it by fire until near midnight; and, when done, the fire or fires have been made more powerful than they ought to be, proving ungenial to the plants that are near the flues. The air, as above directed, having been taken off the house at one o'clock, as soon as the mercury begins to fall in the thermometer, kindle the fire, and, sup-

12*

posing it is anthracite coal, in twenty minutes, with a good
drawing furnace, the heat will operate in the house.   If a
coal fire, kindled about four o'clock, it will require an addition about six, and then may be made up again about nine
or ten, which will suffice until morning.   The quantity
must be regulated by the weather.   If the fuel is wood, it
must be attended to three or four times during the evening; and, when the mornings are intensely cold, a fire
may be requisite.   When there are bad drawing furnaces,
the fires must be made much earlier, perhaps by two or
three o'clock, which will be easily observed by the time
the fire takes effect upon the air of the house.   The temperature ought never to be under fifty degrees of Fahrenheit.

OF WATERING THE PLANTS.

To do this judiciously, is so necessary to vegetation, and
so requisite to understand, and yet the knowledge so difficult to convey to others, (being entirely acquired by practice,) that if the power were in man to impart to his fel-
low-men, he would possess the power of perfecting a
gardener by diction.   However, the hints on this important
point of floriculture will be as clear and expressive as can
at present be elicited.   All plants in this work that are
aquatic shall be specified as such; and those that are arid
shall be duly mentioned.   All others will come in the
medium.

All the plants must be looked over every day, and those
watered that appear to be getting dry on the top.   It must
be strictly observed not to give water to any but such as
strictly require it, and let it be given moderately at this
season.   There is not so much liability to err, at present,
in giving too little, as in administering too much.   Vegetation among the stove or hot-house plants will soon begin
to show, and the soil will become sour if it is impregnated
with stagnant moisture.   Small plants should always be
watered with a pot having what is termed a rose upon it.
The surface of the rose, that is, where it is perforated with
small apertures, ought to be level, or a little concave, which
would convey the water more to a centre, and make neater

work, by preventing any water from being unnecessarily
spilt in the house. The size of the pot will be regulated
by the person to suit the conveniences of the place. Water,
when applied either to the roots or foliage of the plants,
should be about the medium temperature of the house.
Where there are no cisterns, a tank or barrel might be in
the house, in which the water could stand for one night or
more, as is most suitable. When water is given without
being thus aired, it chills the roots, prevents a luxuriant
growth, injures the fresh and healthful appearance of the
foliage, and too frequently gives to all the plants a sickly
hue.

OF INSECTS, THEIR DESTRUCTION, &c.

In this department insects begin to increase by hundreds, and too frequently their ravages are very obvious
before their progress is arrested. We will treat of those
which are most common, under their respective heads, with
their nature and cure, as far as has come under our observation.

Aphis rosæ, of the natural order of Hemiptera, or what
is commonly known by Green Fly, Green Lice, &c., in-
fect plants in general, and are particularly destructive in
the hot-house to *Hibíscus ròsa-sinénsis*, *Asclépias*, *Cràssula coccínea*, *Lantána*, &c., and many other plants of a
free-growing nature. They attack the young and tender
shoots at the point, leaving a dark filthy appearance on the
foliage. Many remedies for their destruction have been
offered to the public by various writers, each equally
secure in his own opinion. Extensive practice alone can
show the most easy and effectual cure. Fumigating with
tobacco is decidedly the most efficacious, and in the power
of any to perform. Take a small circular furnace, made
of sheet iron, diameter at top twelve inches, and at bottom
eight; depth one foot, having a grating in it to reach within three inches of the bottom, which will leave space for
the air to pass, and where the ashes will fall and be kept
in safety, having a handle like a pail to carry it with.
This, or any thing similar, being ready, put in it a few
embers of charcoal, ignited to redness; take it into the

centre of the house, and put therein a quantity of moist tobacco. If it attempts to blaze or flame, sprinkle a little water thereon; and, as it consumes, continue to add tobacco until the house is entirely full of smoke, observing always to do it in still, cloudy weather, or in the evening. If it is windy, the smoke is carried off without having half the effect, and requires more tobacco. The house must be closely shut up. There are several plants whose foliage is of a soft downy nature, such as *Helitròpiums*, *Callacárpus*, *Sálvias*, and many of the *Lantànas*, *Vincas*, with several others that cannot stand strong fumigation without danger. These should be put down in the house, or under the stage. These fumigations will have to be repeated frequently, the time for which will easily be perceived; and, when required, ought not to be delayed. Several species and varieties of the same genus, *Aphis*, can be destroyed in the like manner.

Acaris tellurius, or red spider, is caused by a dry atmosphere, and its havoc generally is obvious before it is arrested. With its proboscis it wounds the fine capillary vessels of the leaves. If they progress in their destructive work, the leaves will prematurely decay. On this appearance, turn up the leaf, and you will see them running about with incredible swiftness. Their body is of a blood colour, and their feet light red. When very numerous, they work thick webs on the under side of the leaf, and frequently all over it, forming a mass of half died plants, decayed leaves, and thousands of spiders. The most effectual remedy is a thorough syringing with water, and profusely under the foliage. This being done every evening, will subdue and eventually banish them. Had the house been syringed two or three times per week, these intruders would not have appeared. It is said by some writers, that watering only reduces them to a temporary state of inaction, and will not destroy them. Laying aside the many prescribed nostrums, we assert that the pure element is the most effectual cure, as well as the most easy to be obtained.*

Thrips, order *Hemiptera*, are insects so minute as

---

* Fumes of sulphur is instant death to them; but it has to be used with great caution and experience.

scarcely to be perceptible to the naked eye. They generally lurk close to the veins of the leaves of plants, and
frequently attack esculents. When viewed through a
glass, they are seen, when touched, to skip with great agi-
lity. The larva is of a high brown or reddish colour. The
thrip has four wings, and walks with its body turned upward. It frequently attacks the extremities of tender shoots
or young leaves, which become shriveled, brown, and will
rub to dust easily between the thumb and finger. When
any leaves or shoots are perceived to be so, if you do not
observe the green fly, expect the thrips. They may be
destroyed by a fumigation of tobacco, in the same manner
as the green fly. By the simple and expeditious method
of fumigation, these insects and several others may be destroyed effectually at any time they appear.

Cocus hesperidus, or mealy bug, has appeared in the
hot-houses about Philadelphia within these few years, and,
if not instantly destroyed, increases rapidly. It is of a
white dusty colour; when broken, of a brownish red, generally covered with down, under which it deposits its eggs;
and they, in a few months, come forth in great numbers.
The cocus generally is of a dormant nature, but in warm
weather they may be seen moving rapidly up the stems of
the plants. Fumigating has no observable effect on these
insects; therefore, as soon as they appear, recourse must
be had to other means. The liquid made from the following receipt is death to any of the *Cocus* tribe: Take two
pounds of strong soap, one pound of flour of sulphur, one
pound of leaf tobacco, one and a half ounce of nux vomica,
with a tablespoonful of turpentine, which boil in four gallons of river water to three; then set aside to cool. When
boiling, stir it well with a stick, continuing to do so until
it is reduced as above. In this liquor immerse the whole
plant, drawing it to and fro gently, that the liquor may
penetrate everywhere. This done, lay the plant on its
side, until it begins to dry, then syringe well with clean
water, and put it in its respective station. Where a collection of plants is free from any insects of the kind, every
plant that is introduced ought to be minutely scrutinized,
that the unclean may be kept from the clean: the above
insect will feed almost on any plant, but indulges on *Crás-*

sulas, any of the bristly *Cáctus, Gardènias,* and in fact whatever is in the way.

Cocus ————, or brown scaly insect, is frequently found on many plants, but we never could perceive that it does any other material injury than soiling them. We have always observed, that it is found in winter to abound in those situations which are most excluded from air; therefore is of less importance than the other species, which eat and corrode the leaves of tender plants. A washing with strong soap-suds will destroy them, or the above liquid will do it more effectually. Tie a piece of sponge on the end of a small stick, and scrub every leaf, stem and crevice. Fumigating destroys the larvæ of this species.

Cocus ————, or small white scaly insect, which generally infests *Cycus, Nèrium, Oleas,* and *Acacias,* &c., may be destroyed by washing as above with a sponge, and a strong decoction of tobacco, using the liquid about the warmth of 100°. Being thus heated, it irritates the insect, when, by easing itself from its bed, the fluid passes under it, and causes immediate death. If it is not thus irritated, it adheres so closely to the foliage, that it will keep you at defiance. The under, or dark side of the leaves is its residence; and we have observed a plant in a house where there was only light on one side, with the dark side literally covered, while the light side was clean. So much for having houses with plenty of light. The effects of this insect are of a corroding nature, extracting all the juice from the leaf; and where they have got to the extremity, the foliage is completely yellow, and of a decayed appearance.

Cocus ————, or turtle insect. We have never observed this insect arrive to any extent. It is the largest of any known among us, and very like a turtle in miniature. On lifting it from the wood, to which it generally adheres, there appear to be hundreds of eggs under it, but fumigating completely destroys the larvæ. In our opinion, this turtle insect is no other than the old female of the brown scaly insect, which swells to a large size before depositing its eggs. We have frequently observed the insect dead in this enlarged state, and question if this be not the last stage of its transmigration. The male insect is winged, and very active in its movements.

Where bulbous roots, such as *Hyacinths, Jonquils, Ixias, Lachenàllas,* &c., are required to be early in flower, they may, during this month, be put in the front of the hot-house and watered freely till they bloom, when they may be taken to the green-house or parlour.

Azaleas, Rhododendron Roses, and some other plants, do admirably to force, and where there is a large stock, a few should be brought into early bloom with the heat of this department.

OF CLEANSING PLANTS, HOUSE, &c.

This subject ought to be kept constantly in view. However correctly every thing else may be executed, without that adorning beauty, cleanliness, all will appear only half done. Therefore let all the dead leaves be picked off every day, the dust and other litter swept out of the house, and, when necessary, the house washed, which will be at least once a week. That the foliage of the plants may always appear fresh, syringe them every morning, when there is the appearance of sun. At present, this will in a great measure keep down the insects, and will prove a bane to the red spider.

Tie up neatly with stakes and threads of Russia mat all the straggling growing plants; let the stakes be proportionate to the plants, and never longer, except they are climbing sorts. Do not tie the branches in bundles, but singly and neatly, imitating nature as much as possible. If any of the plants are affected with the *Cocus* insect, let them be cleansed according to the plan already mentioned, taking particular care also in washing the stakes to which they had been previously tied, and burning all the old tyings, which contain the larvæ of the insect in many instances, especially of *Cocus hesperidus.* It is premised, when any of these things are done, that they will be well done, and not half doing, and always doing. Cleanliness, in every respect, promotes a pure air, which is congenial to vegetation, and will, with other attentions, always ensure a healthful and vigorous appearance in the house.

FEBRUARY.

In the early part of this month the weather generally is
very cold and changeable in the middle states, and strict
attention, with the greatest caution, will require to be paid
to the management of the hot-house. Most of the tropical
plants commence an active state of vegetation; and, if
checked by temperature or otherwise, they will not recover
until midsummer. The thermometer may be kept two or
three degrees higher with fire heat than last month: the
sun will be more powerful, and this will, in a great degree,
increase the vigour of the plants. Air may be admitted
when the thermometer rises to 75° or 80°, not allowing it
to rise higher than the latter. In giving air, let it be done
by the top sashes. It is improper to give it in any way
to cause a current, for the external air is yet very cold,
although the sun is more powerful. An inch or two on a
few of the sashes, as has been previously observed, will be
effectual in keeping the temperature low enough.

With regard to firing, what was said last month may
suffice for this. Always recollect that it is more preferable
to keep out the cold than to put it out. It will frequently
happen in the time of intense frost, that the weather is
dull. In such cases fire in a small degree is requisite all
day.

Heavy snows ought never to be allowed to remain on
the shutters while they are on the house. If the snow lies
on the sashes one day, the internal heat will dissolve some
of it; night coming on, will freeze it to the wood-work,
when it will become a solid mass, and frequently cannot
be separated without much damage. If allowed to remain
on for two days, the plants are very much weakened and
the foliage discoloured. Therefore, let the snow be cleared
off instantly, that no inconvenience may take place.

It will be observed that plants absorb more water this
month than last. The quantity given will require to be
increased, according to the increase of vegetation and the
advancement of the season; but never give it until the soil
begins to dry, and then in such proportion as will reach
the bottom of the pot. The best time to water is after the

sun has got on the house in the morning, observing all the directions given in January.

OF INSECTS, &c.

Perhaps sufficient observations were given under this head last month; but the importance of keeping these disagreeable visitors out of the house constrains us to make a few more remarks. Man cannot be too frequently guarded against his foes, more especially when they are summoning all their forces, and no profession has more than that of the Horticulturist. Let a strict examination be made about the end of the month for the red spider; they will be in operation some weeks before their depredations are observed on the foliage. The under side of the leaf is their resort in the first instance, and on such plants as have been already mentioned.

Observe daily the young shoots, in case the green fly becomes numerous. They give the foliage a very disagreeable appearance, and it is too often intolerable, before their career is arrested. It also takes a stronger fumigation, which has frequently to be repeated the following day to the same degree, much to the injury of many of the plants, and adding to the disagreeableness of the continued vapour in the house.

OF REPOTTING PLANTS.

About the end of the month some of the plants of *Curcúma, Amómum, Kæmpféria, Alpina, Phrynium, Cánna, Zingiber, Hedychium,* and others that are on the dry shelf, will be offering to grow. Let them be taken out of their pots, some of their weakest shoots or tubers taken off, and the strong ones repotted: give gentle waterings until they grow freely, then give an abundance. (Soil No. 17.)

Dionæa mucipula, or Venus fly-trap, grows best in the hot-house, and will, about the end of the month, stand in need of being repotted. This plant is very seldom grown in any degree of perfection, having been always considered

13

a delicate plant in collections. Take it out of the pot just before beginning to grow afresh, and divested of all the soil, leaving only a few of the young roots, (it is a bulb, and will receive no injury by so doing,) put it in new soil; when potted, place the pot in a saucer with one inch of water in it, giving a fresh supply every other day; this being repeated every year, it will grow, flower and seed in perfection. (Soil No. 5.)

Gesnérias, if in small pots, give larger as they advance in growth. This genus requires to have plenty of pot-room to make them flower well. *G. bulbósa*, *G. Zebrina* and *G. Sellòwii* ought to have a situation in every hot-house. They are remarkable for their many brilliant crimson flowers, and continue in flower for a length of time. When the bulbs begin to push, shake them out of the earth, and repot them into smaller pots; and, as soon as the roots reach the side of the earth, which will be in about one month, put them in larger pots, and continue to do so until flowering, which will be about the first of June, observing always to keep the ball of earth entire. *G. Douglásii*, *G. rútilla*, *G. acaùlis*, and some others, are all well worth attention. (Soil No. 11.)

Gloriósas must be repotted in the beginning of this month; *G. supérba* is the most beautiful and curious. The crown of the roots ought to be planted one and a half inch deep, taking care not to break them. Do not water much until they begin to grow. The earth must not have much water. As the plants grow, they will require a more liberal supply; yet it is necessary, at all times, to be moderate in giving it. If well treated, the superb flowers will appear in June or July. (Soil No. 12.)

Gloxìnias are beautiful herbaceous plants, with large showy flowers, requiring soil and treatment similar to (Gesneria). *G. speciósa*, dark blue, *G. speciósa-pállida*, pale lilac; *G. cándida*, pure white, and *G. grandiflóra*, very large light blue, are the finest, although several of the other species are very interesting, especially *G. hirsùta*.

OF CLEANSING PLANTS, HOUSE, &c.

With regard to cleaning the plants. Sprinkling or syringing is at all times, to a greater or less degree, necessary. The plants will, in this compartment, be in their first stage of growth, and, if dust or foulness be permitted to lodge on their foliage, the pores will be obstructed, the plants will become unhealthy, and the growth of insects increased.

Let all moss, litter, decayed leaves or weeds, be cleared out of the house, the earth in the pots stirred up with a round pointed stick, and fresh earth given where required, that the air may operate therein freely.

The house ought always to be sprinkled before being swept, to prevent the dust rising.

Attend to the bulbous roots as directed last month, such as *Hyacinths, Narcissus,* &c.

––––––

MARCH.

IF this department has been regularly attended to, the plants will be in a fresh healthy state. Where there is any sickly appearance, heat has been deficient, or insects of a destructive character are preying upon the plants. Too much water at the root frequently causes the foliage to become yellow. Regular syringing must be continued in the morning, and it is highly necessary that the water that is used should be of the same temperature as the house; and at all times, whatever water is given to the roots, the same must be observed. For airing, see last month, observing, as the season advances, to increase the quantity.

Continue to fumigate when any of the Green-fly appears, (see *January* for directions,) and where there are any of the plants infected with the white scaly insect, clean them as there directed. If overlooked for a few months, they will be increased tenfold. Very frequently, where there are only a few, they are neglected until the plant is overrun

with them, and then it may be said, it is impossible to dis-
lodge them entirely. Clear off all decayed leaves from the
plants which will have made fresh shoots, and the decayed
leaves very much disfigure the whole collection. We
would not have repeated this observation if it was not an
essential point, and one which is so frequently neglected.

OF REPOTTING PLANTS.

Many of the young plants that are growing freely, and
where they may be desired to grow to a large size, should
be frequently repotted to encourage their growth. *Ges-
nèria, Gloxinia,* and others previously mentioned, must
have larger pots, as they require it. Flowering bulbs of
Amaryllis may be brought into the heat to make them
bloom early; before they begin to grow, divest them of the
old soil and put them into fresh: this is particularly necessary, when the bulbs are already in large pots. By thus
renewing the soil, the pots can be used much smaller: they
require plenty of drainage in the pot, and agree best with
(soil No. 12).

Where plants of the dwarf *Musas* are intended to be
grown for fruiting, they must have particular attention in
repotting as they grow; about the first of the month will be
a proper time to begin : copious waterings are daily required
when they are in a growing state. Their soil is No. 12,
with one portion more manure. For farther detail, see
May.

————

APRIL.

WHERE the hot-house has been properly conducted, the
plants generally will have a vigorous and healthful aspect.
An error frequently arises in the conducting of these departments, by inexperienced operators being ambitious of
outstripping their competitors. They keep the house in a
very high temperature, and admit little or no air. Where

such a mode has been pursued, the plants will have got over their first growth, and the foliage looks yellow and decaying; thus throwing the plants into a state of inactivity, when nature herself commences her most active movements. The temperature should not be under 55° in the night, nor much above 75° during the day, without admitting a little air by the top lights. It will not do yet to give air by the front sashes, the wind being cool, and a current in the house would be hurtful. The sun is not so powerful but the heat can be kept down by the air given from above.

Hot-house or tropical plants will not materially suffer with 100° of sun-heat, provided they are not very near the glass; but such an extreme would be injurious to practice.

REPOTTING.

Where there is a general assortment of the Cacteæ tribe, and kept in this department, now is the proper period to give them a general repotting. Of all the tropical floral productions, there is not a family more curious, grotesque, interesting, and beautiful than this; and, what still more enhances their real value, they are in this country of the easiest culture; it is with pleasure that we recommend a few of the grand and the novel, which are faithfully described in the general list given next month. The bottom of every pot must be covered with an inch of pot-shreds, or rough gravel for drainage.

MAY.

VERY few directions for this department remain to be given; except for shifting plants, and a few observations on those that are most desirable for the hot-house; which we will do in this month, considering May and June the best months of the year for that operation.

The days and nights will be very mild by this time, and
the sashes in every favourable day should be opened, both
in front and top, so that the plants may be inured to the
open air, which they will be exposed to by the end of the
month. Leave 'in the beginning of the month the top
sashes a little open every mild night, and gradually, as the
heat increases, leave the front sashes and doors open. Continue to syringe them at least every alternate night, and, if
possible, every night; and give them all, according to their
respective wants, liberal supplies of water every day. Absorption among hot-house plants is as great during this
month as in any period of the year.

OF REPOTTING PLANTS, &c.

It is our candid opinion that this and next month are the
best periods for shifting or repotting all or most of hot-house
plants; the end of August being the time always adopted
around Philadelphia for that operation, (and then they are
done indiscriminately).   We will assign a few reasons for
our practice.

First, that it is not congenial to the nature of these plants
to have their roots surrounded with fresh soil when they
are becoming inactive; *secondly,* that there is not a sufficiency of heat naturally to quicken them to an active state
when they are encouraged; and, *thirdly,* being thus in
new soil while dormant, they have a yellow and sickly
aspect until they begin to grow; and the foliage, thus deprived of its natural vigour, will not appear so healthful
again: whereas, if they are shifted or repotted in this or
next month, at which season they are between two stages
of growth, they immediately, on receiving fresh assistance,
and by the increasing heat of the summer, make new
growths, are perfectly ripened before the approach of
winter, and never lose that vernal appearance they have
attained. These are our reasons, acquired from a close
practice and observation, and are not influenced by the
doings of others which are so much aside. No practical
operator especially, nor, in fact, any individual, ought to be
governed by custom in regard to the treatment of plants,
without having an idea as to why and wherefore, founded

on the principles of nature, and governed by her unerring results.

As many are desirous of having a knowledge of plants before they order them, and likewise which are the finest flowerers and their general character, especially those who are at a great distance, and seldom have the privilege of seeing what is most desirable, our descriptions will be limited, but still will convey some accurate idea of the article described.

Acàcias. Several of these are desirable in the hot-house for the grandeur of their foliage, beauty of flower, and a few of them as specimens of valuable medicinal plants. *A. Houstóni,* now *Annesèia Houstóni,* is one of the most magnificent of the *Mimòsa* tribe, blooming from August to November in large terminal spikes, of a crimson colour, stamens very long and beautiful, leaves bipinnated in pairs. *A. grandiflòra,* likewise given to *Annesèia,* and similar to the former in colour, has very large compound bipinnate leaves, with from twenty to forty pairs. *A. Catèchu,* flowers yellow, wood spiny, leaves bipinnated, about ten pairs. The inner wood of this tree is of a brown colour, from which the *Catèchu* used in medicine is prepared. It is disputed whether *A. véra* or *A. arábica* produces the gum Arabic. We are inclined to think it is the latter, which grows principally on the Atlas mountains. The gum exudes spontaneously from the bark of the tree in a soft half fluid state. There are many others of this genus belonging to the hot-house, but being shy in flowering, are not generally esteemed. Most of the flowers have the appearance of yellow balls of down, and are hermaphrodite. The pots should all be well drained. (Soil No. 1.)[*]

Æschynanthus, about four species, among which *Æ. grandiflorus* and *Æ. parasiticus* are very deserving of culture; they have thick fleshy foliage, are of slender growth, producing orange-coloured tubular flowers in clusters, and require treatment similar to the wax-plant. (Soil No. 2.)

Ardisias, about eighteen species. Plants highly esteemed for the beauty of their foliage, flowers, and berries. The most popular in our collections is *A. crenulàta.* It has rose-coloured star-like flowers, in terminal panicles,

* These numbers refer to the table of soils at the end of the work.

and produces beautiful small red berries, which continue
until other berries are produced the following year, and
frequently there may be seen on one plant the berries of
three successive years, thus being a very ornamental plant
and very desirable. It is vulgarly called the dwarf ever-
bearing cherry. It will keep in a good green-house, but
not grow freely. *A. solanàcea* has large oblong leaves,
narrowed at each end, and bears purple berries; *A. élegans* has entire, oblong, shining leaves; *A. umbellata*,
once *A. littoràlis*, is also a fine plant for an abundance of
flower and beauty of foliage. The flowers are pink, in
large decompound panicles.

Arèca, Cabbage-tree, ten species. They are a kind of
palms, with large pinnated leaves, or properly fronds. In
their indigenous state they are from six to forty feet high,
but in the hot-house they seldom exceed twenty feet. *A.
cátechu* is used in medicine. *A. olerácea* is cultivated
extensively in the West Indies, and the tender part of the
top is eaten by the natives. *A. montanà* is most frequent
in collections. There is no particular beauty in the flowers.
They are all easily grown, if plenty of heat be given. (Soil
No. 12.)

Aristolóchias, Birth-wort. There are several of these
belonging to the hot-house, but none of them deserving
particular observation, except *A. labiòsa* and *A. brasilién-
sis*. The leaves are reniform, roundish, cordate, and amplexicaule; the flower or corolla is of a curious construction,
being incurved, and at the base swelled or saccate, with a
large lip, and all beautifully spotted; colour greenish brown.
They are climbing plants, and require a strong heat. (Soil
No. 9.)

Astrapæas, three species. *A. Wallichii* is a celebrated
plant in Europe, and is frequently met with in our collections. It has a profusion of scarlet umbellated flowers,
with an involucre; has twenty-five stamens united into a
tube, bearing the corolla with five petals; leaves roundish,
cordate, acuminate, very large, with persistent, ovate wavy
stipules. The plant is of easy culture, and grows freely,
wood very strong. (Soil No. 12.)

Bambùsas, Bamboo-cane, two species. Plants of very
strong growth, and are used in the East Indies, where they
are indigenous, for every purpose in the construction of

huts, for furniture both domestic and rural, for fences, boats, boxes, paper, &c. It is frequently used as pipes to convey water. The species thus useful is *B. arundinácea*, which grows to a great height. We do not mention it as interesting in beauty, but as a valuable plant for the many useful purposes to which it is applied. It requires to be kept wet. (Soil No. 15.)

Banistèrias, a genus of about fourteen climbing evergreen plants. Three of them are esteemed, *B. fúlgens*, yellow flowers in racemose spikes, leaves subovate and downy beneath. *B. chrisophylla* has beautiful foliage, as if covered with a shining gold-coloured dust; leaves large, oblong, acute. *B. splèndens*, flowers in spikes of a yellow colour; foliage large and silvery-like; the pots should be well drained. (Soil No. 9.)

Barringtònias, two species. *B. speciòsa* has produced a great excitement among cultivators, and is one of the handsomest plants produced within the tropics. The leaves are large, oblong, acute, shining, with fleshy nerves, tinged with red; the flowers are large, full of stamens with four petals; opens in the evening and fades at sunrise; colour purple and white; grows freely in strong heat. (Soil No. 9.)

Beaumóntias are strong growing climbing plants, with large foliage. *B. grandiflòra* is said to have beautiful large white flowers approaching the *Oleander*. (Soil No. 12.)

Blètias, a genus of about eight species, all beautiful flowering plants. *B. Tankervílliæ* is most superb, a small plant, now (Jan.) in bloom, has upward of fifty full-blown flowers, besides many buds—they are brown, white, and purple, and about two inches in diameter. When out of flower, and the roots become dormant, place the pots in a shady situation; allow the soil to become dry, until the roots begin to grow: as soon as this is observed, repot the plants and expose them fully to the sun, giving plenty of water while growing. *B. Shéppherdii* is a fine pink, and requires similar treatment. (Soil No. 13.)

Bròwneas, five species of splendid plants, but scarce in collections. *B. coccinea* has scarlet flowers in pendulous bunches, corolla semi-double, foliage bipinnate, in three pairs. *B. ròsa*, mountain rose of Trinidad. *B. grandi-*

céps is the finest of the genus, leaves bipinnated; leaflets cordate, acuminate, downy, and pendulous; flowers rose-colour, in large close heads. Drain the pots well. (Soil No. 12.)

Brunfélsias, very fine, free flowering plants, with white, yellowish, or purple flowers. *B. grandiflòra* blooms freely, and is finely scented—a plant before me, now (28th of Jan.) only one foot high, has six full expanded flowers upon it, each fully two inches in diameter. (Soil No. 9.)

Buonapártea júncea, a very curious low growing plant, with long narrow, recurved, round leaves; with spikes of small blue flowers. There does appear to be three distinct varieties in cultivation, but are rarely attainable. (Soil No. 12.)

Búddlea madagascariensis blooms profusely during winter in spikes of orange-coloured flowers, of a kind of honey fragrance—the plant is strong growing, and of the easiest culture. (Soil No. 11.)

Calathèa zebrìna, frequently known as *maránta zebrìna;* it is a plant unique in appearance, having large elongated ovate leaves, beautifully striped with green and dark purple, and called the *Zebra* plant. It has light blue flowers in ovate spikes, about the size of large pine cones. It is an herbaceous plant; but in the warmest part of the hot-house retains its splendid foliage; requires a very liberal supply of water, and ought to be in every collection. (Soil No. 11.)

Cánnas, about thirty species, several of them deserving cultivation both for flower and foliage: they are principally natives of the West Indies, and might all be easily obtained. The finest are *C. gigántea,* has large leaves and orange flowers; *C. limbàta,* flowers scarlet and yellow; *C. discolor,* has large cordate, acuminate leaves of a crimson colour, the flowers are scarlet; *C. iridiflòra,* has large crimson nodding flowers, very different from any of the others, and the finest of the genus. They all, while in a growing state, require a liberal supply of water; and being herbaceous plants, watering ought to be given up about the first of November, and renewed in February, thus giving them a cessation which they require to flower freely; but when water is constantly given, which is the general plan in our collections, they continue to push weak shoots and few flowers. (Soil No. 12.)

Cáctus. This extensive genus is interesting, and varied in character and habit; it is now divided into seven distinct genera, according to their natural appearance and disposition. We will describe a few of each genus, none of which going under the name of *Cáctus*, we will give them the six following, premising that the time is not far distant when this family will be successfully cultivated in every parlour window, and the whole tribe will be sought for with more avidity than any other class of plants that have ever been brought to notice, not even excepting the *Rose.* They require a dry heat, and will grow either in town or country, and are completely adapted for the denizen amateur, and will afford more beauty and interesting display than can be imagined until witnessed.

Mamillàrias, about seventy species, and are those which are covered with roundish bearded tubercles, and with small red and white flowers. *M. coccinea, M. simplex, M. pusìlla, M. cónica, M. stellata,* and *M. acanthòphlegma,* are good species, and will do well with water once a week during summer. (Soil No. 15.)

Melocáctus, seven species, and are those that are roundish with deep and many angles, with spines in clusters on the top of the angle. *M. commùnis* is the Turk's cap, named from having an ovate conate crown upon the top, from which proceed the small red flowers. *M. macránthus* has large spines; *M. pyramidális* is a conical growing species. These require the same treatment as the last. (Soil No. 15.)

Echinocátus, a great number of species; are those that have many deep angles, and have a remarkable swelling, with each parcel of spines; *E. gibbósus, E. crispàtus, E. recúrvus, P. rodànthia,* and *E. scopa,* are curious in appearance, with small white and purple flowers. These three genera in most collections are not well known specifically, but it is easy to discriminate with which genus they are connected. (Soil No. 15.)

Cèreus. This is the most magnificent genus with regard to the magnitude and beauty of the flowers, but not so closely allied in character. It takes in all those of a trailing or erect growing habit, having spines in clusters,

solitary, or spineless.   *C. senìlis* is the celebrated monkey
cactus.   *C. peruviànus* and *C. heptagònus* grow very
erect, and to the height of thirty or forty feet in Peru and
Mexico, where they plant them close together as fences,
and they are in a few years impenetrable.   *C. flagelli-
fòrmis* is a well-known creeping flowering species, has ten
angles; will keep in a good green-house, and produce in
May and June a great number of blooms.   The petals are
of a fine pink and red colour; the tube of the flower is
long, and will stand a few days in perfection, when others
come out successively for the space of two months, and
during their continuance make a brilliant appearance.   *C.
grandiflòrus* is the celebrated " Night-blooming Cereus."
The flowers are very large, beautiful and sweet-scented.
They begin to open about sun-down, and are fully expanded about eleven o'clock.   The corolla, or rather calyx, is
from seven to ten inches in diameter, the outside of which
is a brown, and the inside a fine straw yellow colour; the
petals are of the purest white, with the stamens surrounding the stile in the centre of the flower, which add to its
lustre, and make it appear like a bright star.   Its scent is
agreeable, and perfumes the air to a considerable distance;
but these beauties are of momentary duration.   By sunrise they fade, and hang down quite decayed, and never
open again.*   One of these ought to be in every collection, and, if trained up a naked wall, will not occupy much
room, and grow and flower profusely.   *C. mállisoni* and *C.
scottii* are nearly alike, and have beautiful scarlet flowers:
it has been gratuitously (to say the least of it) called " The
Scarlet Night-blooming Cereus."   *C. speciosíssimus* has
most beautiful large flowers, about six inches in diameter;
the outside petals are a bright scarlet, those of the inside
a fine light purple.   One flower lasts a few days, and a
large plant will produce every year from ten to fifty
flowers, and blooming from May to August.   It has flowered in some of our collections, and is highly esteemed.
C. triangulàris has the largest flower of the *Cacteæ* family;
the bloom is of a cream colour, and about one foot in dia-

---

* They may be preserved if cut off when in perfection, and put
in spirits of wine, in a glass vase, made air tight.   A plant flowered in our collection, in May, 1830, at 12 o'clock at noon—the
only instance of the kind we ever heard of.

meter. In its indigenous state it produces a fine fruit called " Strawberry Pear," and is much esteemed in the West Indies as being slightly acid, and, at the same time, sweet, pleasant and cooling.

Epiphyllums are those species of the Cacteæ family which have flat shoots, or leaves without spines ; from the edges of those leaves the flowers are produced. They are extensively cultivated for their profusion of bloom, and are frequently grafted on *Cèreus triangulàris* and *Perèskia*, which greatly promotes their growth, and prevents them from so easily damping off by over watering. The original species are *È. speciòsum*, pink ; *E. phylanthoìdes* or *Hoók-erii*, white ; *È. alàtum*, white; *È. truncàtum*, scarlet ; flowers tubular, from two to three inches in diameter. The plant is of a very dwarf growth, and much branched ; when in bloom, it is quite a picture, and rendered more beautiful when grafted. There is also a variety of it called *E. truncàtum Àltenstèinii*, the flower of which is rather larger, and is more rosy coloured. *E. Russelliánum* is quite a new species, but has not yet bloomed in our collections ; it is represented as being a beautiful large crimson, and of the *truncàta* habits. *E. Ackermania* has a magnificent large crimson flower. Besides these, there are many superb hybrid varieties, vying with any of the originals. Among them are the following: *E. Hibbèrtii, E. Hoòdii, E. Boydii, E. De vàuxii, E. quillardittii, E. Fèastii, E. Vándesii, E. Mayfly, E. elegantissima*, and *E. Naipèrii*, and no doubt many other varieties and sub-varieties will be continually making their appearance. All the Epiphyllum tribe require a very rich open soil, not of too sandy a nature, as they thereby grow to wood, and bloom but sparingly—give plenty of drainage. (Soil No. 18.)

Opùntias, upwards of fifty species, and are those whose branches are in thick joints, flat, oblong, or ovate ; spines solitary or in clusters. Some of the plants are very desirable for their singular appearance, and some of them, particularly *O. cochinillifera*, are valuable for feeding the Cochineal insect. *O. microdásys, O. feróx, O. lacte-spina, O. sericeá*, and some others, are beautiful plants, and will grow in any kind of soil, but No. 2 will suit them best.

Peréskias. About four species, and those that are of a shrubby nature, producing leaves ; *P. aculeàta* bears a fruit

14

called "Barbadoes-gooseberry." The flowers are very
small and simple, spines about half an inch long, leaves
fleshy and elliptical. (Soil No. 2.)

The whole of the plants in the family of *Cacteæ* require
very little water in winter, and delight in a dry, warm
situation. They do not agree with very frequent repotting; once a year to young plants, and in two or three to
those that are established, with the exception of the large,
free flowering species, which should be repotted once in
two years, and never be allowed to shrink for want of
moisture.

The operation of grafting is very simple, merely requiring an incision to be made, and fitting in it a fresh cutting
of another kind, holding the cutting stationary in the incision half a minute, till the juices of the two adhere together, when it may be said the union is effected, and, in
a few weeks, the new branches will grow freely. We
have seen the *Mammillaria* tribe growing neatly upon the
triangularis, and other species of the *cereus*.

Carissa, a genus of pretty little plants, particularly *C.
spinárum*, which bears a profusion of white flowers like a
jasmine. (Soil No. 4.)

Ceropègia elegàns is the only species of any merit : it
is a thin growing, climbing plant, producing a great profusion of very curious flowers of a greenish colour, spotted
with brown; the interior and tips of the corolla are set
with hairs—it is of very easy culture. (Soil No. 7.)

Caryòta. A genus of palms. *C. ùrens* is an admired
species, produces flowers in long pendulous spikes, which
are succeeded by strings of succulent globular berries. In
its native state it produces a sweet liquor in large quantities, and no stronger than water. (Soil No. 12.)

Caryophyllus aromáticus is the clove tree of commerce.
The whole plant is aromatic, and closely allied to *Myrtus;*
the flowers are in loose panicles, the leaves oblong, acuminate, entire. It is a fine evergreen. Pots must be well
drained. (Soil No. 9.)

Cérberas. About twelve species of strong growing trees,
full of poisonous juice. *C. thevètia* is an elegant plant, with
acuminate leaves, and large, nodding, yellow, solitary fragrant flowers, proceeding from the axil; *C. ahoùai* produces a nut which is deadly poison. *C. odàllam*, once *C.*

mànghas, has large star-like flowers, white, shaded with red. They are principally East India plants, and require great heat. (Soil No. 17.)

Clerodéndrum. This genus contains some very beautiful and fragrant plants; *C. frágrans floré pléno* has a very beautiful head of double white sweet-scented flowers, and does tolerably well as a green-house plant; *C. squamátum* has very showy scarlet flowers. *C. speciosìssimum,* the plant so glaringly figured in some of the English periodicals, is the same as *C. squamátum,* a plant which has been grown in this vicinity fifteen or twenty years. (Soil No. 2.)

Coffèa Arábica. It produces the celebrated coffee, and is a plant universally known in our collections, and of easy culture. The leaves are opposite, oblong, wavy and shining, the flowers white, of a grateful odour, but of a short duration. (Soil No. 17.)

Combrètums. Nine species of beautiful flowering climbing plants, standing in very high estimation. The leaves of the principal part of them are ovate, acute, flowers small, but on large branches, the flowers all coming out on one side of the branch. They have a magnificent effect. *C. élegans,* red; *C. formòsum,* red and yellow; *C. pulchéllum,* scarlet; *C. comòsum,* have crimson flowers in tufts; *C. purpùreum* is the most splendid of the genus. It was first cultivated in 1818, and so much admired that the whole of the species, as soon as introduced, was extravagantly bought up; and none of them has retained their character, except *C. purpùreum,* which is now called *Poivrea coccinea.* The flowers are bright scarlet, in large branches, blooming profusely from April to September, and flower best in a pot. When planted in the ground, it grows too much to wood, carrying a few flowers. This plant ought to be in every hot-house. (Soil No. 13.)

Córyphas, (Large fan Palm,) five species of the most noble and magnificent of palms. *C. ambraculifera,* the fronds or leaves are palmate. In Ceylon, where the tree is indigenous, they are frequently found fifteen feet wide and twenty feet long. Knox says they will cover from fifteen to twenty men, and, when dried, will fold up in the shape of a rod, and can be easily carried about, and serve to protect them from the scorching sun. *C. talìera,* now

Taliera bengalénsis, being stronger, is of great utility for covering houses. They do not grow to such immense extent in artificial cultivation, but require large houses to grow them. (Soil No. 12.)

Crìnums, about one hundred species, chiefly stove bulbs, many of them beautiful. Those that are of great celebrity are *C. erubéscens*, pink; *C. scàbrum*, crimson and white; *C. amàbile*, purple and white; the neck of the bulb of the latter is long, is easily distinguished by its purplish colour, and is unquestionably the finest of the genus. Several specimens of it are in our collections. Their flowers are in umbels, on a stalk about three feet high; corolla funnel-shaped; petals recurved; nearly fifty flowers on each stem, and a good plant will produce three stems in one year. They require large pots to make them flower well, and, when growing, should be liberally supplied with water. (Soil No. 12.)

Cròtons. About twenty-eight species, few of them deserving cultivation; but the genus is celebrated for its beautiful *C. pictus*, leaves oblong-lanceolate, variegated with yellow, and stained with red, flowers small green, or axillary spikes. *C. variegàtus*, variety *latifòlia*, is finer than the original *variegàtus;* the nerves in the leaves are yellow, and the leaves lanceolate, entire, and smooth. To make them grow freely, give them the warmest part of the hot-house, and drain the pots well. (Soil No. 13.)

Cycas, four species, generally called *Sago palm*, as an English name. The plant from which *Sago* is extracted belongs to another genus, (see *Sàgus*.) *C. revolùta* is a well known palm, and will keep perfectly well in the green-house. We have seen a beautiful specimen of it which is kept every winter in the cellar; but those that are kept so cool in winter only grow every alternate year, while those that are kept in the hot-house grow every year, which shows that heat is their element. *C. circinàlis* is a large growing species; the fronds are much longer, but not so close and thick. *C. glaùca* is a fine species; the foliage is slightly glaucous. They require plenty of pot room, are much infested with the small white scaly insect, and ought to be frequently examined and carefully washed as prescribed in January. (Soil No. 12.)

Cypripédium insigne is a very beautiful nepal species

of this curious *Ladies' slipper plant.* The flowers have a
waxy appearance, and very much in shape of an Indian
shoe; the colours are green and purple: it likes a moist,
half shaded situation. (Soil No. 16.)

Cyrtoceras reflexa, or *Hoya coriacea,* a new dwarf wax-
plant of magnificent appearance, either for foliage or bloom,
which it produces in great profusion from the axils of
almost every leaf; it is a native of Manilla; it grows freely
in Soil No. 13.

Dracænas, Dragon-tree, about twelve species of Asiatic
plants, varied in character. *D. Férrea* is plentiful in our
collections, and will keep in the green-house; but the foliage is not so well retained as when kept in the hot-house:
the leaves are lanceolate, acute, of a dark crimson colour.
D. terminális, striped leaved; *D. frágrans,* when in bloom,
will scent the air for a considerable distance, leaves green
and lanceolate. *D. margináta* is rare, yet it is to be seen
in a few of our collections. *D. stricta* is now *Charlwoòdia**
stricta, flowers blush, and in loose panicles. *D. Dráco* is
admired, and the most conspicuous of the genus. (Soil
No. 11.)

Eránthemums, about ten species. *E. pulchéllum* and
E. bicolor are the finest of the genus; the former is in our
collections. Plenty of heat is indispensable to make it
flower in perfection; therefore it should have the warmest
part of the house, and it will produce flowers of a fine blue
colour from December to April. The flowers of the latter
are white and dark purple, with a few brown spots in the
white; blooms from April to August. Drain the pots well,
and give the plants little sun during summer. (Soil No.
11.)

Eugènias, about thirty species, esteemed for their handsome evergreen foliage. This genus once contained a few
celebrated species, which have been divided. (See *Jambòsa.*) The Allspice tree, known as *Myrtus Piménta,* is
now *E. Pimenta;* the leaves are ovate, lanceolate, and,
when broken, have an agreeable scent. There are several
varieties, all of the same spicy fragrance. The plant is in
very few of our collections. *E. frágrans* is sweet-scented;

---

* In honour of Mr. Charlwood, an extensive seedsman of London,
who has made several botanical excursions on this continent.

the flowers are on axillary peduncles; leaves ovate, obtuse. (Soil No. 11.)

Euphórbia, (spurge,) a genus of plants disseminated over every quarter of the globe; a few are beautiful, many grotesque, and several the most worthless weeds on the earth. There are about two hundred species, and from all of them, when probed, a thick milky fluid exudes. Those of the tropics are the most curious, and very similar in appearance to *Cáctus*, but easily detected by the above perforation. There is a magnificent species in our collections, which was lately introduced from Mexico—(see *Poinsettia*.) *E. spléndens* flowers freely from December to May, and is of easy culture. *E. fúlgens*, same as *jaquiniiflòra*, is a plant of a slender willow-looking habit, but produces a profusion of flowers from the axil of each leaf, which renders it very showy. The flowers of the whole genus are apetalous, and the beauty of those described is in a brilliant scarlet bractea, which is very persistent. They must have plenty of pot-room. (Soil No. 9.)

Erythrìnas, (Coral tree,) a genus containing about thirty species of leguminose, scarlet-flowering plants. Several species are greatly esteemed for their beauty and profusion of flowers, which, in well-established plants, are produced in long spikes. *E. corallodéndrum* blooms magnificently in the West Indies, but in our collections has never flowered. Perhaps if it were kept dry during its dormant season, which is from November to January, and when growing greatly encouraged, it might produce flowers. *E. speciòsa* is a splendid flowerer, leaves large, ternated, and prickly beneath; stem prickly. *E. pubéscens* is valued for its large peculiar brown pubescent leaves. *E. princéps* is quite a new species, and is represented as being the finest of all the *Erythrìnas*, and exhibits its rich crimson flowers in great profusion; to make them grow well and bloom freely, they require plenty of pot-room; indeed, while in a growing state, they should be repotted every month. In regard to *E. herbàcea*, which is a native of the Carolinas, and frequently treated as a hot-house plant, it is our opinion that it would be more perfectly grown if planted about the first of the month in the garden; and, when growing, if well supplied with water, it would flower from July to September. About the first of November lift the roots and preserve them in half dry earth. *E. laurifòlia* and *E. cristagálli* are likewise often treated as hot-house plants, and in such situations they cast prematurely their first flowers by the confined state of the air. They will keep in perfect preservation during winter in a dry cellar, half covered with earth, or entirely covered with half dry earth; consequently, the best and easiest method of treatment is, to plant them in the garden about the first of May, and, when growing, if the ground becomes dry, give them frequent waterings. They will flower profusely, three or four times in the course of the summer.

We freely recommend the last species to all our patrons, confident that it will give ample satisfaction, both in profusion of flower and beauty of colour. The soil they are to be planted into should be rich and well pulverized; or, if they are kept in pots, they must be enlarged three or four times, when they are in a growing state, to make them flower perfectly ; otherwise they will be diminutive. (Soil No. 13.)

Fìcus, Fig-tree, a genus containing about fifty hot-house species, besides several that belong to the green-house: greatly admired for the beauty of their foliage. A few of them are deciduous, and all of the easiest culture. We have seen plants of *F. elástica* hung in the back of the hot-house, without the smallest particle of earth, their only support being sprinklings of water every day. *F. brássii* and *F. macrophylla* are the finest-looking species that have come under our observation ; the leaves of both are very large and shading, occupying considerable space. In small collections *F. indìca* and *F. nitìda* are desirable; *F. repèns* is a climbing plant. (Soil No. 13.)

Francìscea, a new genus of plants from South America, containing about four species of profuse blooming plants. *F. Hopeana* and *F. latifòlia* are generally known; the latter possesses all the combined fragrance of the jasmine and jonquil; the flowers are one inch in diameter, of a rich purple fading to pure white, and blooms the whole winter. (Soil No. 9.)

Gardènias, a genus containing about seventeen species, several of them very popular in our collections, going under the name of *Cápe Jasmine*, which do well in the green-house, (see *May*.) The species requiring this department,

and deserving attention, are *G. campanulàta*, of a soft
woody nature, with ovate, acuminate leaves; flowers of a
straw colour, and solitary; *G. amæna*, the flowers are white,
tinged with crimson, terminal and solitary, but seldom
bloom; *G. costàta*, admired for its beautiful ribbed foliage; *G. làcida* has a handsome, ovate, acuminate, shining
foliage, flowers white and solitary; they require to have
the pots well drained. (Soil No. 13.)

Geissoméria longiflòra. This is a new genus, and
closely allied to *Ruéllia.* The species alluded to, is a free
flowerer, blooming from January to May, in close spikes of
a scarlet colour; leaves opposite, ovate, elongate, and shining; the plants must be well drained, and in summer kept
from the direct influence of the sun. (Soil No. 2.)

Helicónia braziliénsis. This very splendid plant is
nearly related to *Strelitzia*, and in splendour surpasses it.
The brilliant scarlet sheath that envelops the flowers, con-
trasts most admirably with its rich green leaves. Give
plenty of drainage to the pots, and, when the plants are
growing, give a liberal supply of water. (Soil No. 17.)

Helitròpiums, about twelve species, of little merit, except
H. peruvianum, H. corymbósum, and *H. grandiflórum;*
these are all very agreeably scented, especially the former,
which is a universal favourite. (Soil No. 3.)

Heritièra littóralis, looking-glass plant. This plant is
unisexual, has beautiful large, ovate, veiny leaves; the
flowers are small, red, with male and female on the same
plant, but different flowers. It requires a strong heat and
plenty of pot-room. How the English name becomes applicable to it, we are not acquainted.

Hibiscus. This genus affords many fine species and
varieties of plants for the hot-house, besides others for
every department of the garden. The most popular in our
collections of the hot-house, is *H. ròsa sinénsis*, with its
varieties, which are magnificent, and flower profusely from
February to September. The single or original species is
also beautiful; the varieties are *H. ròsa sinénsis ràbro
plénus*, double red; *H. r. s. cárnea plénus*, double salmon;
H. r. s. variegàtus, double striped; striped on the back of
the outside petals; *H. r. s. fláva-plènus*, or *carnea*, double
buff; *H. r. s. làtea plènus*, double yellow, or rather sulphur. The plants grow freely, and produce their flowers

three or four inches in diameter, from the young wood; the leaves are ovate, acuminate, smooth, entire at the base, and coarsely teethed at the end. All the varieties are of the same character, and highly deserving of a situation in every collection. There is said to be a double white variety, which we doubt. *H. mutàbilis flòre plèno* is a splendid plant, of strong growth, and will, when well established, flower abundantly, if the wood of last year is cut to within a few eyes of the wood of the previous year; the flowers are produced on the young wood, and come out a pale colour, and change to bright red, and about the size of a garden Provins rose ; leaves downy, cordate, angular, five-lobed, acuminate, and slightly indented. *H. lilliiflòrus* is a new highly esteemed species; the flowers are various in colour, being pink, blush, red, and purple. The leaves vary in character, but are generally cordate, crenate, acuminate; the petioles are brown, and the whole slightly hirsute ; is deciduous, and requires to be kept in the warmest part of the house. (Soil No. 9.)

Hóyas, wax-plant, seven species. All of them are climbing succulents, requiring plenty of heat and little water. *H. carnòsa* is the finest flowering species of the genus, and known in our collections as the wax-plant; the leaves are green and fleshy; the flowers are mellifluous, five-parted, and in pendulous bunches, slightly bearded, and have every appearance of a composition of the finest wax; of a blush colour. *H. crassifòlia* has the best-looking foliage, and the flowers are white. The former will keep in the green-house, but will not flower so profusely. (Soil No. 2.)

Ipomæas, a genus of tropical climbing plants, nearly allied to *Convolvùlus*, but of greater beauty. *I. Jálapa* is the true jalap of the druggists, but not worthy of any other remark. *I. Horsfállia* has brilliant rosy crimson flowers, which it is almost entirely covered with from December to May. *I. rugosa* has a profusion of large rosy lilac flowers. *I. multiflòra*, blush and lilac. *I. Learii* produces a profusion of large blue flowers; they are all very showy and beautiful ornaments for either the hot-house or the flower garden. (Soil No. 13.)

Ismène amáncaes, or *Pancràtium amáncaes*. This profuse yellow flowering bulb is richly deserving of cultiva-

tion, and should be kept in the house all summer, repotting
it as often as the roots touch the interior side of the pot,
giving it plenty of water when in a growing state; but
when dormant, it must be kept dry till it offers to grow:
when well treated, it will bloom repeatedly during summer.
(Soil No. 12.)

Ixòras, a genus of fine flowering plants, and does extremely well in our collections in comparison to the state
they are grown in England. The genus specifically is
much confused among us, either from error originating
with those who packed them for this country, or after they
have arrived. *I. purpùrea*, leaves oblong, ovate, blunt;
flowers crimson; it is now called *I. obovàta*. *I. crocàta*,
leaves oval, lanceolate, narrowing toward the stem, smooth
underside of the leaf; the nerves are very perceptible; flowers saffron-coloured, and very profuse. *I. ròsea*, leaves
large, regular, oblong, a little acute, very distant on the
wood, central nerve strong; flowers rose-coloured in large
corymbs, branching finely; *I. bandhùca*, leaves very close
to the stem, ovate, acuminate; nerves straight, middle
nerve stronger than any other of the genus; flowers scarlet.
I. blánda, leaves small, lanceolate, ovate; flowers blush,
cymes branching in three. *I. dichotìma*, leaves largest of
the genus, ovate, acuminate, undulate footstalk three-
eighths of an inch long; whereas, none of the leaves of the
other species have footstalks of any length; it is now called
I. undulàta; flowers are white. *I. grandiflòra*, leaves
ovate, elongate, sessile; flowers scarlet, in crowded round
corymbs; is called *I. coccìnea* in the Botanical Magazine,
by which it is known in our collections, and we think is
the same as *l. strìcta*. *I. flámmea* and *I. speciòsa*. *I.
fúlgens*, same as *I. longifòlia* and *I. lanceolàta;* foliage
glossy; flowers scarlet. *I. Pavétta*, the flowers are white
and sweet-scented, the leaves of all the species are opposite; there are a few other species that we are not thoroughly
acquainted with, but have been thus explicit to prevent
error as far as possible in this beautiful genus. They are
all evergreen, low growing shrubs; the plants grow best in
Jersey black sandy earth, but flower most abundantly with
Soil No. 10.

Jambosas, about twelve species, which have been principally taken from *Eugènia*, and contains its finest plants,

and is a splendid genus of evergreen shrubs. *E. Jámbos* is now *Jambòsa vulgàris*, which flowers and fruits freely in our hot-houses. The fruit is about an inch in diameter, eatable, and smelling like a rose, hence called "Rose Apple." The petals of all the species are simple, and may rather be considered the calyx; the beauty of the flowers is in the many erect spreading stamens, either straw, white, rose, or green colour. *J. malaccénsis*, Malay Apple, is greatly esteemed for the delightful fragrance of its fruit. We frequently see *J. purpuráscens*, which is a native of the West Indies, going under *J. m.*, which is an Asiatic species, with white flowers and entire oblong leaves; whereas, the leaves of *J. p.* are small, ovate, acuminate; the young shoots and leaves are purple. *J. macrophylla*, white, and *J. amplexicaùlis*, green, have very large oblong, lanceolate leaves, and are of a strong, woody habit. They are all easy of culture. (Soil No. 11.)

Jasmìnum, Jasmine, is a favourite genus of shrubs, for the exquisite fragrance of its flowers, of which none are more delightful thán *J. sàmbac* or Arabian Jasmine. There are two other varieties of it, *J. s. múltiplex*, perfectly double; and *J. s. trẏfòliatum*, double Tuscan Jasmine. The latter requires a great heat to make it grow and flower freely. There is also a semi-double variety in cultivation. *J. hirsùtum* has cordate downy leaves; flowers many, in terminal sessile umbels. *I. paniculàtum*, white, flowering in terminal panicles from March to November; leaves smooth, oval, obtusely acumínate; *plant scarce.* *J. simplicifòlium* is in our collections under the name of *J. lucidum;* plant spreading; leaves oblong and shining. *J. multiflòrum* is a profusely flowering and beautiful species. There are several others, all with white flowers, and generally easy of culture. (Soil No. 11.)

Játropha, Physic-nut, is a genus of six strong growing shrubs, natives of the West Indies. *J. multifida* and *J. panduræfòlia* have the handsomest foliage, and both have scarlet flowers: the appearance of the foliage of this genus is the only object: the flowers are small, in coarse disfigured panicles, and several of the species have not been known to flower in artificial cultivation. The seeds of *J. cùrcas* are often received from the West Indies; the leaves are cordate, angular and smooth. *J. manihot*, now *Ma-*

nihot cannabìna, is the Cassada root, the juice of which, when expressed, is a strong poison. They are all easy of culture: want of strong heat in winter will make them cast their leaves, but does them no other injury. (Soil No. 17.)

Justícia. A few species of this genus are fine showy hot-house plants. *J. coccínea* has large terminal spikes of scarlet flowers, blooming from December to March, and is a very desirable plant, of easy culture, and should be in every collection; it is apt to grow spindley, if not kept near the glass. *I. picta*, with its varieties, *I. lúcida* and *I. calyctrìcha*, are fine shrubby species. *I. speciòsa* is a beautiful profuse purple flowering plant. (Soil No. 11.)

Kæmpfèria, an Asiatic genus of tuberose rooted plants; none of them in our collections, except *K. rotúnda;* the flowers come up a few inches above the pot, without the leaves, in April and May, and frequently sooner; they are purple and light blue, partially streaked and spotted; leaves large, oblong, purplish-coloured beneath. The roots, when dormant, ought to be kept in the pot without watering, otherwise they will not flower freely. No bulbs nor strong tuberose rooted plants will flower in perfection if kept moist when they are not growing. (Soil No. 17.)

Lantàna, a genus of twenty species, all free-flowering shrubs; the flowers are small, in round heads blooming from the axils, in yellow, orange, pink, white and changeable colours; principally of a rough straggling growth, and are not esteemed. However, *L. sellòi*, light purple; *L. mutàbilis*, yellow, orange and pink; *L. bícolor*, white and pink, and *L. fucáta* (or *Douglásii* of some), lilac and white. These are very handsome growing plants, and will even keep in a good green-house; but in such case will only bloom in summer. They will not bear a strong fumigation; therefore, when the hot-house is under that operation, they must be set down in the pathway, or other low part in the house. (Soil No. 9.)

Latànias. This genus contains three species of handsome palms. *L. barbònica* is one of the finest of the *Palmæ*, not growing to great magnitude; the leaves or fronds are plaited flabelliform, leaflets smooth at the edge, footstalk spiny, and the plant spreading. *L. rùbra*, fronds same as the former, but leaflets more divided and serrulate; footstalk unarmed: foliage reddish. *L. glaucophylla*, same as *L. rùbra*, only the foliage glaucous. They are all valuable plants, and are obtained by seed from the East Indies. They require plenty of pot room. (Soil No. 12.)

Laúrus. This genus, though of no beauty in flower, is generally admired in collections for its fine evergreen foliage, and aromatic or spicy flavour, and several trees are important in medicine. The most esteemèd are given to a genus named *Cinnamomum*, as has been observed in the green-house, (see *March.*) *L. Chloróxylon* is the Cogwood of Jamaica. *L. pérsea* is now *Pérsea gratíssima*, Alligator-pear, a fruit about the size of a large pear, and greatly esteemed in the West Indies ; the plant is generally known in our collections. *C. vérum* is the true Cinnamon of commerce.

The part taken is the inside of the bark when the tree is from five to eighteen years old. The leaves are threenerved, ovate, oblong ; nerves vanishing toward the point, bright green above, pale beneath, with whitish veins. This plant ought to be kept in the warmest part of the hot-house. *C. cássia* is frequently given under the former name, but, when compared, may be easily detected by the leaves being more lanceolate and a little pubescent. They both make handsome plants, but require great heat. Drain the pots well of the delicate sorts. (Soil No. 13.)

Magnifera, Mango tree. There are two species. *M. índica* is in our collections, and bears a fruit which is so highly esteemed in the East Indies, as to be considered preferable to any other except very fine pine apples. The leaves are lanceolate, and from six to eight inches long, and two or more broad. The flowers are produced in loose bunches at the end of the branches, but of no beauty, and have to be artificially impregnated, or it will scarcely produce fruit. The shell is kidney-shaped, and of a leathery crustaceous substance. They contain one seed, and in their indigenous state are more juicy than an apple. Drain the pots well, as the roots are apt to get sodden from moisture. The other species goes under the name of *oppositifòlia*, but we question if it is not only a variety, for it has every character of the one just described. (Soil No. 11.)

Malpíghia, (Barbadoes-cherry,) about eighteen species, all beautiful evergreen trees or shrubs. They are easily

15

distinguished by having bristles on the underside of the leaves. These bristles are fixed by the centre, so that either end of it will sting. We are not aware of any other plant being defended in this manner. *M. ùrens* has oblong, ovate leaves, with decumbent stiff bristles; flowers pink. *M. aquifòlia* has lanceolate, stiff, spiny leaves, and we think the most beautiful foliage of the genus. *M. fucàta* has elliptical shining leaves, with lilac flowers. *M. glàbra*, leaves ovate, entire, smooth; flowers purple. They all have five rounded clawed petals. The last species is cultivated in the West Indies for its fruit. The pots must be well drained. (Soil No. 17.)

Merica, a genus of hot-house plants, closely allied to *Iris*, between which there is no distinction in the leaves. The flowers of *M. cœrùlea* are beautifully spotted with light and dark blue, the scape many-flowered. *M. Sabìni* has flowers similar, but not so dark in colour. *M. North-iàna* has splendid white and brown spotted flowers, spathe two-flowered. These plants, when growing, require a liberal supply of water, and should be greatly encouraged by frequent potting, to flower well. (Soil No. 12.)

Melàstoma was once an extensive genus, on which the natural order *Melastomaceæ* is founded; but is now much divided into other genera contained in the natural tribe *Micomeæ*. There are about thirteen species remaining in the genus. They now display great unity of character, and many of them may be considered very ornamental. The finest are *M. heteromàlla*, bluish purple, and an abundant bloomer; *M. malabàthrica*, rose-coloured; *M. sanguínea*, lilac; *M. splendens*, large violet; and *M. àspera*, rose. There is a plant in several of our collections known as *M. purpùrea* and *M. tetragòna*, which is *Ossæa purpuráscens ;* leaves ovate, lanceolate, acuminate, five-nerved, pilose; the footstalk and nerves underside of the leaf covered with brown hairs; stem four-sided; flowers purple. All the species are easy of culture. *M. nepalénsis* is a green-house plant. (Soil No. 1.)

Mandevilla Suaveòlens, or *Chili Jasmine:* this beautiful climber is a native of South America; the flowers are in clusters and nearly bell-shaped, white, and of exquisite fragrance; the bloom is produced on the extremity of the shoots. After the flowering season the plants should be pruned back to within a few eyes of the preceding year's wood. (Soil No. 13.)

Mùsa, (Plantain tree,) contains eight species, and is greatly esteemed in the East and West Indies for the luscious sweet flavour of its fruit, which can be converted into every delicacy in the domestic cookery of the country. *M. paradisìaca* is the true plantain tree, has a soft herbaceous stalk, fifteen or twenty feet high, with leaves from five to seven feet long, and about two feet wide. *M. sapiéntum* is the true banana tree; habit and character same as the former, except it has a spotted stem, and the male flowers are deciduous. The pulp of the fruit is softer, and the taste more luscious. *M. rosàcea*, *M. coccìnea*, and *M. chinènsis*, are more esteemed in artificial cultivation for their flowers, and for being smaller in growth. *M. Cavendìshii* produces immense clusters of ripe and well-flavoured fruit, plants only four feet and a half high; will yearly produce about eighty pounds. *M. dàcca* is another dwarf species, and in 1838 ripened a cluster of fruit in the Royal Botanic Gardens of Edinburgh, which weighed fifty pounds. These dwarf Bananas are now being cultivated in Europe expressly for their fruit, which is very delicious when perfectly ripened. They are Chinese plants, and will soon be introduced into the West India Islands, where they will entirely supplant the large varieties.

Myrtus Piménta, or, more properly, *Piménta Vulgáris*, is the Jamaica pepper or allspice; there is no beauty in the flowers—the leaves are highly aromatic, and it is a handsome evergreen. (Soil No. 9.)

Nepénthes, (Pitcher-plant.) There are two species of this plant. *N. distillatòria* is an esteemed and valuable plant in European collections, and we are not aware of there being any in this country, except in Philadelphia. The leaves are lanceolate and sessile; from their extremity there is a spiral, attached to which are long inflated appendages that are generally half full of water, which appears to be confined within them by a lid with which the appendages are surmounted; hence the name of pitcher plant. We have never observed the lids close again when once open. Writers have called it an herbaceous plant, but it is properly a climbing shrub. The pot in which it grows should be covered with moss, and the roots liberally sup-

plied with water every day. It delights to be in a moist
state. The flowers are small, and in long spikes. The
plant is of easy culture, and even rapid in growth : a plant
with us, only nineteen months old, is now five feet high.
(Soil No. 5.)

Pancràtium is a genus of hot-house bulbs, and now only
contains five species. They are all free-flowering. Several of them are handsome and fragrant. *P. maritimum*
and *P. verecúndum* are the finest; the flowers are white,
in large umbels; petals long, recurved, and undulate. *P.
littoràlis*, *P. speciòsum*, and *P. caribæum*, are now given
to the genus *Hymenocàllis*, and are fine flowering species.
Care must be taken not to give them water while dormant.
The soil ought at that time to be in a half dry state. They
are in flower from May to August. (Soil No. 12.)

Pandànus, Screw Pine. There are about twenty species
in this genus, several of them very interesting, but none so
greatly admired as *P. odoratissimus*. The leaves in established plants are from four to six feet long, on the back
and edges spiny; are spreading, imbricated, and embracing
the stem, and placed in three spiral rows upon it. The
top soon becomes heavy when the plant throws out prongs
one, two, or three feet up the stem in an oblique descending
direction, which take root in the ground, and thus become
perfectly supported. It is cultivated in Japan for its delightful fragrance, and it is said, "of all the perfumes, it is
by far the richest and most powerful." *P. útilis*, red
spined. We question this species, and are inclined to believe that it is the former, only when the plants are newly
raised from seed, the spines and leaves are red, changing
to green as they become advanced in age. The plants
are easy of culture, and will grow almost in any soil. (Soil
No. 12.)

Passiflóra, "Passion-Flower, so named on account of its
being supposed to represent in the appendages of its flower
the Passion of Jesus Christ." There are about fifty species, all climbing plants, that belong to the hot-house. Many
are of no ordinary beauty ; a few species are odoriferous;
others bear edible fruits, though not rich in flavour. *P.
alàta* is in our collections, and greatly admired; the flowers
are red, blue, and white, beautifully contrasted, and flower
profusely in pots. *P. racemòsa*, red flower. *P. cærúleo-*

racemósa, purple. *P. quadrangulàris* has beautiful red
and white flowers. The plant is in several collections, but
has seldom flowered; it requires to be planted in the ground
to make it flower freely, and it will also produce fruit. *P.
picturàta* is a scarce and beautiful various-coloured species.
P. kermesina, bright rosy crimson, and, beyond all question, the most profuse flowering species now in cultivation,
and will do well in a good green-house. *P. Loudònii*,
bright crimson; *P. edúlis* is cultivated for its fruit. There
are many other fine species, but these are the most esteemed sorts; and, when well established, will flower profusely from May to August. They are desirable in every
collection, and will take only a small space to hold them,
by training the vines up the rafters of the hot-house. (Soil
No. 13.)

Phœnix, Date-palm, about eight species, principally
Asiatic plants. The foliage is not so attractive as many
others of the palm family, but it is rendered interesting by
producing a well-known fruit called Date. *P. dactylifera*
will do very well in a common green-house. In Arabia,
Upper Egypt, and Barbary, it is much used in domestic
economy. *P. paludósa* has the most beautiful foliage,
and the best habit. The flowers are diœcious. (Soil No.
12.)

Plumbágo rósea is a pretty free-blooming plant, with
continued profusion of red flowers; it requires plenty of
heat and a good drainage. (Soil No. 11.)

Plumèrias, above twenty species. Plants of a slow
growth, robust nature, and are deciduous. The foliage is
greatly admired. The plants are shy to flower, but are
brilliant in colour. *P. acuminàta* has lanceolate, acute
leaves, flowers corymbose and terminal. *P. tricolor* has
oblong, acute, veiny leaves; corolla red, yellow and white.
This and P. *rubrá* are the finest of the genus. They
ought not to get any water while not in a growing state.
(Soil No. 11.)

Poinséttia pulcherrìma. When well cultivated, this

---

* Named by Professor Graham, of Edinburgh, in compliment
to the Hon. J. R. Poinsett, (late secretary of war,) who introduced the plant in 1828 to this country from Mexico, while he was
Minister Plenipotentiary to that Republic. He also, at the same
time, introduced a rich and valuable collection of Cactæa.

is truly the most magnificent of all the tropical plants we
have ever seen; from December to April it is crowned with
flowers, surrounding which, are bright scarlet whorls of
bracteæ, frequently measuring twenty-two inches in diameter. To grow it to such perfection, we treat it as follows: in April we cut the young wood down to within two
inches of the wood of the preceding year, and reduce the
ball of earth, putting it into a smaller pot. About the end
of May we plant it in the open ground, in light rich soil,
giving it one or two waterings after planting. During
summer it will grow three or four feet; about the end of
September, it is carefully lifted and potted into a large-
sized pot, and put into the hot-house, carefully shading it
for a few days—when it requires no more attention except
a regular supply of water, and to be kept in a temperature
of from 55° to 75°. There is also a pale yellow bracteced
variety; but we are not aware of its being for sale in this
country. When the plant is grown in pots during summer, it must be repotted every month to encourage its
rapid growth. (Soil No. 18.)

Polyspòra axillàris, once called *Caméllia axillàris*,
though in appearance it has no characteristic of a *Caméllia*,
and has been frequently killed in the green-house by being
too cold for its nature; leaves oblong, obovate, toward the
extremity serrulate. The leaves on the young wood are
entire. Flowers white; petals a little notched. It is
worthy of a situation in every collection. (Soil No. 11.)

Pterospérmum, five species of plants that have very
curiously constructed flowers, of a white colour, and fragrant; the foliage is of a brown rusty nature, and, before
expansion, silvery-like. *P. suberifòlium* is in several of
our collections, and esteemed. *P. semisagittàtum* has
fringed bractæa; leaves oblong, acuminate, entire, sagittate
on one side. (Soil No. 11.)

Rhápis, a genus of palms that will grow very freely with
heat and room at the roots. *R. flabellifórmis* is an erect
growing palm, with a spreading head. It is a native of
China. (Soil No. 12.)

Rondelétia speciósa is a new and rare plant, in every respect equal, if not superior, to *Ixòra còccinea;* its large
corymbs of orange-red flowers have a very striking appear-

ance, and it is easily cultivated in soil No. 1. It should have frequent repottings when growing.

Ruéllia. There are a few species, very pretty free-flowering plants, of easy culture. *R. formòsa*, flowers long, of a fine scarlet colour; plant half shrubby. *R. fulgida* has bright scarlet flowers on axillary long stalked fascicles. *R. persicifòlia*, with unequal leaves and light blue flowers, is now called *R. anisophylla.* (Soil No. 10.)

Russèlia júncea, a slender plant of an upright habit, producing, when well-grown, a profusion of scarlet tubular flowers, about one inch long each: it is of the easiest culture in soil No. 19.

Sàgus, Sago-palm. We are of opinion that the true palm from which the sago of the shops is produced, has not been introduced into our collections. It is very rare in the most extensive collections of Europe, but it is not so fine a plant as the one we have under the Sago, which is placed in the natural order of *Cycadeæ;* and Sagus is in that of *Palmæ.* The finest of this genus is *S. vinifera* and *S. Rúmphii.* They grow to a great height; even in artificial cultivation they may be seen from ten to twenty-five feet. We have not introduced them here for their beauty, but to prevent error. (Soil No. 12.)

Solándra, a genus of four species, remarkable for the extraordinary size of their flowers, and are considered beautiful. *S. grandiflòra* and *S. viridiflòra* are the best two. The plants will bloom well if they are restricted in pot room, and are only introduced as being worthy of cultivation. If they are repotted once in two or three years, it is sufficient, except where the plants are small and want encouragement. (Soil No. 13.)

Strelitzia, a splendid genus of noble-looking plants, all of which do perfectly well in the green-house, except *S. augùsta*, the flowers of which are pure white; the leaves are very large, being nearly six feet long and eighteen inches wide, and assume the appearance of the Banana tree: it requires great space for its roots. (Soil No. 12.)

Stephanotus florabundus, a new and splendid evergreen climber, with dark green thick leaves like a luxuriant wax-plant, producing large bunches of pure white fragrant flowers; of easy culture in soil No. 13.

Swietènia, (Mahogany tree,) the wood of which is cele-

brated in cabinet-work. *S. mahógoni,* common. This tree
varies much in general appearance, according to soil and
situation. The leaves are pinnated in four pairs; leaflets
ovate, lanceolate ; flowers small, white, in axillary panicles.
S. fubrifùga, leaves pinnated, in four pairs ; leaflets elliptical; flowers white, in terminal panicles. The wood of
the last is the most durable of any in the East Indies.
They are fine plants, and require heat and pot room to produce flowers. (Soil No. 15.)

Tabernæmontàna, a genus of little beauty, except for
one or two species. A plant known in some collections as
Nèrium coronàrium, is now, and properly, *T. coronària.*
The variety *flòre plèno* is the one most deserving of culture, and will flower profusely from May to August ; the
flowers are double white, fragrant and divaricating. The
plant will lose its foliage if not kept in a strong heat ;
therefore place it in the warmest part of the hot-house. *T.
densiflòra* is a fine species, but very rare. Drain all the
plants well, and keep them in the shade during summer.

Tecòma, a genus of plants closely allied to *Bignònia,* and
are free-flowering; several of them much esteemed. *T.
móllis, T. digitáta,* and *T. splèndida,* are the most beautiful of those that belong to the hot-house. They have
large orange-coloured, tubular, inflated, ringent flowers, in
loose panicles. There is a plant known in our collections
as *Bignònia stáns,* which is now *T. stàns;* has pinnated
leaves, with oblong, lanceolate, serrated leaflets; flowers in
simple terminal, raceme, and of a yellow colour, and sometimes known by Ash-leaved *Bignònia.* It will always
have a sickly aspect, if not well encouraged in light rich
soil. Drain the pots well, as much moisture disfigures the
foliage. (Soil No. 10.)

Thrinax parviflòra is a fine dwarf palm of the West
Indies, with palmated fronds, plaited with stiff, lanceolate
segments. The plant is of easy cultivation, and will grow
in any soil. (Soil No. 12.)

Thunbérgia, a genus containing six climbing plants of
a half shrubby nature. Some of them have a fragrant
odour. *T. coccínea,* red ; *T. grandiflòra,* blue; *T. fràgrans,* white sweet scented; *T. aláta* has pretty buff and
purple flowers, which are in great profusion. The latter
makes a very pretty annual in the flower garden, with its

beautiful white variety, forming an elegant contrast. If sown in May, they will bloom from July until killed by frost. (Soil No. 13.)

Tradescántia discolor. Purple-leaved spider wort. This is an herbaceous plant, and is only cultivated for its beautiful purple foliage. It has curious small white flowers. (Soil No. 10.)

Uránia speciósa, a gigantic-looking plant closely connected to *Musa,* from which it differs in habit by the large leaves being more erect: to grow it luxuriantly, give it plenty of heat, water, and pot room. (Soil No. 12.)

Zàmia, a genus of plants in the natural order of *Cycadeæ.* Several species of them are admired. *Z. média, Z. furfuràcea, Z. ténuis, Z. integrifòlia,* are the most showy that belong to the hot-house. The whole genus is frequently kept in this department. They are all plants of a slow growth, and the beauty is entirely in the pinnated fronds, with from ten to forty pairs of leaflets. The pots must be well drained. (Soil No. 11.)

Those genera of plants which we have enumerated under the head of repotting in this or next month, are composed of the finest hot-house plants that have come under our observation. There are perhaps a few of them that are not to be found in the United States, or even on our continent; but the great object, in a choice collection of plants, is to have the finest from all parts of the known world. There are many plants whose nature does not require much support from soil, which is frequently observed in those that are mentioned. And there are many hundreds of plants desirable for beauty, ornament, and curiosity, which would take volumes to specify and describe. In fact, every year brings many · *new* things, and frequently both *new* and splendid, either in flower, fruit, or foliage.

We have previously observed, that plants ought not to be flooded with water when newly potted, as it saturates the soil before the roots have taken hold of it; and that the best draining for pots is small gravel or pot-shreds broken fine. We wish it to be understood that, when plants are repotted, any irregular branch or shoot should be lopped off that cannot be tied to advantage. And repotting may take place either before or after the plants are exposed to the open air, according to convenience.

OF BRINGING OUT THE HOT-HOUSE PLANTS.

Where the hot-house is very crowded with plants, the best method to have them exposed without danger is, to take out those of the hardiest nature first, that have no tender shoots upon them, thereby thinning the house gradually. This may be done from the sixteenth to the twentieth of the month, which will admit of a free circulation of air among those that remain. All may be exposed from the twenty-fourth to the twenty-eighth of the month. This is a general rule, though in some seasons there may be exceptions. Having previously given all the air possible to the house, that no sudden transition take place, which would make the foliage brown and otherwise materially injure the plants, choose calm days for the removing of them.

There are few plants while in pots that agree with the full sun upon them ; or, if the plants receive the sun, the pots and roots ought not. The best situation for them is on the north side of a fence, wall, house, or other building, where they are excluded from the mid-day sun, and they should stand on boards or gravel, with the tallest at the back, firmly tied to a rail or some other security, to prevent them from being overturned by high winds. Make a fanciful bed, and cover it with sand or coal ashes, for the reception of the smaller plants, and setting them thinly and regularly thereon, is preferable to crowding them with the taller sorts. And it may be desired to have some of the plants plunged in the garden through the flower borders. Of those that are so treated, the pots must be plunged to the brim, and regularly turned round every two weeks, to prevent the roots from running into the earth. If the roots were allowed to do so, it might for the present strengthen the plant, but ultimately would prove injurious.

Where a sufficiency of shade cannot be obtained, it would be advisable to go to the expense of a very thin awning, that would not exclude the light, but merely the powerful rays of the sun, attending to roll it up every evening. Plants will keep in beautiful order by the above method, which amply repays for the trouble or expense.

Avoid putting plants under trees; comparatively few thrive
in such situations.

When they are thus exposed to the open air, it will be
very little trouble to give them a gentle syringing every
evening when there is no rain, and continue your usual
examinations for insects: when they appear, resort to the
prescribed remedies. *Green-fly* will not affect them, but
the thrips may. Give regular supplies of water every
evening, and again in the morning to all that require it,
carefully examining those that are in small pots.

SUCCULENTS, OR THE CACTÆA TRIBE.

The *Céreus Mammallària*, and *Opúntia.* Divisions of
this family are, in their indigenous state, exposed on rocks,
hilly lands, and arid situations, being at all times fully exposed to the sun : still, with us, we find that they thrive
best with a partial shade, though we have frequently seen
them doing well when fully exposed to the influence of the
sun; but where they are to be kept out of doors all the
season, be careful in choosing for them an airy situation,
and never allow the pots to become saturated with moisture.

The habits of the *Epiphyllum* tribe are entirely different; they are generally parasites, growing on the branches
and about the roots of decayed trees; consequently, they
are often much shaded, and they evidently show it, for they
still delight to be shaded from the direct rays of a noon-day
sun. If they are kept in the house through the summer
months, take some whiting, and make a thin white-wash,
and put it on the inside of the glass, which will be found
an agreeable and effectual shade; but where time and
means are at hand, a thin awning, of gauze or muslin, is
preferable, provided it is regularly rolled up when the sun
is not powerful.

JUNE AND JULY.

As the plants of the hot-house are all exposed to the open air, the directions will include both months. If the repotting is over, as recommended last month, all the attention they will require until the end of August is, the administering of water at the roots, and by the syringe overhead. It will be impossible to say how great are their wants, these depending entirely upon the nature of the plant, the situation, and the season; but never neglect to look over them every evening, and after dry nights they will need a fresh supply in the morning, observing to give to none except they are becoming a little dry. Make weekly examinations for insects of any description, and when they appear, have them instantly destroyed.

Always after heavy rains look over the pots, in case water should be standing in them, which would injure the roots. Where any is found, turn the pot on its side, and, in a few hours, examine the draining which is defective; small pots in continued rains should be turned likewise.

Tie up all plants and shoots to prevent them from being destroyed by the wind, and be attentive to pick all weeds from the pots. Turn round all the plants occasionally, to prevent them from being drawn to one side by the sun or light.

AUGUST.

The plants of the hot-house that were repotted in May and June, according to the directions therein given, will, at present, be in an excellent state of health, provided they have got, at all times, the requisite supplies of watering. And as we already have been very explicit on that subject, more remarks now would be merely repetition.

REPOTTING.

If any of the repottings were neglected during May or June, let it be done about the first of this month. Let young plants that are growing freely, where the roots have filled the pots, and the plants required to grow, have pots one size larger. In turning out the ball of earth, keep it entire, not disturbing any of the roots.

OF PAINTING, REPAIRING AND CLEANSING THE HOUSE.

The necessary repairs of the hot-house are too often put off to the last day or week; and then with hurry are super-ficially attended to. Previous to the first of September, have all the wood-work painted, (which ought to have one coat every two years,) and the glass all neatly repaired. Have the flues and furnace examined ; plaster over all rents and make good every deficiency. Give the flue a thick coat of lime white-wash. Have the walls, shelves and staging properly painted. If there is a tan-bed, have that renewed ; take out what is most decayed, using two-thirds new tan, which must be dried at least three days in the sun before it is housed, and carefully protect it from rains.

16

SEPTEMBER.

DRESSING THE PLANTS.

HAVING last month put the house in complete order, all that remains necessary to be attended to, is the state of the plants and pots, which should be regularly examined, and of those where the roots fill the soil, a little may be taken off the top, supplying its place with fresh earth, thereby giving what is called a top-dressing. Give each that re-quires it a sufficient rod, tying the plant neatly thereto; minutely scrutinize each for insects, and where they are detected, have them eradicated.

Finally, wash all contracted foulness from off the pots, at the same time pick off any decayed leaves; thus all will be in perfect order to take into the house. If any plants have been kept in the hot-house during summer, they must like-wise go through the same operation.

OF TAKING IN THE PLANTS.

From the 16th to the 24th, according to the season, is the proper time to take in the hot-house plants. It is pre-ferable to have them what might be deemed a few days too early, than have them in the slightest degree affected by cold.

Commence by housing the largest first, and those that stand farthest in the house, observing to place the most ten-der sorts nearest the heat or warmest part of the house. For observations on them, see *May*. In regard to arrange-ment, that must be according to the taste of the operator. We may observe, that in a small collection it is better to have them in a regular than in a picturesque form. A dry shelf is indispensable in this department for placing on it all herbaceous plants, such as *Cánna Hedychium, Zingi-ber, Kœmpféria,* &c., the watering of which from this time should be gradually suspended, that they may have their required cessation to make them flower well. This shelf

may be in any situation; one in darkness, where other
plants will not grow, will answer perfectly well. If there
is a bark bed, do not until the end of December, plunge
any of the pots therein. If any plants of the *Poinséttia*
are in the ground, have them carefully lifted and shaded
from the sun.

GENERAL OBSERVATIONS.

The plants being now all under protection, they must
have as much air as possible admitted to them every day,
by opening the doors, front and top sashes, closing only at
night. The syringings must be continued, and care taken
that plants of a deciduous or herbaceous nature are not
over-watered. The tuberous species might be kept almost
dry. Some practical men of sound science repot these
plants in this month into fresh soil, and allow them to stand
till January almost without water. We have never adopted this method with any description of plants, but do not
doubt of its success with that genus.

See that the ropes and pulleys of the sashes are in good
order, and fit to stand all winter.

OCTOBER.

VERY few directions remain to be given to the department
of the hot-house. The supplies of water for this and the
two succeeding months are, according to the state and nature of tropical plants, more limited than at any other period
of the year. This is the first month of what may be called
their dormant state. Observe the herbaceous plants, that
they are set aside as soon as their foliage decays, in case
of being too liberally supplied with water. Airing is
highly essential about this period, that the plants may be
gradually hardened; but guard against injuring them.
The temperature should never be under fifty degrees:
when the days are cool and the wind chilling, airing is not

necessary; and, when air is admitted, always close up
early in the afternoon, while the atmosphere is warm, to
supersede the necessity of fire as long as possible. If, at
any time, you have recourse to it in this month, use it with
great caution.

Examine all the shutters and fastenings, and see that they
are in good substantial order, and, where deficient, repair
them instantly, that they may be in readiness. Remove
all leaves, and give syringings in the morning of sunshine
days, twice a week. Clear off, sweep out, and wash clean,
that every part may be in the neatest order.

The succulent tribe will not require water more than
once a week, or once in two weeks. If any of them have
ripened seeds during summer, wash such carefully from
the pulp, and lay them past till the first of January, when
they may be sown on the surface of sandy soil, and gently
pressed down. Water them very carefully as they require; cover the pot with a piece or pane of glass, which
will greatly assist their vegetating. In a few weeks they
will make their appearance; and, when they are one-quar-
ter of an inch high, plant them out into other pots and
fresh soil. In a few months they will make wonderful
progress in growth, and, in the following year, will require
to be potted singly, and treated as recommended for established plants.

NOVEMBER.

The essential points to be attended to in the hot-house
during this month are, *fire*, *air*, and *water*. The former
must be applied according to the weather, observing not to
allow the temperature to be under fifty degrees, and it
ought not to continue long at that degree; fifty-two degrees
being preferable. The shutters should be on every night
when there is any appearance of frost, and taken off early
in the morning. Admit air in small portions every day
that the sun has any effect and the atmosphere mild, observing that the temperature of the house be above sixty

degrees previous to admission. Shut all close early in the afternoon, or when any sudden changes occur.

OF A CISTERN AND WATER.

In watering, it is important to have the water of the same temperature in this department as the roots of the plants. To have this, there are two kinds of cisterns or tanks that might be adopted ; one may be sunk in the house under ground, either closely plastered, or lined with lead, and neatly covered up, having a small perpendicular pump therein, or placed so that the water could be lifted by hand. The other might, where convenience will admit, be placed over the furnace, either in the back shed, or inside of the house, and the water could be drawn off this by a stop-cock. These can be supplied, in part, with rain water, by having spouts round the house to lead into the cisterns, supplying any deficiency from the pump. Thus water of a congenial temperature may be always at hand, which is of great importance to the healthful constitution of the plants. The water must now be given in moderate portions, examining the plants every day. Be careful in watering bulbs, as the smallest supply is sufficient for them at present. Succulents will require a little every two weeks, except they are over the flues, when they may have some every week.

Constantly clear off all decayed leaves, and carry them out of the house, which sweep and wash clean, and keep all in the neatest order.

DECEMBER.

THE uncertainty of the weather in this month requires the operator to be constantly on guard, to ward off danger, either from frost, snow, or cutting winds. The temperature observed last month must be continued, but not exceeded, which would cause premature vegetation, of which the result and effects have already been observed. Always

kindle the fires in time, to prevent the heat from being
lower than what has been mentioned, lest a severe frost
should take place, as then a considerable lapse ensues
before the fire has any effect; and if the wind blows high,
the result might be injurious, unless the house be very
close.

OF SHUTTERS.

The benefit of these in severe weather is of material
service, for the preservation of an even temperature in the
house during the night, when changes are not observed;
but they ought never to remain on through the day, when
the fire can be properly attended to. If the front and the
lowest sash of the roof are covered with these, it is generally sufficient. They should be made of three-quarter
inch boards, closely grooved together, having a cross bar in
the centre, and one at each end and each side, which will
make them substantial. If they are frequently painted
with care, they will last many years. Snow ought not to
be allowed to lay on these while they are on the glass, for
reasons that we have assigned. See *January* and *February*.

Some adopt double panes of glass to supersede the use
of shutters, which they think are attended with considerable labour, (at the most only fifteen minutes a day, while in
use.) The sash frame is made a little deeper, so as to
allow half an inch between the panes of glass. The one
is glazed from the out and the other from the inside. It
appears to answer the purpose tolerably well, but the glass
must be both fine and even on the surface, lest a lens should
be produced, which would scourge the plants. We are
almost confident that we have seen this effect in some instances. There must be a small hole about an eighth of
an inch in both ends of each row of glass, to allow a current to dry up the moisture that may arise. Double sashes
during the severe months are frequently used; but shutters
are preferable to either.

OF PLACING BULBS, &c., IN THE HOT-HOUSE.

If any *Hyacinths* or other Dutch roots are wanted to flower early, a few of them may be put in the hot-house near the front glass, which will greatly tend to forward their time of flowering. By having some brought in every two weeks, a continued succession of bloom will be kept up.

GENERAL OBSERVATIONS.

If there is a tan-bed in the house, and it was renewed in September, the pots should now be half plunged therein. The violent heat will partly be over, and the plants are not so liable to suffer at root in this as last month. It will in part prevent the plants from being affected by sudden changes of temperature. Be attentive in keeping all insects completely under. This is the period that these are most neglected, but by attending to the modes of their destruction, as already given, no species of them will either be hurtful or unsightly. Syringe the plants about twice a week, and always remember that decayed leaves or litter of any description, do not beautify healthy plants, neither do they form a part of a well kept hot-house.

ORCHIDEOUS EPIPHYTES OR AIR PLANTS.

Before we close the hot-house subject, it may be interesting to some of our readers to know the nature and character of a few of the most desirable of those tropical parasites, that have within these few years caused so much excitement in Europe. In several instances, houses upward of two hundred feet long have been erected for their exclusive culture, and unless they do thus have an apartment adapted to their nature, no success will attend their cultivation. They grow only in a very humid atmosphere, kept at a temperature of from 70° to 100°, and also in a partially shaded situation : it is only under such treatment that we have had any prosperity in blooming these pecu-

liarly beautiful and interesting plants.   Annexed are the
names of a few that are of the easiest culture and most
profuse of flower :

Brássia maculàta, greenish yellow, spotted with purple.
Catasètum trifidúm, greenish yellow, spotted with dark
    brown.
Cáttleya críspa, white and purple, and is considered a su-
    perb plant.
Cáttleya labiàta, rose and rich purple, striped and spotted
    with carmine.
Cáttleya Forbésii, yellow, white, green and rose-coloured,
    fine.
Dendròbium cucullátum, rose and pale yellow.
Dendròbium speciosùm, pale yellow flowers, in great pro-
    fusion.
Epidéndrum cucullátum, dark brown, with yellow, is a
    very constant bloomer.
Gongóra atropurpùrea, dark purple ; the plant must be
    suspended in a pot or small box.
Gongóra speciósa, yellow, with black spots.
Maxillària Loddgèsii, orange flowers in long racemes.
Maxillària pícta, yellow, beautifully spotted with red and
    crimson; it is in the mornings *only* delightfully
    fragrant.
Oncìdium críspum, brownish copper colour, and profuse
    flowering.
Oncìdium papílio, bright yellow, spotted with rich brown.
Oncìdium lurídum, flowers of a brownish-green.
Renànthera coccinea, a very superb scarlet flowering plant,
    but does not bloom very freely ; it grows in moss,
    and must be suspended in a pot or tied to a piece of
    stick.
Stanhòpia grandiflòra has delicate, white, sweet-scented
    flowers.
Stanhòpia insignis, yellow and white, spotted with purple,
    and delightfully fragrant.
Vánda Roxbùrghii, flowers pale yellow.
Zygópetalums, all very beautiful flowering, generally of a
    yellowish green colour, spotted with brown.   They
    require to be kept in a hot dry atmosphere.

Orchideous epiphytes generally grow upon trees, in the recesses of damp tropical forests, establishing themselves in the forks of the branches, and even upon rocks, stones, or decayed trees. Shade, therefore, is essential to their welfare; consequently, never permit them to be exposed to violent sunshine. They require but little water at the roots, provided the atmosphere they grow in is very humid. The best soil for them is a sandy, turfy peat, containing a large portion of fibrous matter; mix with this pieces of pot-shreds or cork, and be careful not to place the plant deep in the pot; they will also grow on blocks or sticks of wood. Although we use and prefer small boxes (about six inches square) made of cork, in which they grow finely and bloom profusely. With some of the strong-growing kinds, we use, in addition to the above soil, a little leaf-mould, using always plenty of drainage. The house we cultivate them in has an eastern aspect. Shade can easily be given to them by having creepers trained up the rafters of the house, or an occasional large plant, placed in such a situation as will afford most shade during mid-day; and it must be observed, that, although the plants are fond of moisture, they never thrive, except the water has a free passage from their roots.

THE

AMERICAN FLOWER GARDEN

DIRECTORY.

GREEN-HOUSE.

ON THE CONSTRUCTION OF A GREEN-HOUSE.

In many respects, the construction of the Green-house
will be the same as the Hot-house, but might be made
much more an ornamental object, and could be erected
contiguous to the mansion-house, with large folding doors
to open at pleasure, and be connected with the drawing-
room or parlour. The extent may vary according to the
collection to be cultivated.

It was formerly the practice to build these houses with
glass only in front, and even to introduce between the windows strong piers of brick or stone; but this is now abo-
lished, and has given way to a more light and ornamental
style, by which cheerfulness and the desired utility are
better consulted. There should be conveniences for the
admission of air in the highest part of the house, that a free
current may be obtained whenever desired, which is an
essential point.

GREEN-HOUSE.

JANUARY.

THIS compartment requires particular attention, in order to preserve the plants in good health, and carry them through this precarious season of the year. A little air must be admitted at all convenient times. An hour or two at mid-day will be of the utmost importance in drying up damp and clearing off stagnated air, which is a harbour for every corruption. The top sashes being let down or turned a few inches, in mild days, (that is, when there are not high and cutting winds), from ten or eleven o'clock to two or three, according to the intensity of the frost, will renovate the interior air of the house and harden the plants. When the weather will permit, let the front sashes be opened about one inch or more. An assiduous, experienced hand will never omit an opportunity.

With regard to fire heat, the temperature must be regulated to suit the nature of the plants in a general sense; so let the mercury, or spirits of wine, of Fahrenheit's thermometer, be from 35° to 50; if it begins to fall, give a little fire heat. No doubt we have seen the thermometer much lower in the green-house than the above, even as low as 24°, without any immediate injury; but it was in an extensive collection, where the most hardy of the plants were selected into one house. Many boast how little fire they give their green-house, and how cold it is kept, not observing the miserable state of their plants—inexperience causing them to think that the least fire heat will make them grow, and would rather look on naked stems than healthy plants. The above temperature will not, in exotics, cause premature vegetation, but will cause the plants to retain the foliage requisite to vegetative nature. A high temperature is not necessary for the generality of green-house plants; on the contrary, it might very much injure them.

OF WATERING.

In this month very little is requisite, and must be given with great caution. Few plants will require much, and some hardly any; but all must be attended to, and have their wants supplied. Some will need it twice, some once a week, and some in two weeks, according to their shrubby and woody nature. Herbaceous and deciduous plants will seldom need water. Perhaps, from the shedding of the foliage to the commencement of vegetation, three or four times will be sufficient. Particular attention should be paid to the state of health and of growth, in which the plants respectively are, in the application of water; otherwise much mischief may be done, and many entirely ruined.

Green-house plants being now in an absolutely inactive state, require little more water than merely to keep the earth about their roots from becoming perfectly dry, by occasionally applying a very small quantity at the root; and, if done with a watering-pot, as described under this head in the hot-house of this month, very little will be spilt in the house to increase dampness, which, if it does appear, by any of the leaves of the plants becoming musty, they must be instantly picked off; and, if it increases, give a little fire and air. Succulent plants will not need any water during this month, unless omitted in December.

CAMELLIA JAPONICA.

This magnificent and attractive flower, with all its splendid varieties, will, about this time, begin to open its beautiful flowers. But for this admired genus of plants, our green-houses, at this season, would be void of allurement. It is, in this country, subject to red spider, and more especially in the city, which appears to be from the nature of the air. The effects of the spider on these plants, if not prevented, would prove fatal; as, from appearance, many have died by it in several collections. If it has reached a great extent, the leaves are brownish, having the appearance of being decayed, or scorched with the sun.

17

In taking hold of the leaf, it feels soft, and altogether seems to have lost its nutritive substance; and, when the young foliage expands, it becomes covered with dark brown spots, and finally very much disfigured; and, when in this state, the red spider is severe, and, ultimately, death ensues.

If any of the plants are affected as above described, take a sponge, and wash every leaf minutely with soft water, and syringe them with water three or four times a week, which will clean them. All the young foliage will be healthy, and that which has been affected will fall off. However, prevention is better than cure; and if the *Camelias* are properly syringed every evening during summer, and once or twice a week during winter, they will never be subject to the ravages of that destructive insect.

Tie up any of the flowers that are expanded to stakes, in case of accident; and, in syringing, observe not to let any water fall on the flowers, as it causes premature decay and change of colour.

OF ORANGES, LEMONS, &c.

As there will perhaps be more leisure in the green-house this month than in any other during the winter, it is presumed that there will not be a moment lost. If any of the trees are infested with insects, these, being now in their inactive state, may be more easily destroyed than at any other time. It is the brown scaly insect that generally infests them. For treatment, see *Hot-house, January.* The plant or tree, after being washed, before it becomes dry, will require to be syringed with water, otherwise the dust will adhere to the glutinous particles of the soap. Set the plant in an airy situation to dry, in case of damp. There are several others subject to this insect, such as *Myrtles, Oleas, Oleanders,* &c., which treat in the same manner. Be careful that these trees are not over-watered; if the soil is moist, it is sufficient.

OF CAPE BULBS, &c.

If there are any out of the ground, it is time that the whole were potted, such as *Lachenàlia, Wachendórfia, Eùcomis, Ixia, Gladìolus,* with several others. Keep them in the shade until they begin to grow; then put them on shelves near the light. Those that are growing must be kept in front of the house, to prevent them being weak. *Wachendórfia* has a beautiful large red tuberous root, and requires a pot about six or seven inches deep.

OF HYACINTHS AND OTHER BULBOUS ROOTS.

All these roots must be carefully examined. In case slugs or nails are preying upon the embryo of the flower, some of those that are farthest advanced may be put for a few weeks in the hot-house. It will greatly accelerate their flowering, but they must be brought out again before the florets expand, and carefully tied up, leaving room for the increase and extension of the flower stem. Give them plenty of water, and if saucers can be placed under them to retain it, it will be of advantage. Change the water every week on those that are in glasses, and keep all the growing bulbs near the light. *Narcissus, Jonquils,* &c., may be similarly treated.

FEBRUARY.

THE directions given last month respecting the airing and temperature of the house may still be followed, differing only in admitting air more freely as the season advances, and according to the power the sun has on the glass, which now begins to be considerable.

If the weather is tolerably mild, air may be admitted in time of sunshine, so as to keep the mercury as low as 50°, but be cautious in cold, cloudy, frosty weather. It is a practice with many in such weather to keep the shutters on the house night and day, for the space of a week, and sometimes more, never entering it; and, when the weather has induced them to look in, they find that the frost and damp have made many lifeless subjects; whereas, had the house and plants been attended to, in taking off the shutters, and giving a little fire when requisite, all would have been in safety, and many plants that cannot be replaced still in the collection.

When watering, strictly adhere to the directions of last month, except with *Geraniums*, and other soft wooded plants, which require a little more water towards the end of the month. If the days are mild and sunny about eight or nine o'clock in the morning, all the plants would be benefited by a gentle syringing, which retards the progress of insects, and accelerates vegetation.

Succulents, such as *Cáctus, Mesembryánthemum, Áloes, Furcrœas, Crássulas, Cotylèdons*, &c., will very seldom need water, at the same time keep them from getting as dry as powder.

OF ORANGES, LEMONS, &c.

Similar treatment to that recommended last month will do for this. Where the soil in the tubs or pots requires to be enriched, take of bone-dust or shavings, and fresh sheep dung, equal quantities; put the mixture into a large tub or barrel, until one-third full; and fill it up with water. Stir it well two or three times every day till it ferments, then give each tree one good watering with the compound. Continue to mix up afresh, and let it stand another week, and so on until all the trees requiring it are watered. This watering will greatly enrich the soil and invigorate the roots.

OF CAPE BULBS, &c.

The bulbs of *Ferrària undulata*, and *F. antheròsa*, that were taken out of the pots in October, will now require to be planted. Five-inch pots will be large enough for good roots. The grand criterion for planting bulbs is when there is a protuberant appearance about the bottom, or root part of the bulb, showing by a principle of nature, the true time for transplanting. When bulbous roots of any description appear above ground, they ought to be placed in an airy situation. They are very frequently placed under other plants, by the inexperienced, until they show their flowers, and then brought to the light, having weak flowers, and comparatively of momentary existence.

Hyacinths, Narcissus, Gladiolus, Ixia, &c., having flower stems, ought to have support, to prevent accident, especially the two former; keep them nigh the glass, and water freely. Change the water regularly once or twice a week in the bulb glasses, observing that their roots are never allowed to become matted with fetid water. Any of the above plants that are in flower might, if desired, be taken into the drawing-room or parlour, washing the pots clean, and putting saucers under them, keeping therein a little water. Twice a week the decayed ones can be taken out, and supplanted with those that are coming into bloom.

CAMELLIA JAPONICA

Will, in this month, show a profusion of flowers; and, where there is a variety, they have truly a magnificent appearance. From a good selection, endless varieties, by seed, of exquisite beauty, might be obtained by attention to the following rule: The best to select for bearing seed are *Single white, Antoniana, Grandiflòra, Waratah, Carnation Waratah, Rubricaulis, Donkelaari,* and, in many instances, the pistil, or pistillum of *Variegata, Pompone, Pœoniflora, Intermedia* and *Hosackia* are perfect, with several others. When any of the above are newly expanded, (*Waratah* is most perfect about one day before full expansion,) take a fine camel-hair pencil, and put it gently on the farina or pollen, from the double sorts, which is a yellow substance on the anthers; and, when ripe, appears in thousands of small particles. Then, with this on the pencil, dust it lightly on the stile of those intended to carry seed. Between the hours of ten and twelve in the

17*

forenoon is the most proper time for the operation; the seed will be ripe in September or October, which will be taken notice of, and directions given. For other particulars on cleaning and syringing, see *January* under this head.

OF SHIFTING, &c.

The best time to repot *Camellias* is in October or November, or just when they are done flowering, which will be before they begin to grow. There are, though not frequently, some flowers after the young foliage begins to appear, and probably it would be better to discriminate the time by the buds offering to push, which will answer to those that have no flowers as well as those that have. The most general time in shifting *Camellias* is in August and September, indiscriminately with other plants; and, if then not very gently handled, bad roots eventually are produced. Frequently very fine plants have been killed by probing, and breaking the young fibrous roots, thus causing mortification.

In the process do not, by any means, break or bruise any of the roots; and do not give large pots, with the idea of making them grow fast: it acts on most plants diametrically opposite to what is intended. A pot one or two inches wider and deeper than the one they have been in previously, is sufficient. Healthy plants, under five feet, will not require shifting oftener than once in two years; from five feet upward, in three or four years, according to the health of the plants. This treatment, in the opinion of some, will appear insufficient for their support: it will be found enough with a top-dressing every year to keep them in a healthy flowering condition, the soil being according to our description.

On turning the plant out of the pot, it may easily be observed if the soil has, in any degree, been congenial to it; for, if so, the roots will be growing all round the ball; if otherwise, no roots will appear.

Therefore, with a blunt pointed stick, probe away all the bad earth, until you come to the roots; then put the plant in a pot about one inch in diameter larger than the combined roots, previously putting a few small pieces of broken pots, or clean gravel, to drain off the superabundant moisture, and give light waterings, as the roots in this case will grow but slowly.

Top-dress all that require shifting, probe out the soil down to the roots, and by the side of the pot, taking care not to break the fibres ; then fill up with fresh earth, watering gently with a rose on the watering-pot to settle it.

OF CLEANING, &c.

If any of the plants require cleaning, either by fumigation or otherwise, let it be done before the young foliage appears, according to the directions heretofore given. Likewise tie neatly all that require it, clean and top-dress those that will not be shifted, having every plant, and all in the green-house, in perfect order before the throng of spring commences. The weather will now admit, in very fine mornings, of the plants being syringed, which may be done between seven and eight o'clock; and the path or pavement should be washed out once a week, which is a great improvement to the appearance of the whole interior.

In winter when any glass is broken, it should be immediately mended. Broken glass in cold nights causes a very destructive current of air. It should always be made water tight, for if the drops fall into the pots upon the roots, they will frequently prove fatal to the plants ; therefore care ought to be taken during rain to remove those that stand in any manner exposed.

MARCH.

THE plants in this compartment will begin to assume a different aspect, and air must be admitted every day if practicable, giving large portions in sunshine by the sashes regularly over all the house, opening those of the front a little, and likewise the doors in fine mild days. To perform this judiciously, give a little about eight or nine o'clock, more at ten, and the whole from eleven till twelve o'clock, shutting again by degrees.

Fire heat will now be dispensed with, but in frosty nights have the shutters on about sundown.   The sun is now powerful, and the house can be early shut up in the afternoon, and will gain as much natural heat as will keep up the required temperature, viz., 36° to 45°.   Perhaps there may be uncommonly cold weather: at such times be attentive to ward off danger by applying artificial heat.

OF WATERING.

Look over the pots and tubs at least every alternate day, to see where water is wanted.   In watering, too much caution cannot be used, especially during winter and the commencement of spring.   It was observed last month what would be the effect of too much water.   It may be remarked, that if the exterior of the pot is very damp, the soil inside is too wet, and, in that state; is uncongenial to vegetation, which now begins to start, and ought, by all possible means, to be encouraged.   People may be frequently observed watering all plants indiscriminately, not taking the trouble to look into or feel the state of the soil in the pots or tubs, and thus, by going over them three or four times in this manner, will be sufficient to put the plants in such a state, that they will not be recruited for some months.   Hence the reason of so many sickly plants.

Caméllias, where there are collections, will continue to flower.   Treat them according to the directions given last month.

OF ORANGES, LEMONS, &c.

Be sure they are not too wet, as too much humidity as well as aridity causes their foliage to have a yellow appearance, with this difference, that in the former case the foliage is the same to the touch as when green ; but in the latter, it is soft and dry.   We have observed trees in tubs and half barrels, with holes all round their sides.   This is a

ludicrous idea, having the appearance of keeping the
water from reaching the bottom of the tub or barrel. For
the best kind of tub for large trees, see *August* under this
head. If any of the trees have stunted, straggling, or
irregular heads about the end of this month or beginning
of next, head or cut them down to the shape desired. The
old wood will push fresh shoots. You may cut close, or
shorten less or more, according as you desire young shoots
to arise; at the same time observe that you do not cut below
the graft or inoculation. Trees thus headed down should
be kept until May, and then planted in the garden, (see
May,) or, if that cannot be done, turn it out, and reduce
the ball of earth by probing with a pointed stick all round
the sides and bottom of the ball, cutting off any very matted
roots. If any of the roots are decayed, cut them into the
sound wood. By being thus reduced, it will go into the
same pot or tub, if not a less one. Having a good supply
of fresh earth ready, put a few inches in the bottom of the
pot or tub, place the tree therein, and fill all around, at the
same time pressing it down with the hand or a stick. Give
very little water until there are signs of vegetation.

MYRTLES, OLEANDERS, &c.

These, with similar exotics, may be treated as above. If
any of them have been infected with the scaly insect, after
heading down, &c., scrub the remaining stems with a strong
decoction of tobacco, heated to about 100°. Afterward
clean with soap and water.

GERANIUMS.

These will be growing freely. Keep them in airy
situations, so that they may not grow too weak, and flower
imperfectly. To flower these plants strong and of good
colour, they must not be crowded together, neither far from
the light, and have plenty of air admitted to them when
the weather is favourable. Keep them free from the green-
fly, by fumigating frequently.

HERBACEOUS PLANTS.

Plants of this character will, by the first of the month, begin to grow. The best time to divide and fresh-pot them is when the young shoots are about one inch above ground. See under the head *Shifting* in this month.

OF CAPE BULBS, &c.

Cape Bulbs, such as *Lachenàlias, Oxalis, Ixias, Gladìolus, Watsònias, Babiànas*, &c., will, in many of the species, be showing flower. Keep all of them near the glass, to prevent them from being weak and unsightly.

Hyacinths, Tulips, Narcissus, &c. Those that have been kept in the green-house during winter will be in great perfection. Have all the flower stems tied up neatly to small stakes, (which, if painted green, will look much better,) and keep them from the direct rays of the sun. The front of the house, perhaps, will be the best situation. They must be freely watered while in flower. Where there is convenience, it will be essential to keep the pots in saucers containing water: it will strengthen both stems and flowers, and likewise preserve them longer in perfection. Those that are blooming should be put aside, and watered sparingly, until the foliage begins to decay, when the pots may be laid on their sides to ripen the bulbs.

REPOTTING.

We have always considered that this month is the best period for repotting the generality of Cape and New Holland plants, and more especially those that you are desirous of encouraging. Large plants of the *Citrus, Myrtus*, and *Oleánder* tribes may be deferred till August: these are of a strong, robust habit, and will not be affected at that period; and they will then be out of doors, and more room can be had for the operation, but by no means defer repotting your *Acacias, Erìas, Leptòspermum, Epácris*, &c.; and, for the guidance of our more inexperienced friends,

we give a descriptive list of many of the finest, with a faint
outline of their characters and general treatment, which
will prove a desideratum for those who are inexperienced,
and strangers to the beauties, pleasures, and arts of exotic
flora culture.   Therefore, if you have any of the following
plants that you are desirous of encouraging, they should
be repotted this or next month at the latest.   Large plants
will not require it, if they were done in August.   Pots one
size larger than those that they are in, are sufficient.

Acàcias and *Mimòsas* being now united into one genus,
there are above two hundred species.   About one hundred
and thirty belong to the green-house.   Among such a
beautiful family, both for elegance of flower and beauty of
foliage, it will be difficult to specify the most handsome
and desirable for this department.   *A. dealbàta, A. glaucé-
scens, A. verticillàta, A. florabúnda, A. diffùsa, A. armàta,
A. decipiens, A. fragràns, A. pulchélla, A. lophántha, A.
decúrrens, A. pùbescens, A. myrtifòlia, A. conspìcua, A.
lineáris,* &c.   These will afford a great variety of foliage,
and are very desirable, flowering principally in winter, or
early in spring.   The flowers of those belonging to the
· green-house are of a yellow or straw colour; the most of
those that are red or purple, with the celebrated medicinal
species, belong to the hot-house, for which see *May.*
There are some of the species very subject to the white
scaly insect, which must be attended to, that they may not
get to any extent.   (Soil No. 1.)

Agapánthus, three species.   *A. umbellàtus,* with bright
blue flowers, is very celebrated, and well known in the
collections of the country.   There is a variegated variety
of it highly desirable, the foliage being white striped, and
frequently the flower stem and the flower *A. álbidus* has
pale white flowers, and as yet rather scarce.   They have
very strong roots, and require plenty of freedom.   Plants
are always large before they flower, and when the pots, by
frequent shifting, become inconvenient, the plant should be
divested of all the earth, and, if too large, divide it, cutting
off the strongest of the fibres; then they will admit of being
put into smaller pots.   If the above operation is performed
in August or September, it will not retard their flowering,
which, when well grown, is very handsome, the flower
stem arising about three feet, and crowned with twenty or

thirty blossoms, continuing to bloom successively. (Soil
No. 12.)

Achimenes. About eight species, the type of this new
genus has been long known in our collections, under the
name of *Trevirània coccinea*, now *A. coccinea*, flowers
bright scarlet; *A. longiflora*, large blue; *A. grandiflora*,
fine rose; *A. hirsuta*, bright rosy purple; *A. rosea*, profuse flowering, and *A. picta*, the foliage of which is beautifully variegated and striped. They have all scaly tuberous roots requiring the pots to be kept entirely dry during
winter; in this month they should be taken from the old
soil and planted into fresh, giving gentle waterings till they
begin to grow. They delight in a warm close moist atmosphere, and will bloom freely from July to October. (Soil
No. 10.)

Aloe. Nearly a hundred species of grotesque looking
succulent plants, and are principally natives of the Cape of
Good Hope, and, consequently, will do well in the warmest part of the green-house, although, when convenient,
they frequently get a situation in the hot-house. *A. vulgàris*, known as *A. barbadénsis*, has orange yellow flowers; *A. obliqua*, now called *Gastèria obliqua; A. dichó-
toma*, and *A. variegàta*, which is perhaps the finest of the
genus: the leaves are beautifully striped, and commonly
known as the partridge-breast Aloe; flowers scarlet and
green. They ought to have very little water; once a month
is sufficient. They would grow without it, and several of
them would also grow by being suspended in the house,
without earth or any substitute about their roots, by being
frequently sprinkled with water. Few of them are admired for the beauty of their flowers, but the whole are
considered curious. They flower from May to September.
(Soil No. 9.)

Alonsòas, five species, all soft-wooded, small, shrubby
plants, with scarlet flowers. *A. incisifolia* is known among
us under the name of *Hemimeris urticifólia*, and *A. lineàris*
as *H. lineàris*. If well treated, they form very handsome
plants, and flower freely. They will not bear strong fumigation; and, when the house is under that operation, they
must be put on the floor of the green-house, where they
will not be so much affected. They flower from April to
August. (Soil No. 9.)

Alóysa citriodòra, known in our collections as *verbena triphylla.* The flowers are small, in long spikes of a pale lilac colour: the celebrity of the plant is in the delightful odour of its foliage, which is linear, lanceolate, and ternate. It is of very easy culture, and has been known to survive winter in the open air in Philadelphia. Where large plants are desired, they should be planted in the ground during summer, and lifted in November, and put in a dry cellar or under the stage in the green-house. Before they begin to grow in the spring, trim the plants into a neat shape. (Soil No. 9.)

Alstræmèrias, about sixteen species, all exceedingly desirable, and many of them particularly beautiful; such are —*A. áurea,* golden flowered; *A. acutifòlia,* scarlet; *A. Hookerii,* rose-coloured; *A. pelegrina,* elegantly spotted; *A. pulchélla,* red flowered, and will grow six feet high, having its shoots crowned with a profusion of flowers; *A. psittacìna,* red, yellow and green; *A. tricólor,* black, white and yellow ; very beautiful. They have, generally, tuberous roots, and should be potted into fresh soil as soon as they show symptoms of growth, and they will require repotting about every month previous to flowering, taking care never to break the ball of earth while they are in a growing state. (Soil No. 10.)

Amaryllis. This is a genus of splendid flowering bulbs, containing about eighty species and one hundred and forty varieties. They are natives of South America, but more than one-half of them are hybrids grown from seed by cultivators. They are generally kept in the hot-house, but in our climate will do perfectly well in the green-house ; and we have no doubt that in a few years many of them will be so acclimated, as to keep as garden bulbs, planting about the end of April, and lifting them in October. As the beauty of these plants is in the flowers, it will be proper to give a small description of a few of them. *A. Johnsòni,* the flowers are a deep scarlet, with a white streak in the centre of each petal, four bloom on a stem of about two feet, each flower about six inches in diameter: a bulb well established has two stems. *A. regìna,* Mexican Lily, has large scarlet pendent flowers, tube of the flower fringed-like, with three or four on the stem. *A. vittàta* is an admired species with scarlet flowers, striped with pure

18

white: there are two or three varieties of it; corolla campanulate, three or four on the stem, about three inches in diameter; petals a little undulate. *A. fùlgida,* flower scarlet, large, tube striped, petals acute, two flowers on the stem. *A. áulica* is one of the most magnificent, has from two to four flowers about seven inches in diameter, erect on a stem about two and a half feet high; six petals, strongly united to the capsule, bottom of the petals green, connected with spots of dark crimson, which spread into fine transparent red, covered with rich tints, nerves very perceptible, anthers bold; it is called Crowned *Amaryllis.* *A. psittácina,* Parrot Amaryllis, is scarlet striped with green, two or more flowers on the stem, each about five inches in diameter. There are several varieties of it; the best that we have seen are *cowbèrgia* and *pulverulènta.* A bulb known in our collections as *A. purpùrea* is now *Vallótta purpùrea,* has beautiful erect scarlet flowers, three or four on the stem, each about four inches in diameter. There are three varieties of it, differing only in habit. *A. longifòlia* is now *Crìnum capénse,* and is perfectly hardy; flowers pink, inclining to white, in large umbels, leaves long, glaucous, and is a desirable garden bulb. *A. longiflòra striàta* has pure white flowers with bright pink stripes, and each flower is about seven inches long; it was introduced from South America by Mrs. R. Alsop, and is a most superb flowering bulb. *A. solandriflòra,* large red; *A. Augùsta,* buff and orange; *A. elegáns,* red and green, and many other superb kinds, especially the hybrid sorts; from *Johnsòni* there are above twenty cultivated varieties; from *formòsa* about twelve; and from *Griffini* about ten, all of them esteemed. Where they have been kept in the earth in which they were grown last year, the ball ought at this repotting to be reduced; when the bulbs are in a growing state, they ought to have plenty of water, and be fully exposed to the sun, so that the foliage may have its full influence, and as the roots grow to the outside of the earth, give them another and a larger pot. They must have plenty of drainage, and be kept from heavy rains. We prefer growing them in the green-house all summer, or into frames under glass: about the end of October the watering must be gradually withheld, and by the middle of November put the bulbs where they will be

kept dry till February or March next, when they must be
again potted (in soil No. 12).

Aòtus, two species, both fine leguminose plants. *A.
villòsa* is a native of Van Dieman's Land, and *A. virgàta*
is from New Holland. The former is preferable. Both
have yellow flowers, and are small evergreen shrubs. (Soil
No. 1.)

Araucària. This noble genus contains four species,
which are without exception the most noble plants we are
acquainted with, for the beauty of their foliage and symmetry of their growth, that belong to the green-house. *A.
excélsa,* Norfolk Island Pine, has leaves closely imbricated
as if with a coat of mail, and are imperishable. *A. imbricàta,* Chile Pine, is one of the grandest of trees, and is the
hardiest of the genus; grows in the open air with me; the
leaves are also closely imbricated. The other two species
are rarely seen even in European collections. The foliage
of either of the species will adhere to the wood many years
after the plant is dead. They are all highly valued: the
pots must be well drained; for if the plants get much water
while dormant, the foliage becomes yellow, and never attains its beautiful green colour again; otherwise they are
easily grown. (Soil No. 11.)

Arbutus, ten exotic species and six varieties. They are
generally hardy in England; but we question if they stand
out in the middle states. *A. unìdo rùbra* has the finest
crimson flowers; *A. serratifólia,* the largest panicles; and
A. andràchne, the finest foliage; and very profuse of
bloom. They flower in nodding panicles; *A. canàriensis*
has very neat pink flowers. They bear a pretty fruit
similar to a strawberry; hence it is called strawberry tree,
and the fruit will remain on the bush a long time. They
are very fine evergreens, and if any of them become acclimated, they will be a great acquisition to our gardens. In
the southern states they make lovely evergreen shrubs.
(Soil No. 9.)

Aster argophyllus, or musk plant, has no beauty in its
flowers, but is esteemed by some for its musky flavour
when the leaves are gently rubbed. Leaves ovate, lanceolate, and silky beneath: the plant is of strong growth. (Soil
No. 9.)

Aùcuba japónica is the only species. The flowers are

small and almost insignificant, colour purple; but the
foliage is a desirable object, being yellow spotted, or
blotched. It is tolerably hardy, and withstands our winters. It prefers shade, and, if the situation were such
when planted out, it would grow more freely. The hot
rays of the sun are very prejudicial to its growth. It is an
evergreen shrub, and very desirable. (Soil No. 2.)

Azàleas. The Chinese varieties of *Azàlea índica* are
almost without an end; we might properly say that they
are without end; but the finest we have seen are those we
shall enumerate. The one that has been longest known
in the collections of this country is *A. índica*, a most splendid shrub, with red flowers and dark spots. *A. índica
àlba*, the flowers of the purest white, rather larger than the
former. *A. índica purpùrea plèno*, double purple. This
variety is not so fine as many of the others. Properly it
is not purple, or, if it may be termed so, the colour is very
light, and the flower irregular. *A. índica phœnícea*, rich
purple and a free grower. *A. índica smithii*, of the
French, and *A. índica purpùrea* of the English, are alike,
pale lilac and very profuse of flower. *A. índica coccínea*,
bright scarlet, a superb variety, and extremely abundant of
bloom. *A. índica flore variegàta* flowers beautifully variegated, pink and white. *A. lateritia*, salmon colour, *fine*.
A. Williamsii, bright, rich crimson. *A. Powleii*, rosy
purple. *A. Copeii*, bright rose. *A. Danielsiana*, bright
red. *A. índica cárnea*, delicate flesh colour. *A. índica
nova blanc*, white with a greenish yellow spot on the upper
petals. *A. índica, elegàns*, bright rosy purple, a very profuse flowerer and of a neat habit. *A. índica Gillinghàmia*,
very large lilac, and of a strong habit. *Azàlea sinénsis* does
not belong to the *índica* tribe; it is of a hard woody nature,
flowers of a golden yellow, in large clusters; it no doubt will
prove a hardy species. The varieties and sub-varieties of
índica will, in a few years, be so numerous, that the greatest
difficulty will be to keep clear of those that are not decidedly
distinct: to obtain this object our own feeble exertions will
be industriously applied. We might have named a few
other varieties, but they so nearly approach some of the
above, that it is better to avoid them. A choice selection
of the Chinese Azalea ought to be in every green-house;

they are all easy of culture, and bloom freely from February to May. The pots must be well drained and shaded from the sun during summer, though the tops of the plants do best to have the full rays, to which we have them fully exposed, and find that by such treatment they are every year completely covered with their flowers, and grow more stiff in habit than when the whole plant is shaded. They should be repotted as soon as done flowering in soil No. 6, when they are flowering plants, and in soil No. 5, when young plants.

Bánksias. There are about thirty-two species, all curious in flower, and handsome and various in foliage; flowers in large heads of cone shape, anthers mostly green, and continue a considerable time in flower; produces a cone in shape of a pine, but not imbricate. The substance is as hard as bone, and contains many seeds. A cone of *B. grándis* in our possession weighs one pound and twelve ounces, and contains about one hundred and seven seeds. Those most admired for the foliage are, *B. dentáta, B. æmúla, B. serráta, B. latifólia, B. grándis,* which is the largest. *B. speciósa* has the longest foliage. *B. Cunninghámii, B. spinulóse, B. palludósa,* and *B. repéns,* these will afford a good variety. *B. verticilláta* is entirely different in appearance from the others.

They must be well drained, and placed in an airy part of the green-house. Great care should be taken that they do not get too dry, for they seldom recover if allowed to flag for want of water. This genus is named in honour of Sir Joseph Banks, a distinguished promoter of the study of natural history. (Soil No. 6.)

Barósmas, above ten species of pretty plants, separated from *Diósma. B. serratifólia,* white; *B. pulchélla,* purple; *B. fœtidíssima,* blush; *B. odoráta,* white; and *B. dioíca,* pink, are the finest. (Soil No. 8.)

Beaufórtias, only two species. *B. decussáta* is splendid; the flowers come out of the wood with stamens in fine parcels, colour bright scarlet, foliage decussate, oval, and many-nerved, bloom persistent, and much esteemed. *B. spársa,* in flower similar to the other; colour light pink, foliage scattered, both of easy culture, and flower abundantly. (Soil No. 8.)

Begònias, a few species, are desirable for the green-

18*

house especially. *B. incarnàta*, flesh colour, and blooms during winter; *B. zebrina*, zebra-like, very pretty; they are of a soft woody nature, and should be kept in the warmest part of the green-house. (Soil No. 9.)

Benthàmia fragiféra. This beautiful new plant will make a splendid hardy evergreen for the southern states, where it will produce its pale white flowers in July, and an abundance of fruit very much like strawberries, of a slight acid taste: but we are doubtful if it will fruit in our green-houses, unless greatly encouraged. (Soil No. 9.)

Blètia hyacinthìna is the only species belonging to the green-house, once known as *Cymbidium hyacinthìnum.* It is herbaceous, and before it begins to grow, divide the root, putting the best into six-inch pots. The spike of flowers are hyacinth-like, and of a beautiful purple, flowering from April to July. (Soil No. 9.)

Bouvàrdias, two species. *B. triphylla* is well known among us, has brilliant scarlet flowers, and, when well grown, will flower beautifully from May till September. To keep the plants, they should be frequently renewed; otherwise they are liable to grow straggling, and become subject to the small white scaly insect. *B. jacquìnæ* we suspect has got confounded with the former, being very little different, except the foliage, which is more pointed. They flower from the young wood, and throw their foliage in winter. (Soil No. 3.)

Borònia is a beautiful genus of New Holland plants, contains about nine species; most of them have been universally admired; the flowers are star-like, rose-coloured, and some of them sweet-scented. *B. pinnàta* grows and flowers freely. *B. serrulàta*, foliage serrated and very crowded, bearing the flowers on the extremity of the shoot, and does extremely well in this country; the flowers are bright rose, and sweet-scented. *B. alàta* has a fine appearance, and grows handsomely. The foliage is winged and pinnate, strong-scented; of a hardy nature, and easy culture. They are in flower about April and May, and continue a considerable time; are subject to mildew if not frequently syringed: drain the pots well. (Soil No. 8.)

Brachysèmas, two species, both evergreen climbers. *B. latifòlium* has the best foliage, and large purple leguminose flowers. *B. undulàtum*, flowers yellow, and more

plentiful than the former, continuing in long successions.
The pots require to be well drained; very few plants of
either in the country. (Soil No. 6.)

Brugmánsias, two species of strong, coarse-growing
plants, requiring great nourishment to flower them well.
B. suavéolens has very large white flowers, about five
inches in diameter, and sweet-scented. *B. sanguínea* has
flowers with a green thorax; the brim of the corolla is of
a dark orange colour. If this plant is kept in the hot-
house, it will drop its flower buds. They must have very
frequent repottings, and be liberally supplied with water
while growing. (Soil No. 18.)

Brúnias, about ten species, have heath-like foliage,
very fine, generally, on close observation, found to be three
cornered. The flowers are white and globular, the plants,
when young, are very handsome; the finest are, *B. nodi-
flòra, B. lanuginósa, B. comòsa, B. abrotanoídes,* and *B.
formòsa.* They require an airy situation, and, in summer,
to be protected from the powerful rays of the sun. Drain
the pots well. (Soil No. 6.)

Brunsvìgias are all large bulbs from the Cape of Good
Hope, and will keep in the green-house during winter, but
are better where they can obtain a situation in the hot-
house. It is a splendid genus, containing about ten species. Some of the bulbs grow to an enormous size, and all
of them, while growing, require a liberal supply of water;
but when dormant, it must be wholly withheld, and they
should have large pots, to make them grow and flower in
perfection. *B. multiflòra,* flowers scarlet and green; the
leaves lay on the surface of the pot. *B. laticòma,* flowers
pale purple. *B. Josephinæ* has splendid rose-coloured
flowers, and the most admired species of the genus; the
foliage spreading, half erect, and glaucous; flowers numerous, and in large umbels, on a stem two feet high, blooming successively: there is a variety that has striped flowers.

Several other species have been given to different
genera. *B. falcàta* is now *Ammócharis falcàta; B. margináta,* now *Imhófia;* and *B. cilliàris* is now *Buphóne
cilliàris.* They all flower in umbels, on stems from six
inches to two feet; flowers lily-like, with six petals. (Soil
No. 12.)

Burchéllias, two species. *B. capénsis* is a beautiful
dwarf evergreen shrub, with tubular orange-coloured flowers, in large terminal clusters; when well treated, grows
and flowers freely, and highly deserving of attention. *B.
parviflòra* differs from the above in the flowers being
smaller and paler, and the foliage more pointed. (Soil
No. 10.)

Cactus : for descriptions of, see hot-house in May.

Calceolària. This genus of glants has undergone a
complete revolution. Within these few years hundreds of
superb hybrid varieties have been brought to notice, many
of them truly splendid. With us the herbaceous kinds are
very delicate during summer; they are generally all cut off
by our intense heat, or severe droughts. The shrubby
varieties appear to withstand the vicissitudes of our climate
better, though, as yet, we confess we are not even altogether successful in their summer culture. However, a
few of them have done well, and are *C. angustifòlia*, bright
yellow, and in great profusion; *C. jupìter*, brown and yellow; *C. marjoriána supèrba*, nearly scarlet; *C. smìthii*,
red and yellow; *C. ignèa*, bright crimson; *C. méteor*, dark
crimson; *C. Vulcan*, dark red; *C. maculata*, superbly
marked with red or crimson. There are many others of
very great merit of the shrubby kinds cultivated in Europe,
such as whites of different shades, dark crimsons, with
white capes, and others blending into almost every description of colour and character. Any quantity of new sorts
may be obtained by cross impregnation between any two
of very different colours: the seeds will ripen in July, when
they may be sown on light soil, and they will flower the
following season. Flowering plants require to be greatly
encouraged, and must be shaded during summer from the
violent noon-day sun. (Soil No. 10.)

Calothámnus, four species. This genus is named in
allusion to the splendid appearance of the branches, covered with scarlet flowers of curious construction, which
come out of the old wood. All the species are of easy culture, and very like dwarf pines. *C. quadrifìda* has the
largest flowers; *C. clavàta* the most abundant. They are
all evergreens, and flower from April to November, and
are very desirable in a collection. (Soil No. 6.)

Callicóma serratifòlia, the only species, and remarkable

for tufted yellow heads of flowers, which come out at the axils, and continue from May to July. The foliage is ovate, lanceolate, deeply serrated and opposite. (Soil No. 6.)

Caméllias. There are about eight distinct species of this plant, known in our collections; and the varieties of *japonica* approach to one thousand, to which many are yearly added; but, unfortunately, their merits are not fully scrutinized before they are sent forth to the floral world, under names representing and expressing every quality that is grand or beautiful in floral imagination. Such has been the rapid increase of varieties in Europe, and even in this country, that, in many instances, three or four distinct plants have come out under the same name; consequently, a great confusion of names has been the result, which has caused much difficulty in attaining the best of the names. The collections of this country were kept comparatively *pure* till within the last few years, when the anxiety of our cultivators to obtain variety caused them to import from the French and German markets, which has thrown the nomenclature into an almost impenetrable chaos. But still we can unite in saying, "What species of plant is there which better merits the intelligent and vigilant care of the amateur and horticulturist?" The elegance of its form, the beautiful verdure of its foliage, and the pure and brilliant colours of the large and elegant flowers, sufficiently justify the admiration of all. In fact, we may say, there is not a green-house in which this lovely plant has not found a place, where it stands in the first rank of floral population. To give a full description of all the varieties we know would occupy this volume. However, we will give lucid details of nearly one hundred of the finest we have seen in cultivation. But, in regard to the shades and spots of colour, we must throw ourselves on the charity of our readers; for many sorts are very capricious in that particular, though styled self-coloured, may come spotted, and even those that are generally spotted sometimes show themselves of one colour.

Caméllia euryoídes, flowers small, single white, and a little fragrant; plant of a slender growth.

C. oleíferia is cultivated principally in China for the oil

which is expressed from its seeds, which is much used in
the domestic cookery of the country; flower single white.

C. Sesánqua, Lady Banks's. The foliage of this species
is very small, and paler, and the green not so fine as any
of the others. It seeds freely, and is often used as the
female parent in producing new varieties; flowers small,
white, and single, with many anthers. There are a semi-
double and double variety of it of the same colour.

C. sesánqua rósea, or *mallifòra* of some, double pink,
small flowers, but in very great profusion; the plant is of a
free, upright growth. The flowers are of about four weeks'
duration: it is very much esteemed.

C. kissii. Small single white: the only species that is
a native of Nepaul.

C. reticuláta was brought from China by Capt. Rawes
in 1822. The foliage is very characteristic, being stiff and
flat, distinctly serrated, nerves deeply sunken; flowers
bright rose, of a loose form, and above six inches in diameter, semi-double. From present appearance, it will never
be so plenty as many of the others, being tardy of propagation; only a few eyes on the extremity of each shoot
make young wood, and, if these are cut off, the plant does
not seem to push afresh. *Magnificent.*

C. japónica, small, single, red. It is supposed that this
is the type of all the garden cultivated varieties of the
Caméllia, though some are inclined to think that it is a
variegated or striped species, not yet introduced, that has
been the origin of so many beautiful Chinese sorts.

The following are supposed to be its varieties:

C. aitònia. This variety is a beautiful specimen of a
single flower, affording a development of the organ of fruc-
tification; the petals are delicately penciled, and the
anthers very bold, colour pink, and the flower very large;
grows freely, and, in our opinion, is surpassed by none of
the single sorts for raising fine new varieties, if impregnated with the pollen from double flowers. *Good.*

C. alba-plèna, common double white, is admired by the
most casual observer, and is generally considered a very
superior flower, from the purity of its whiteness and the
abundance of its large flowers, which are closely and regularly set with round petals. The foliage is large, and the
plant grows freely; we have seen one shoot grow two feet

in one summer. It was imported into Europe from China, among the first of the varieties, about eighty years ago. *Magnificent.*

C. semplex* *álba*, single white. It is mentioned somewhere as being very sweet-scented, though not very perceptible to us. The foliage and wood are very strong, the fine-striped sorts have been raised from it; consequently, it is particularly desirable as a stock to grow new varieties from. Its flowers are large and abundant. *Good.*

C. althæflóra, hollyhock flowered, is a great beauty, with large double dark red flowers; the veins are very prominent, petals frequently irregular; foliage large, smooth, and very dark green, and is much esteemed. *Fine.*

C. anemoneflòra, or *Waratah* (from the centre petals, having the appearance of the Waratah plant, *Telopia speciosissima*). This variety is very characteristic, both in flower and foliage. The flower is dark crimson, with five regular large outside petals; those of the centre are very small and neatly plaited, with the stile (female organ) prominent; the foliage is large and oblong, nerves very smooth, and the wood strong, bark light. Had this kind not been found, we would have been deprived of many most splendid varieties which have originated from it, and we have no doubt they may become as diversified as the roses of the garden : this variety, in a collection, for that alone is invaluable. It seeds freely, and the pollen of any of the others applied to the style of this, will produce a new variety, which seldom fails of being double, provided the pollen is from a double variety. It must be applied the first day that the flower is expanded, for the bloom is only of a few days' duration. Those that are not acquainted with the buds of this *Caméllia*, will take them to be dead, because, before expansion, they are very dark brown, and have a dried appearance. *Superb.*

C. anemoneflòre rosea, fine rose, the exterior petals are large and well rounded, the interior very full of small short petals, flower very persistant—foliage large, cordate, acuminate. *Superb.*

---

* We have now, 1839, in flower, a single white, very similar to this, which we have raised from the seed of *Dahliaflora*, a good double red variety; it, therefore, appears impossible to predict their character from the parent that produced the seed.

C. amàbile. This exceedingly perfect flower was raised
from seed by J. B. Smith, Esq., of this city; it is regularly imbricated, the extreme petals are bright rose,
shading to delicate pink, and then again shading in the
centre to light red. The plant is full of foliage and of excellent habit, flower about three and a half inches in diameter. *Magnificent.*

C. atrorùbens, Loddiges' red, is a good variety; colour
dark red, outside petals large, inside small and irregular,
forming a very distinct character; foliage stiff; grows freely
and flowers well; and of long duration. We have seen a
flower stand fresh on the plant two months; however, that
cannot be a rule, as it depends on the situation. *Good.*

C. aucubafòlia, bright rose, perfectly double, three and
a half inches in diameter, a free bloomer—foliage large,
cordate, pale green, and sometimes spotted like Aucuba
japonica. *Good.*

C. augústa, cherry red, large, finely double, centre petals
rather irregular—foliage dark green. *Good.*

C. américana, blush, medium size, finely cupped form,
generally spotted with rose, an American seedling by Mr.
Dunlap, of N. Y. *Magnificent.*

C. Bealiana, or *Leana Superba*, dark crimson, very
large, superbly double, cup form. *Magnificent.*

C. candidìssima, purest white flowers, very large, four
inches or more in diameter, full and most regularly imbricated, and resemble very much the *old double white*, though
more perfect in form—leaves rather small, of an elongated
form, smooth and pale green, often spotted with yellow.
The plant is of vigorous growth, and a Japan variety.
Magnificent.

C. cárnea, frequently known as Middlemist's blush.
Double pink, one of the original varieties, and frequently
produces seeds, from which many very fine varieties have
been obtained; grows freely. *Good.*

C. chalmerii perfecta, delicate waxy rose, perfectly imbricated form, flower medium size, very persistent, foliage
pale green, plant of regular pyramidal growth. *Magnificent.* An American seedling in the possession of Mr. Wm.
Chalmers, gardener to Geo. Pepper, Esq.

C. chandlerii or *versicòlor*, perfectly double, colour
vivid red, with occasional splashes of pure white; the

flowers vary, and are often only red—they are of long,
duration, from six to eight weeks; foliage large and dark
glossy green. *Magnificent.*

C. clàveàna, large, irregular, double flower, of a bright
cherry red colour: plant of rather slow growth, but a profuse bloomer. *Superb.*

C. coccinea, deep cherry red, a double flower of about
three inches in diameter; plant of a very neat growth, and
a most profuse bloomer; it frequently produces seed.
Good.

C. colvillea, pale blush, with rose spots and pink stripes,
is partially anemone formed; but very compact and of free
growth; leaves cordate. *Superb.*

C. concinna, deep cherry red, a very perfectly imbricated double flower, about three and a half inches in diameter; foliage generally a little undulated, wood slender.
Superb.

C. conspìcua, (Loddigies,) a shrub of strong handsome
growth, with large dark green foliage; flower very double;
five inches in diameter; bright orange red, hemispherical
shape; petals erect, and appear as if three or four flowers
were united; it is profuse of bloom and very conspicuous.
Magnificent.

C. coronàta, shrub of stiff growth; foliage pale green;
flower large, irregular, and double, of a clear pink colour;
four inches in diameter. *Very good.*

C. crassinérvis, a good improvement on the original
anemoneflòra or *Waratah,* and has much the same habit.
Superb.

C. curvatifòlia, leaves narrow and pointed; plant of
good habit; flower pure white; regular and very double,
petals disposed in a regular rosette, about three and a half
inches in diameter. *Superb.*

C. decóra, pale rose, flower perfectly double, four and a
half inches in diameter, three rows of exterior petals, those
of the centre short and thick, containing a few concealed
stamens—foliage large glossy green. *Magnificent.*

C. Derbyàna, very bright dark red, flower finely double
cup-shaped, petals bold and broad spoon-shaped : a striking
flower, often over four inches in diameter—foliage of a very
beautiful green. *Superb.*

C. Donkelàri, bright red, variegated and sprinkled with
19

pure white, three rows of large petals about one inch broad
and two inches long: centre full of stamens, flower fully
four inches in diameter; leaves about two inches broad and
four inches long; this will be an elegant variety to seed
from, and is of Chinese origin. *Magnificent.*

C. *delectìssima*, white, profusely striped with rose, exterior petals large and round; those of the interior are closely
set; flower nearly four inches in diameter; leaves very
large, ovate, acuminate. *Superb.*

C. *Duchess of Orleans*, rose white, beautifully spotted
or striped with rose, perfect form, large, a free bloomer.
Magnificent.

C. *dorséttia* or *parthoniàna*, of the Belgians; leaves flat
and closely set, of a dark shining green, flower very large,
nearly five inches in diameter, of a pale red, mixed with
rose and white, petals closely imbricated, irregular, and
numerous; those of the centre small. *Magnificent.*

C. *eclìpse* or *Préssi*, of the English, or *impérialis* of the
French; flower pure white, with rose stripes, four inches
in diameter; irregular, full, and double, with a few stamens
appearing among the petals; the whole flower forms an
arched centre, almost hemispherical; leaves long and
pointed, of a clear rich green: we have seen flowers of this
plant entirely rose. *Magnificent.*

C. *élegans*, (Chandler's,) flower rosy red, fading to
nearly white in the centre; three and a half inches in
diameter, exterior petals large and rounded; those of. the
interior very numerous, and beautifully harmonize; forming, as it were, a depressed sphere; a profuse bloomer, and
of a neat habit. *Magnificent.*

C. *elàta*, violent crimson, spotted with white, flower
three and a half inches in diameter, perfectly imbricated
to the very centre, and of the most perfect double, foliage
dark green, plant of a good habit. *Magnificent.*

C. *elphingstònia*, red spotted with white, frequently
four inches in diameter, exterior petals very large, regularly graduating to the centre, which cover a few hidden
stamens, foliage dark green; plant of a fine habit. *Magnificent.*

C. *Esthèrii*,* foliage nearly three inches wide and five

* Grown by J. B. Smith, Esq., of this city, who is a very success-

inches long, finely serrated—nerves prominent; flower, when well grown, is five inches in diameter; colour pure white, spotted, and striped with rose and pink, petals broad, bold, erect, and closely set; the bloom, when fully expanded, forms a perfect hemisphere, and contains a few hidden stamina; it is the finest and largest of all the striped varieties, and is a profuse bloomer. *Magnificent.*

C. exímia, (Chandler's,) flowers bright crimson, four inches in diameter, of a perfect double imbricated form, foliage light green and deeply serrated, nerves smooth; it is of free growth, but with us does not bloom freely. *Magnificent.*

C. Fáirlea: foliage large, ovate, acuminate; of a smooth shining dark green; flowers nearly four inches in diameter, of a rich crimson, marked with pure white, very double. *Superb.*

C. Feastii, pure white, with a few spots of rose fully double, imbricated, very distinct, foliage dark green, of free growth. *Magnificent.* A seedling by Mr. Feast, of Baltimore.

C. fimbriàta: fringed white. The size, shape and set of the flower same as *alba-plena,* and the white as pure, with the edges of the petals deeply serrated, or rather fringed; is equally as free in flowering, though not so strong in growth. It is universally admired, and in great demand. *Magnificent.*

C. flavéscens, or *incárnata.* Lady Hume's blush, and by some called *buff.* It is a very double flower, beautifully regular and imbricated, and frequently hexangular, or star-like; the bottom of the petals is most delicately tinged with blush; on looking into it, it shows more like a blush vapour than nature, and is a great favourite, and deservedly so: flowers and grows freely; foliage rhomboid, elongate, nerves very visible, surface smooth and pale green, distinctly serrate, growth strong and erect. *Magnificent.*

C. flórida. Flower clear cherry red, large, frequently above four inches in diameter; very persistent; exterior petals large and well rounded; the interior small and closely set, rising in the centre: it is a profuse bloomer; foliage

ful amateur cultivator, and has raised some of the finest seedling Camellias that are at present known.

dark green. The plant is of a neat and regular habit. *Magnificent.*

C. Flóyii, one of the most noble of the Camellias, both in flower and foliage; leaves three inches wide, and nearly five long; smooth, dark green, plant of strong growth; flower five inches in diameter, of a perfectly double form; the extremity is cherry red, diverging to a pale rose in the centre; the exterior petals are bold, round and elegant, of a cup shape when newly opened. It is frequently sold in Europe under the imposing name of *Frederic the Great*, though grown from seed by Mr. Floy, of New York, who has been very successful in producing several other esteemed sorts. *Magnificent.*

C. Fórdii, a free-growing plant, with lively green foliage and graceful habit; flower dark rose, three inches and a half in diameter, perfectly double, and regularly imbricated, forming a symmetrical bloom. *Magnificent.*

C. formósa, foliage very dark green: flower fully four inches in diameter, of a dark rose colour, regularly double, petals large and erect; interior shortened, covering a few stamens. *Superb.*

C. frankofórtensis, or *Wellingtoni*, a plant of a very compact habit; flower three inches and a half in diameter, beautiful rose, occasionally spotted with white. *Magnificent.*

C. fúlgens, flower three inches and a half in diameter, and very bright double crimson, approaching to *C. atrorubens*, but more brilliant; petals regularly decreasing to the centre; foliage a lucid green, very smooth; young wood and wood buds have a red appearance. We have no doubt but it will occasionally seed; if so, it will be a first-rate breeder. *Superb.*

C. Gilèsii, or *Nancy Dawson.* The leaves are large, ovate, oblong and pointed; flowers above four inches in diameter, of a fine dark red colour, often striped with white, and is " distinguished for fragrance as well as beauty." *Magnificent.*

C. grunèlla, foliage oval and acute, of a deep glossy green, flower white, three inches and a half; rather irregular, but perfectly double, a profuse bloomer, and of good habit. *Superb.*

C. Hendersòni, raised by the celebrated camellia grower, Mr. Henderson, of Woodhall, Scotland. It is a large flower, four inches and a half in diameter, beautifully imbricated, and perfectly double, of a bright rose colour, foliage round, ovate, and distinctly serrated. *Magnificent.*

C. Hampsteadii, large rosy crimson, quite double, with bold petals, foliage dark green, heart-shaped, a free grower. An American seedling sent out by Messrs. Ritchie and Dick.

C. Henri Favre, a beautiful rose colour, of French origin, perfectly double, being similar to *Landrethi.* A free bloomer, foliage pale green. *Magnificent.*

C. Hosàckia, large dark crimson, nearly five inches in diameter; flower rather flat, petals numerous, regularly decreasing to the centre, which has an occasional speck of white. It does seed, and will prove a first rate variety for that purpose; foliage long and pointed, rather drooping; is of a free growth and bloom. *Superb.*

C. imbricàta, foliage very large, three inches wide and four and a half long, of a pale green, often marked with white; flowers rich crimson, almost invariably marked more or less with white; they are full four inches in diameter; the petals are round, and regularly disposed, and imbricated on each other, gradually decreasing to the centre, forming a most perfect flower. The plant grows freely, and blooms profusely; no collection can be perfect without it. *Magnificent.*

C. intermédia is a sport from *S. pæoniflòra;* it is a very large blush, beautifully suffused with rose. *Magnificent.*

C. invincìble, or *punctàta,* flower three inches and a half in diameter, rose ground, marked and striped with cherry red; the circumference petals are broad and convex; those of the centre small and erect. This Camellia sometimes produces flowers entirely red or rose-coloured; it is of free growth; leaves round, acuminate, and of a dark green. *Superb.*

C. Jeffersoni, rosy crimson, perfectly imbricated to the centre; flower of medium size; foliage shining green, three to four inches long, and two wide. A seedling by Dr. J. S. Gunnell, of Washington city. *Magnificent.*

C. kermosìne, leaves long and narrow, strongly nerved, of a pale green, bud depressed at the extremity, flower cherry red, double, petals rather numerous, among which are a few stamens. *Very good.*

19*

C. Landréthia, or *Jacksònia*, very beautiful pink, fading to the centre, a perfectly double and finely imbricated flower, about four inches in diameter, a free bloomer, and a plant of good habit; leaves ovate, acuminate, pale green. We have seen the flower profusely spotted with white. This elegant Camellia was grown from seed by D. and C. Landreth, and bloomed first in the spring of 1829. *Magnificent*.

C. latifòlia, leaves three inches wide and four inches and a half long, point recurved, a fine glossy green; flower cherry red, cup form, interior petals irregular, festooned and curled, those of the exterior bold and round, about three inches and a half in diameter. *Superb*.

C. minùta, plant vigorous, leaves nearly orbicular, and three inches and a half long, very shining and nerved flower three inches in diameter, of a beautiful cherry red, petals regularly imbricated, and arranged into a vase form; the centre is of a vivid red. *Superb*.

C. mutàbilis travèrsii, foliage very large and almost cordate, plant of an elegant and free growth, leaves rather reflexed and of a lively green, nerves very conspicuous, flower four inches and a half in diameter, regular, and very double: it opens a delicate rose, and soon changes to a violet purple, shaded with a faint line of white, an unique plant and flower. *Magnificent*.

C. myrtifòlia, known in some collections as *involùta*. There are two varieties of it, major and minor; the former is certainly the best, and has a very handsome, large and regular red flower; the centre frequently is pink and purple; it is much the shape of *double white*, only the petals are more cupped. The flower is of considerable duration. The foliage, though small, is much larger than that of any of our common myrtles, which might make many mistake its character; and another prominent feature is, the leaves are much recurved and shining; plant pendulous, of a pale green. *Magnificent*.

C. nivàlis, flower large white, very pure, having three rows of large round exterior petals, the centre irregularly filled with small petals, showing a considerable quantity of stamens, foliage very dark green, plant of a good habit, and will make an excellent variety for producing new sorts. *Superb*.

C. pæoniflòra: bright pink, large flower, fully four inches in diameter, two rows of circumference petals; those of the centre numerous, very close, erect, and in the form of a sphere; plant of slender growth; leaves two inches broad and three inches long, of a delicate green. *Superb.*

C. Palméria álba: leaves two inches broad and three long, rather reflexed, of a very dark green—is a plant of neat habit, an¹ profuse in blooming—flowers finely double, clear white, about three and a half inches in diameter; petals bold and round—regularly imbricated, though not closely set; is a very graceful flower, and has been sold in England as *C. Candidissima,* which is a superior article, and even figured in the Florist's Magazine as such. There is also another flower by this name, but very inferior, being only semi-double. *Superb.*

C. Palmer's perfection, dark crimson, inclining to purple, very large, perfectly double, and of handsome form; a free bloomer. *Magnificent.*

C. Párksii, or Park's rose striped; pale rose marked with white; flower about four inches in diameter; petals large, round, and irregular; centre showing a few stamens. This flower is to some sweet-scented—leaves two and a half inches wide and three and a half inches long; roundish, oval, and slightly acuminate—deeply separated; plant of a stiff growth. *Superb.* (There is a French Parksii: *single crimson.*)

C. Philadélphica, (Smith's,) flowers four and a half to five inches in diameter; the circumference petals large and round; those of the interior smaller, with a little convexity, perfectly double, colour changeable, bright crimson, spotted with white; dark rose, fading to the centre, or all crimson: even the same plant producing all the variety; plant of an upright branching habit; leaves ovate, acuminate, of medium size, and a very dark dull green; bloomed first in 1834, when only two years from the seed, and the flower was then four and three-quarter inches in diameter. *Magnificent.*

C. picturàta: leaves three and a half inches wide and four and a half inches long, of a bright green; flower four inches in diameter; spherical and extremely double; petals of the centre irregular and closely folded; those of the periphery or circumference, round and entire, of a pure white, occasionally striped with red—a few hidden stamens—plant of an elegant habit. *Magnificent.*

C. pompónia, or Kew blush, flowers over four inches in diameter; white, with a tinge of blush at the bottom of the petals, which has a good effect in setting off the flower. They frequently bloom all blush, having one or two rows of guard or outside petals; those of the inside are short, stubby, and generally irregular, continues long in flower, yellow anthers among the short petals, and seeds when the female organ is perfect; foliage similar to *pæoniflòra,* a very fast grower, and flowers freely. *Superb.*

C. Pràttii;* flower bright rose, full four inches in diameter, frequently every petal having a white stripe from the apex to the base, very closely and regularly imbricated to the very centre : in every respect equally as well formed as *C. imbricata;* leaves two and a half inches wide and four inches long, of a rich smooth green—is a plant of free growth and profuse flowering; bloomed first in 1836. With pleasure we say, it is our first seedling of merit. *Magnificent.*

C. Punctàta, see *Invincible.*

C. Prince Albert, pale rose, striped with bright red, very distinct; a Chinese variety perfectly double, a large flower; petals rather short in the centre. *Magnificent.*

C. Queen of England, dark rosy crimson, with an occasional spot of white; large, imbricated and fully double. *Magnificent.*

C. rósa sinénsis, a large double flower, four inches in diameter; colour bright rosy pink, petals long and full, closely imbricated to the centre: a very distinct variety, with beautiful dark green shining foliage, two inches wide and three and a half long; grows and flowers freely. *Magnificent.*

C. rósea, (*China,*) petals regularly and perfectly imbricated, flower frequently star-shaped, like *Hume's blush,* about three inches in diameter; colour bright rose, changing to rosy purple; foliage pale green; leaves one and a half inches wide and three inches long; plant of slender

---

* In compliment to our late and esteemed patron, H. Pratt, Esq., of Lemon-Hill.

habit, though well formed, and a profuse bloomer. *Magnificent*.

C. rùbra-plèno, or Greavill's double red, is a strong growing and free flowering variety. The flowers are large, irregular, and very double, and are of long duration; foliage of a yellowish green, leaves two inches wide and three inches long; plant of a stiff habit. *Superb*.

C. Róssii; buds very pointed; flower four inches in diameter; petals of the periphery large, graduating smaller to the centre, though a little irregular, perfectly double, colour red, with an occasional tinge of white; foliage dull green, ovate, acuminate, pointed, and pendent; plant of a good habit and free of bloom. *Superb*.

C. Saccoi, bright rose, imbricated form, very perfect, fading to pale rose, a free bloomer. *Magnificent*.

C. Sherwoodii, rosy crimson, frequently spotted with pure white, very double, petals reflexed when fully open, a free grower and profuse bloomer. *Magnificent*. A seedling by Mr. Sherwood, of Laurel Hill.

C. sesànqua rosea. See among the species.

C. speciòsa is a most splendid variety, has been called *Chinese striped Waratah*. The guard petals are large, round, and bold; colour crimson with stripes of white; the centre is full of irregular small petals, and spotted; the foliage three inches wide and four inches long, and more heart-shaped than any of the others; grows freely, flower persistent, four inches in diameter, and highly esteemed, and considered one of the finest of the coloured *Caméllias*. *Magnificent*.

C. spicàtum; foliage very dark shining green; leaves two and a half inches wide and four inches long, very pointed; flower bright red, nearly four inches in diameter; circumference petals large and round, gradually diminishing to the centre, and concealing a few stamens: the plant grows and flowers freely, and is of an upright branching habit. *Superb*.

C. spléndens; rosy red, flower full and bold, nearly four inches in diameter; petals few, but very large and round, lying gently over each other, showing a few stamens in the centre—is very attractive and conspicuous in a collection; foliage dark green, ovate, acuminate. *Superb*.

C. spoffòrthiana; foliage deep plain green, acutely ser-

rated, plant handsome and vigorous; flower three and a
half inches in diameter, of a pure white, with an occasional
red stripe; petals rather irregular, full and double, though
showing a few stamens. *Superb.*

C. spofforthiana cárnea; flower larger than the former,
otherwise very similar. *Superb.*

C. swéetia vera; leaves three inches long and four
inches wide, distinctly serrate, of a fine shining green,
plant of an upright free-growing habit; flower nearly four
inches in diameter, with three rows of circumference petals
—rose white, sprinkled with bright red; those of the centre
small and erect, concealing a few sterile stamens. *Magnificent.* There is a spurious plant out under this name,
which is very inferior.

C. tricòlor; foliage pale green, two inches wide and
three and a half inches long, distinctly serrated, with the
nerves very prominent; flower full four inches in diameter
—semi-double; petals large and round—very beautifully
set; colour white, shaded with various shades of red, rose,
&c. A superb variety to produce seeds, having the female
organ very perfect, and was introduced from China by Dr.
Siebold. *Superb.*

C. triùmphans; foliage dark green: leaves roundish
oval, slightly pointed with nerves, and serratures very distinct; flower nearly four inches in diameter, of a bright
cherry red, shaded with rose; petals regular, round, and
large, a little recurved at the extremity, and gracefully imbricated to the centre, which is occasionally striped with
white: the plant is of a good habit and free growth. *Magnificent.*

C. variàbilis: this is a sportive variety of *C. pæoniflòrà,*
with flower and foliage of same character; frequently
blooming rose-striped, or marked with pink, blush, &c.
Magnificent.

C. variegàta is one of the old standard varieties, and
very much esteemed. It is striped with red and white;
sometimes the ground is red, with white streaks or blotches,
and *vice versa;* nearly four inches in diameter, petals large
and round, rather loose, centre showing a number of stamens; foliage very fine dark green, three inches wide and
four inches long. We have had seed from it. Plant of a
good habit and a profuse bloomer. *Superb.*

C. Walbánkiana; foliage pale green, two inches broad
and nearly four inches long; plant of rather loose habit;
flower greenish white, full four inches in diameter; petals
large and oval, irregularly tufted, showing a number of
stamens, though very double. We are inclined to believe
that this is the *lútea álba* of some catalogues. *Superb.*

C. Wárdii; very dark green foliage; leaves rather
cordate and undulate, of a coriaceous texture; plant of a
branching stiff habit; flower full three inches in diameter,
very persistent—circumference petals large and round;
those of the interior small, round, and closely set, rather
flattened, colour vivid crimson. This fine variety is another
by Mr. Floy, of New York. *Superb.*

C. Wóodsii; foliage light green; leaves two inches wide
and four inches long; plant of a rapid growth and regular
shape; flower four and a half inches in diameter, of a bright
rose-colour; petals large and rounding in the periphery;
those of the centre rather irregular—perfectly double, and
blooms with difficulty. We have observed it to bloom
finest when a gentle heat was applied, or when the plant
flowered in March or April. *Magnificent.* (Soil No. 11
for the whole family.)

There is another Camellia named *Wóodiana,* with foliage
very similar to the former, but the flower is cherry red and
only semi-double. We beg to observe that, in giving descriptions of the camellia, we have invariably, as far as
known, described the best variety, where there were several
varieties under one name. The new varieties in this beautiful family of plants are increasing with astonishing rapidity. The seedlings of this country alone, would of themselves form a collection of every shade and colour, though
many of them are almost alike, especially among the whites
and reds—nearly fac-similes except in foliage. The description of such we have carefully avoided. Indeed, we
boldly assert, though an extensive cultivator of over two
hundred varieties, that there are not more than one hundred varieties known worthy of a passing remark, except
for their deformed character.

Carmichælia austràlis, the only species, has very curious foliage, which the lilac leguminose flowers come out
of, and continue from April to June. (Soil No. 6.)

Ceanòthus azùreus is the only species of the genus

worth cultivating; it blooms profusely from May to July, and has considerable attraction with its brilliant blue spikes of small flowers. (Soil No. 6.)

Chorizèmas, about ten species, foliage very variable; flowers small and papilionaceous, often very profuse ; colour red and yellow; though small, they are very neat. *C. nàna* and *C. ilicifòlia* are pretty ; but nothing of the kind can exceed *C. ovàta* and *C. Henchmanii*, with their beautiful scarlet blossoms, which are in great profusion; if grown from seed, they will flower freely the second year ; drain the pots well. (Soil No. 6.)

Cineràrias, Cape aster, about twelve belong to the greenhouse. They are herbaceous, or half shrubby, soft wooded plants. *C. speciòsa, C. amelloìdes,* (now called *Agathæa cœléstus,*) *C. purpùrea,* and *C. lanàta*, are among the finest of the species; flowers blue or yellow; the latter is considered the handsomest of the genus. The exterior petals are bright purple, and the interior ones white, and, with *A. cœléstus*, flowers most of the year; flowers syngenesious and star-like. The herbaceous species must be treated as previously mentioned for that kind of plant. The new hybrids of this genus are rivaling the species, both for beauty of colour and size of flower; among these are *C. Kingii, C. triumphant, C. cœlestis, C. ignescens, C. Hendersònia,* and *V. Waterhòusia.* (Soil No. 12.)

Cinnamòmum camphòra is the camphor tree of commerce; is an excellent evergreen, but has no beauty in its flower. The foliage, when bruised, has a camphorated odour. (Soil No. 10.)

Cistus, or Rock rose. There are above thirty species, principally natives of Europe, consequently hardy there, and form a great ornament to their gardens, being very abundant and various in flower; but with us they will not stand the rigour of winter. We have no doubt, however, but, through time, some kinds may be grown that will withstand the greatest cold of the middle states ; they are low shrubby plants, of easy cultivation. *C. ladaniferus, C. sàlignus, C. populifòlius, C. undulàtus,* and *C. formòsus,* are perhaps the best : the flowers are of short duration, frequently only for one day ; but the quantity makes up this deficiency, being constantly in flower in May and June, and sometimes flower again in autumn. *C. crèticus* is most productive of the gum laudanum, which is secreted about its leaves and branches. The flowers are generally five-petaled, and some of them large and showy; centre full of stamens. (Soil No. 3.)

Citrus. This genus contains the most grand and noble of fruit-bearing trees: Loudon says, "The golden apples of the heathens, and forbidden fruit of the Jews, are supposed to allude to this family." They are all handsome ever-green shrubs or trees, bearing highly odoriferous flowers and beautiful golden fruit. In cultivation, the orange fruit is dry and more insipid than in the tropics, but the lemon is far superior in its quality. The varieties of orange are extensive, nearly eighty kinds being cultivated in Italy; but, with us, the sweet, sour, and rough-skinned are the principal sorts, and more recently we cultivate the manda-rin, otaheitean, and other beautiful dwarf Chinese varieties; also, the striped-leaved varieties of Bergamotte. The lemon are nearly as numerous, though not so apparently distinct; it is very valuable as a cultivated fruit, and should be in every green-house or conservatory. The lime and the shaddock should not be overlooked, as they are very orna-mental, especially the latter when it arrives at a fruit-bear-ing state. (Soil No. 18, when young plants, and when fruit-bearing keep from it the portion of sand.)

Clématis, Virgin's Bower. There are only six of these belonging to the green-house, all climbing plants. *C. aris-tàta* and *C. brachiàta* are the best; flowers in racemose clusters, pure white; foliage small; and natives of the Cape of Good Hope. The foliage of *C. aristàta* is cord-ate and blotched. Some of the hardy species and varie-ties make beautiful plants for the green-house, such as *C. flòrida, C. siebóldi* and P. *cærùlea;* they are profuse bloomers and free growers. (Soil No. 3.)

Clerodéndron frágrans múltiplex, frequently known under the name of *Volkamènia japónica,* which is a very different plant, and not supposed to be in this country. It keeps in a good green-house, and flowers well, frequently blooming during winter, and, if planted in the garden dur-ing summer, will flower superbly. The flowers have a delicious fragrance; if the foliage is rubbed with the hand the smell is not so pleasant. The leaves are large, round,

20

ovate and tomentose; flowers corymbose, compact and terminal. (Soil No. 12.)

Cléthra arbórea and *C. arbórea variegáta* are both fine shrubs; the latter is preferable; leaves are oblong, acuminate and serrated, having a gold-coloured edge; flowers white, downy, in large branching racemose spikes, and sweet-scented; grows freely. (Soil No. 2.)

Cliánthus punicens,* or Glory flower. This magnificent plant a few years ago produced great excitement among European cultivators, which consequently reached this country. The plant sold at extravagant prices, and cost the writer upwards of fifty dollars to introduce a living plant of it, which was done three years ago. The plant has been cultivated in pots, and has not yet given general satisfaction; the leaves are smooth, pinnated, of a delicate green, consisting of eight pairs and an old one; the stem is of a soft woody nature; the splendid large scarlet, leguminose, pea-like flowers grow in clusters, hanging down from the axils of the leaves on the lateral branches; each flower is about two inches long. To have it in perfection, it must be grown in large pots, or planted in the ground in the conservatory or green-house, or even a good pit would do; it is a native of New Zealand, and is tolerably hardy in the south; it makes a magnificent hardy shrub. (Soil No. 10.)

Clivea nóbilis, a tuberous herbaceous plant, closely allied to *Brunsvigia*. The flowers are said to be very splendid; colour scarlet and green: although it has been in the country several years, we are not aware of its ever having bloomed. (Soil No. 11.)

Cobæa scándens, the only species. It is a climber of very rapid growth, has been known to grow above two hundred feet in one summer; large bell-shaped flowers; when they are newly expanded, they are of a pale green colour, and change to dark purple: will grow in the garden during summer, bearing a continual profusion of flowers, but will not stand frost. When this plant becomes too large in the

---

* A plant five feet high, and only eighteen months old, now in the beautiful conservatory of Gen. R. Patterson, of this city, has upward of fifty racemes or clusters of flowers, varying from five to nine on a raceme, and will be in full bloom in a few weeks; this is the finest specimen we have heard of in this country.

house, do not cut it close to the root, except there is a
young shoot arising to carry off the superabundant sap, for
the old wood will not push, which will soon cause a mortification.

The best method to adopt in such a case is, to turn back
a shoot, and lay it in the ground to root, when it will become a young plant, which should always be done as soon
as it appears unsightly. It does best to be planted in the
ground, but will not give any satisfaction as to flowering in
a pot. It will flower as an annual if sown in pots this
month, and placed in a warm room or hot-bed, and planted
into the garden about the middle of May; it seeds freely.
(Soil No. 11.)

Coronilla, a very few are fine species in the green-
house. *C. glaúca* is a celebrated plant among us, as a
free and early flowering shrub. *C. valentiana* and *C.
viminális* are equally so, flower from April to June, colour
yellow; papilionaceous flowers in clusters; agree best in
summer with partial shade. Drain the pots well. (Soil
No. 12.)

Corrèa, five species and several varieties, all very pretty
dwarf shrubs, and flower profusely; foliage ovate, cordate,
and either rusty or downy beneath. *C. álba* and *C. rúfa*
have both white flowers a little tubular. *C. pulchélla* is
a very handsome, erect growing plant; flowers large and
tubular, of a bright red colour, and grows freely. *C.
speciòsa* has been long admired as a splendid free-flowering plant; flowers same shape as *C. pulchélla*, but more
elongated; colour red and yellowish green. *C. virèns* is
a very free grower, flowers same shape as the last two,
colour entirely green. The last three mentioned are abundant flowerers, when the plants are well established; having a continued succession from November to June, possessing the valuable requisite of flowering through the
winter, and ought to be in every collection. They require
an airy situation and the pots to be well drained. The
plants in summer must not be fully exposed to the sun.
(Soil No. 6.)

Cràssula. This genus has now no plant in it attractive
in beauty. Several beautiful plants in our collections belong to *Róchea* and *Kalosánthus*. There is a strong growing succulent plant, known in our collections as *C. falcàta*,

which is *R. falcàta.* It seldom flowers; the minor variety
blooms profusely every year from May to August, and has
showy scarlet flowers in terminal panicles. The plants
known as *C. coccinea* and *C. versicolor* are now given to
the genus *Kalosánthus.* The flowers of the former are
scarlet, wax-like, terminal, and sessile; those of the latter
are rose and white, also wax-like, and are both desirable
plants, requiring very little water during winter. (Soil
No. 18.)

Cratàgus. There are none of these belonging to the
green-house; but there is a plant in the collections, known
as *C. glabra,* which is *Photínia serrulàta,* a native of
China, and is a very handsome plant, has long foliage,
deeply serrated, very shining. *P. arbutifòlia,* a native of
California, and is the finest of the genus; flowers in large
dense panicles, foliage larger than the former, and not so
deeply serrated; they are both comparatively hardy, and
we soon expect to see them acclimated. (Soil No. 11.)

Crínum, several species do well in the green-house,
especially *C. Mexicánum, C. capense,* and *C. ascótica:*
they require considerable pot room to make them do well.
(Soil No. 12.)

Cròwea saligna is among one of the finest plants of New
South Wales. It flowers at the axils of the leaves, colour
pink, with five petals, connected by entangled hairs; in
flower from April to December, and frequently through the
winter; foliage lanceolate, and a fine green. The plant
grows neat, and requires an airy situation: drain the pots
well. (Soil No. 1.)

Cunónia capnésis, the only species, and a handsome
shrub, with large pinnated shining leaves, beautifully contrasted by numerous dense elongated branches of small
white flowers, and twigs of a red colour, having more the
habit of a tropical than of a Cape of Good Hope plant.
(Soil No. 2.)

Cupréssus may be desired in collections, as erect and
handsome growing evergreen shrubs. *C. lusitánica* the
famed cedar of Goa; *C. péndula* and *C. juniperoídes* are
the most desirable; the flowers are insignificant and yellowish; we have no doubt they may prove hardy. *C.
lusitánica* is the handsomest tree of the genus. Its abun-

dant, very long dichotomous branchlets distinguish it from all the evergreens of the conoferious tribe. (Soil No. 11.)

Cyrtànthus, a genus of Cape bulbs, containing nine species, and will do very well in the green-house, but we find the assistance of the hot-house a great advantage. They are closely allied to *Crìnum.* The tubes of the flowers are long and round, with various shades of orange, yellow, red, and green. *C. odòrus, C. striátus, C. obliquus,* and *C. vittàtus,* are the finest. When the bulbs are dormant, which will be from October to January, they should not get any water; before they begin to grow, turn the bulbs out of the old earth, repotting it immediately. At this time they should be potted with the bulbs of earth entire, which will cause them to flower stronger. (Soil No. 12.)

Dampièras, four species. The genus is named in honour of Captain W. Dampier, a famous voyager, has Lobelia-like flowers, either blue or purple. *C. purpùrea, C. undulàta,* and *C. stricta,* are the finest; the former two are shrubby; the latter is herbaceous; they all flower freely. (Soil No. 6.)

Davièsias, above ten species, principally natives of New South Wales, all yellow papilionaceous flowers. *D. ulicìna, D. latifòlia, D. aciculàris,* and *D. incrassàta,* are very fine species, flower and grow freely, and require to be well drained; bloom from April to August. (Soil No. 6.)

Dillwynias, above twelve species, and plants very little known. *D. cineréscens, D. floribúnda, D. teretifòlia,* and *D. phylicoides,* are desirable plants; flowers small, papilionaceous, and colour, yellow and red. They are very liable to suffer from too much wet; while dormant, therefore, the pots must be effectually drained. (Soil No. 6.)

Diósmas. This pretty genus of heath-looking plants has recently been very much divided by botanical professors. The genera that they have been given to are *Adenándra, Acmàdenia, Agathósma,* and *Barósma.* However, we incline to adhere to the original name, and recommend *D. capitáta, D. oppositifòlia, D. rùbra, D. álba, D. fragràns, D. uniflora, D. serratifòlia, D. speciòsa,* and *D. pulchélla.* They are all profuse blooming plants, with generally small flowers of a white lilac or pink colour. It is supposed that the dried leaves of *pulchélla* are used by the Hottentots as powder to mix with the grease with which

20*

they anoint their bodies. Some travelers assert that it
gives them so rank an odour, that they sometimes could
not bear the smell of those who were their guides. In fact,
the foliage of all, if rubbed by the hand while on the plant,
has a very strong smell, some of them very agreeable,
others disagreeable. They are all evergreen small neat
growing shrubs. They require, while growing luxuriantly,
to have their young shoots topped to.make them bushy;
drain all the pots well, and keep them in airy situations,
and not crowded with other plants, or they will become
slender and unsightly. (Soil No. 6.)

Diplàcus puniceus. This shrubby (*mimulus*) plant was
introduced by Mr. Nuttall from California, by seeds, in
1836, and sent by us to England in 1837. The flowers
are of a scarlet orange, about one inch and a half long, and
produced in pairs; from the axils of the leaves, on young
wood, the plant requires considerable nourishment; for the
more rapid it grows, the more profuse are its flowers, which
bloom from May to September, and are rather showy. In
the southern states it will prove a hardy shrub, blooming
nearly the whole year. (Soil No. 12.)

Dracæna, or Dragon tree. The *D. austràlis* and *D.
férrea* will keep in the green-house, and are attractive
plants for their foliage, especially the latter, which is of a
purple crimson and very unique; the flowers are on large
terminal spikes. (Soil No. 11.)

Doryànthus excélsa, a *Yucca* looking plant belonging to
the natural order of Amaryllidea; the leaves arise from the
root, and are about three inches wide and three feet long;
the flowers are bright crimson, surmounted on a stem about
twenty feet high. The plant does not bloom till it is of
considerable size. (Soil No. 10.)

Dryándras. This genus is closely allied in character
and habits to *Bánksia*, and contains above sixteen species.
D. nivea has most beautiful foliage, very long and deeply
indented. *D. formòsa* has a scent like the fruit of an
apricot. *D. nervòso, D. floribúnda, D. armàta, D. plu-
mòsa, D. Baxtèri, D. nervòsa,* and *D. falcàta,* are the
most conspicuous, and all highly desirable plants in collections. They are very delicate of importation; flowers are
straw and orange-coloured, and thistle-like. Seeds in

small cones. Treat them the same as directed for *Bánk-sias.* (Soil No. 6.)

Dyckias, two species of very curious growing plants, of a dwarf habit with bright orange flowers; they may be cultivated with the aloe tribe, to which they have a similarity. *D. rariflòra* and *D. ramotiflòra;* the latter is in the country. (Soil No. 18.)

Echevèria, a genus of succulent plants chiefly from Mexico and California. *E. grandiflòra,* flowers green and red. *E. pulverulènta,* flowers red. The foliage of this species is delicately covered with powder, which gives it a very beautiful appearance. *E. bicòlor* is also a pretty species: they require to be kept very dry during winter. (Soil No. 10.)

Edwárdsias, about four species, very beautiful foliaged plants, and have very curious yellow flowers, but do not flower until the plant becomes large. *E. grandiflòra, E. chrysòphylla,* and *E. micròphylla,* are the best, and are tolerably hardy, though doubtful of ever being acclimated. The flowers are leguminose, foliage ovate, pinnate, from eight to forty on one footstalk, and appear to be covered with gold dust. The hardier they are grown, the more visible it will appear. (Soil No. 11.)

Elichrysums. This genus is now extinct, and two splendid species of it given to others. *E. proliferum* is now *Phœnàcoma prolifera,* and has beautiful purple rayed flowers, and highly esteemed: the foliage small, round, ovate, smooth, and closely imbricated. *E. spectábile* is now *Aphélexis hùmilis,* has pine-like foliage, and large light purple flowers; care must be taken that they are not over-watered; drain the pots well. (Soil No. 6.)

Enkiánthus, only two species, both very fine. *E. quinqueflòrus* has large ovate, acuminate foliage, flowers pink and pendulous; very handsome. *E. reticulátus,* the foliage is netted, and the flowers blush: they are liable, when dormant, to suffer from wet. Be sure to drain the pots well, and be sparing in water while in that state. (Soil No. 11.)

Epácris, above twelve species, and all very ornamental. *E. grandiflòra* has been celebrated ever since it was known; the foliage is small, flat, and acuminate; flowers tubular and pendulous, bright crimson, with a tinge of

white, and very abundant, in flower from January to June.
E. pulchélla is likewise a most beautiful plant ; foliage very
small and closely set, flowers pure white, and in long
spikes, sweet-scented. *E. impréssa,* foliage impressed,
and flowers of a rose colour. *E. paludòsa,* flowers white,
grows and flowers very handsomely, and is very fragrant.
E. purpuráscens rùbra is a variety, with good bright red
flowers. *E. pallida,* rose coloured, long tubular flowers.
E. nivalis, rosy white. *E. Townii,* beautiful rosy blush
colour. These with several others are very desirable.
They are mostly erect growing plants; flower from January till August, and a rough, turfy, sandy soil is found
most congenial. They are natives of the mountainous
districts of New South Wales. The pots must be well
drained ; the roots will run with avidity among the pot-
shreds. (Soil No. 6.)

Ericas, heath. There are in cultivation in Europe
above five hundred and fifty species and varieties of this
magnificent genus. About sixty years ago it consisted
only of a few humble British plants, with the heath of
Spain, *E. Mediterrànea,* which is at present most common
in our collections, though in a few years we may expect to
see it supplanted by others more splendid.

In their native countries they are adapted to a great
many useful purposes. In the north of Britain the poorer
inhabitants cover their cabins or huts with heath, and build
the walls with alternate layers of it and a kind of cement
made with straw and clay. They likewise brew ale and
distil spirits from the tender shoots ; and it has been known
to be used in dying, tanning, and many other useful domestic purposes. Encomium on their beauty is not requisite; they are almost as diversified in colour as colour itself.
Many are graceful and elegant ; hundreds are pretty ; a
few noble and splendid ; others grotesque, curious and
odoriferous. To cultivate and propagate them is considered
one of the most delicate branches of floriculture. Nevertheless, it has been said by a scientific writer, that " those
who complain of the difficulty of growing the heath, are
ignorant people, who have never had a heath to grow." The
most splendid collection in Europe is under the care of Mr.
M'Nab, of the Royal Botanic Garden, Edinburgh, where.
there are two large houses devoted to their culture ; and

through the whole year a continued profusion of bloom is kept up. Some of the plants are eight feet in diameter, and fourteen feet high. The soil used is a coarse sandy peat. Pots drained with potshreds, and pieces of freestone are put down the sides of the large pots and tubs : where these can be had they are essential to the culture of mountainous plants, preventing them from being saturated with moisture, or from becoming dry, thus keeping the roots in a medium state; for if once the roots are allowed to get thoroughly dried, no art of the gardener can recover them. This may be the true reason why they are said to be difficult of cultivation.

In the summer season the pots must be kept out of the violent sun, for in a few hours the pot would become heated, dry the roots, and cause death, or a brownness of foliage which would never again become natural. In winter, too, much fire heat will also hurt them. They only require to be kept free from frost, need a great deal of air, and plenty of light; consequently, should be placed near the glass, that they may have the benefit of all the air that is admitted. Their flowers are as varied in shape as variety or colour, but they all partake of a wax-like nature, and are very persistent. (Soil No. 5 for young plants : when older, No. 6 will do better.)

The finest and most select varieties that appear to withstand the severity of the summer, are the following :

WHITE FLOWERS.	YELLOW FLOWERS.	RED FLOWERS.
Arborea,		*Bélla,*
Bowieàna,	*Capitàta,*	*Canaliculata,*
Cáffra,	*Epistóma,*	*Curviflòra rùbra,*
Confèrta,	*Grandiflòra.*	*Grácilis,*
Jesminaflòra,		*Ignèscens,*
Margaritácea,	SCARLET FLOWERS.	*Plukenétii,*
Odoràta,		*Pinèa,*
Pellúcida,	*Ardens,*	*Mediterránea.*
Phylicòides.	*Coccinea,*	
	" *grandiflòra,*	PURPLE FLOWERS.
	Vernix coccinea,	
	Véstita coccinea.	*Amœna.*

Denticulàta,	VARIOUS CO-	*Crúenta supèrba*.
Fasciculàris,	LOURS.	*Rúbida*,
Hispidúla,		*Tubiflòra*,
Mammósa,	*Abetina*,	*Ventricòsa supèrba*.
Pubèscens,	*Báccans*,	
Tenèlla.	*Cerinthòides*,	

Eriabòtrya japónica, Loquat, or *Mespìlus japónica*, is a fine plant, with large lanceolate, distinctly serrated leaves, white underneath; small white flowers on a racemose spike, and produces a fruit about the size of a walnut, of a fine yellow blush colour, and of tartish flavour. If it flowers in the autumn, it will require the heat of a hot-house to ripen the fruit. It is of very easy culture, and its noble aspect is never passed unobserved. It is perfectly hardy in the southern states, and forms a handsome evergreen. (Soil No. 11.)

Eròdiums, Heron's bill. There are about thirty species, all of a geranium character, and there are among them some very pretty flowering, soft woodéd, shrubby, herbaceous, and annual plants. Only a few of them belong to the green-house, of which *É. incarnàtum, E. crassifòlium*, and *E. laciniàtum*, are the finest; culture similar to *Gerà-nium*. The flowers of these are scarlet, pentapetalous and veiny. (Soil No. 10.)

Erythìina cristágálli, or Coral plant. If this magnificent scarlet flowering plant is desired to be kept in a pot or tub, it must have a repotting every month till September: to keep it in fine blooming condition, it is worthy of *extra* care, as it will bloom three times during the season, if well treated. (Soil No. 18.) For other methods, see Flower Garden for April, May and November.

Escallònia, a shrubby genus, of about ten species, of rather neat blooming plants, of a strong shrubby habit. They require great encouragement to flower them well, if kept in pots: the best mode of treatment would be to plant them in pits with other half hardy shrubs. *E. rùbra*, red flowering; *E. glandulósa*, white; and *E. bìfida*, pink, are the finest. (Soil No. 12.) They are perfectly hardy south of Virginia, and we are not certain but they may become acclimated here.

Eucalyptus, above fifty species of them, and the tallest

growing trees of New Holland; foliage very diversified, generally of a hard glaucous texture. From their rapid growth, they soon grow higher than the loftiest house. The most conspicuous are, *E. cordàta, E. rostràta, E. radiàta, E. pulvigéra, E. glòbifera, E. pulverulénta,* and *E. resinefera.* In Van Dieman's Land, a manufactory has been established, where a tannin is extracted from many of the species. The last-mentioned produces gum like that which the druggists call *Kino.* They ought not to be too much fostered, as it would in some degree retard their growth. They are of a very hardy nature. When large, the plants will flower freely, and are similar in flower to *Myrtle;* many stamina, proceeding from a hard nut-like capsule. (Soil No. 6.)

Euónymus. One or two of this genus have been recently introduced from China, and are found to be very ornamental, in having beautifully variegated, or rather margined foliage. *E. japònicus áureas* has golden-edged leaves, and *E. japònicus argénteus** has silvery-edged foliage ; the flowers have no beauty ; the leaves are ovate, acuminate, about one inch and a half broad and two inches and a half long. (Soil No. 11.)

Eupatòrium. There is only one species deserving of cultivation in the green-house; flowers syngenesious, white, and in large flattened panicles ; very sweet-scented. The plant, when growing freely, in the beginning of summer, should be topped, which would make it more bushy; if not, it is apt to grow straggling. Known in our collections as *E. elegáns.* (Soil No. 3.)

Eutáxias, two species. *E. myrtifòlia* is a most beautiful free-flowering evergreen shrub; foliage small, but very neat; flowers leguminose, small and very many; colour yellow and red; grows freely. The young plants should be frequently topped, or they will grow naked and unsightly. *E. pùngens,* similar to the other except in foliage. They flower from March to June, and ought to have a place in every green-house. Culture very easy. (Soil No. 6.)

Ficus, a few species, are good plants for this department,

---

* This plant is in some collections as a variegated leaved camellia, and is perfectly hardy with us.

especially *F. elástica;* leaves smooth, shining green, frequently six inches wide and twelve long: this is the plant that produces the gum elastic, or Indian rubber. *F. austràlis* is also an excellent evergreen, with elliptic dull green foliage; very rusty underneath; they grow almost too freely. (Soil No. 11.)

Fúchsia, or Ladies' Ear-drop. There are an endless variety of this lovely genus of deciduous small shrubs now cultivated, but there are only a few, to surpass the common and celebrated *Cóccinea:* true, many have been, and are, represented as far surpassing it, but, when brought to the test, they are, in some particular, found wanting. However, among the many, *F. glóbosa, F. chauverii, F. exoniensis, F. elegans superba, Champion Britannia,* and *Stanwelliana.* These are very superb, dark varieties; some of the flowers are two and a half inches long and two inches in diameter. The following are light coloured varieties, indeed nearly white, with a purple or pink centre, forming a beautiful contrast with the deep crimson and purple sorts; *F. rosea alba, F. bicolor, F. Queen Victoria, F. chandlerii, F. venus victrix, Conspicua arborea,* and *Snow Ball.* To grow these in perfection, they require to be very frequently shifted, as they advance in growth till you have them in pots ten inches wide. Just now I have plants only six months from the cutting that are four feet high and sixteen feet in circumference, loaded with thousands of flowers, and are the admiration of every beholder. They require liberal supplies of water. *F. fúlgens* is a distinct species; the foliage is very different from any other sort; leaves of a well-grown plant are four inches wide and five inches and a half long: the flowers are from two inches and a half to three inches long, of a pink and scarlet colour, and the plant is nearly tuberous. We would recommend our readers to grow them from seeds when obtained: it is well known they will produce variety, and it is even supposed by some that the seeds of *F. coccinea* have produced by hybridizing nearly all the varieties of the present day, which exceed one hundred: most of the flowers are a bright scarlet, the stamens are encircled with a petal of bright purple, and are of very curious construction; they bear a dark purple berry, and are of the easiest cultivation; but during summer the pots must be carefully kept from the sun, although the plants will not be affected by it. If the plants are young and growing freely, we find that a deluge of rain, and afterward a hot day, is their instant death. Some of them do tolerably well when planted in the flower-garden early in May. (Soil No. 10.)

Fabiána, a genus of new plants that will prove entirely hardy in the southern states; they are upright growing shrubs, with delicate foliage. *F. imbricàta* is the most popular, producing a profusion of white tubular flowers about an inch long, of easy culture in soil No. 12.

Gardoquìa Hookèri, a very pretty dwarf plant—native of the Floridas: it blooms profusely from June to October; flowers are about one inch and a half long, of a tubular labiate form, of a bright orange colour; it is easy of culture in soil No. 1.

Gelsèmium nitidum, Carolina jasmine, a most beautiful climbing evergreen, flowering shrub. In the months of April and May it produces many large yellow trumpet-like blossoms of delicious fragrance. If much encouraged in growth, it will not flower so freely. (Soil No. 6.)

Genísta: a few of these are very pretty free-flowering shrubs. *G. ramòsus*, *G. canariénsis*, *G. tricuspidáta*, *G. cuspidòsa*, and *G. umbellàta*, are the finest green-house species. All of them have yellow leguminose flowers in great abundance; leaves small, lanceolate. (Soil No. 1.)

Gnaphàlium, everlasting. There are above ten species, most of them very splendid, persistent flowers. *G. eximia* has briliant red flowers. *G. spiràlis*, *G. speciosissima*, *G. frùticans*, *G. oriantàlum*, and *G. imbricàtum*, are all very fine; pots must be well drained. (Soil No. 8.)

Gnídias, about ten species of pretty green-house shrubs. *G. símplex*, *G. serícea*, *G. imbérbis*, and *G. pinifòlia*, flower the most freely; flowers straw colour, tubular, and corymbose. *G. símplex* is sweet-scented, leaves small; the pots must be well drained, and care taken that they do not get either too wet or too dry, for the roots are very deli-cate. The plants must be kept near the glass, or they will be drawn weak. (Soil No. 6.)

Gortèria personàta is the only species that belongs to this genus, and is an annual. There are several plants in our collections known as *Gortèrias*, but which properly are *Gazània*, of which there are five species. *G. rìngens*,

21

when the flowers are fully expanded, (which will only be
while exposed to the sun, closing at night and opening
again with the influence of the sun's rays,) is a great
beauty. The rays of the flowers are bright orange, and
the centre dark purple. *G. pavónia* has handsome foliage; flower similar to *G. ringens,* except the centre of
the flower being spotted, and is thought to be the finest,
but does not flower so freely. *G. heterophylla* is of the
same character, except the foliage, which is variable, the
colour orange and vermilion. They are dwarf-growing
plants, and during the months of July, August, and September, are liable to damp off at the surface of the earth,
from the action of heat and too much water. Pots must be
well drained, and the plants kept partially in the shade.
Their flowers are syngenesious, and about two inches in
diameter. (Soil No. 9.)

Grevilleas, about thirty species. A few of them very
handsome in flower and foliage, among which are *G. puni-
cea; G. acanthifolia,* (beautiful foliage;) *G. concinna,* very
pretty straw and rose-coloured flowers; *G. juniperìna,*
green and straw-coloured; *G. lineàris,* white flowers. The
flowers of the whole are curious, though not very attractive. Some carry their flowers in racemose spikes, others
on flowering branches, which are recurved; the petals are
very small and rugged; the stile longer than the appendage. They grow freely, flower and ripen seeds; all evergreen dwarf shrubs. (Soil No. 1.)

Habránthus, about ten species of small South American
bulbs, nearly allied to *Amaryllis. H. Andersònii, H.
versicolor, H. candìda,* and *H. robusta,* are fine; they are
in colour yellow, blue, white, and lilac. We have very
little doubt but these bulbs will do to plant out in the garden
in April, and be lifted in October. Keep them from frost.
Thus treated, they are very desirable. (Soil No. 12.)

Helychrysums, above forty species, chiefly belonging to
the green-house, all everlasting flowers. *H. grandiflòrum,
H. arboreum, H. fràgrans, H. adoratìssimum, H. fruti-
cans,* and *H. fùlgidum,* are all very esteemed species,
mostly with soft downy foliage. The pots should be well
drained, and the plants kept in an airy situation, as they
suffer from the least damp. If the flowers are cut off before they fade, they will retain for many years all the

splendour of their beauty; but if allowed to decay on the plant, they will soon become musty, and all their colour fade. (Soil No. 6.)

Hibbértias, about ten species. Three of them are known to be fine climbing evergreen shrubs, namely, *H. glossulariæfolia;`H. dentàta; H. volùbilis*, if closely approached, has a disagreeable smell; *H. fasciculàta, H. salígna*, and *H. pedunculàta*, are evergreen shrubs; they have pure yellow flowers of five petals, blooming from May to September. (Soil No. 12.)

Hòveas, about eight species, pretty plants of New South Wales, blue pea-flowering evergreen shrubs; the finest are *H. panòsa, H. atropurpùrea, H. lineàris, H. rosmarinifòlia, H. longifòlia*, and *H. Célsii*, which is the most superb, and flowers in abundance. They grow and flower freely; the pots should be drained. (Soil No. 6.)

Hypéricums. St. John's wort, about twenty species. A few of them are very showy, and, with few exceptions, have yellow flowers. *H. monógynum, H. balearicum, H. floribúndum, H. canariénse, H. ægyptìacum*, and *H. cochinchinênse*, which has scarlet flowers, are among the best, and all of them flower freely; five petals, filaments many in three or five parcels. They are all of very easy cultivation, and bloom generally from April to September. (Soil No. 11.)

Hydrángea horténsis is a well-known plant, and much esteemed for its great profusion of very elegant, though monstrous, flowers. They are naturally of a pink colour, but under certain circumstances of culture they become blue. If grown in brown loam with a little sand, they will preserve their original colour; but if grown in swamp earth with a little mould of decayed leaves, they will become blue.* The swamp earth and vegetable mould being more combined with aluminous salt than brown loam, is the cause of the change: and, when first found out, (which was merely by chance,) was thought a great wonder. It must have a very plentiful supply of water when in flower, which is produced on the shoots of the previous year.

---

* Mix the iron sparks, from the blacksmith's shop, with any kind of soil, and they will be a beautiful blue. One and a half quarts to a bushel will do.

They will neither grow nor flower well if they are not
kept constantly in the shade. When kept in the sun, the
foliage is very brown; and by being neglected in watering,
we have seen the flowers completely scourged. *H. japónica,* a new variety with pink flowers, a little fragrant.
Being tolerably hardy, when the winters are mild, by a
little protection in the open air, they will flower profusely;
the flowers will be very large, and in bloom from June to
October. They are deciduous, soft-wooded shrubs.

Ilex, Holly, of *I. aquifòlium.* There are above one
hundred of them in cultivation in Europe, differing in vari-
egation, margin, shape, and size of the leaves; some are
only prickly on the margin of the foliage, others prickly
over all the surface. In Europe they are all hardy, but
with us few or none of the varieties are so. If they become acclimated, they will be a great ornament to our
gardens, being all low evergreen shrubs. The most common and conspicuous varieties are the *hedge-hog, striped
hedge-hog, white edged, gold edged,* and *painted;* the
flowers are white and small, berries yellow or red; they do
not agree with exposure to the sun. *J. Cassine* and *J.
vomitòria* have very bitter leaves, and, though natives of
Carolina, we have to give them the protection of a green-
house. It is said that at certain seasons of the year the
Indians make a strong decoction of the leaves, which makes
them vomit freely, and after drinking and vomiting for a
few days, they consider themselves sufficiently purified.
(Soil No. 15.)

Illiciums, Anise-seed tree, three species. *I. floridànum*
has very sweet-scented, double purple flowers, and the
plant grows freely and systematically if properly treated,
and deserves particular attention. *I. parviflòrum* has small
yellow flowers; *I. anisàtum* is so very like *I. parviflòrum*
in every respect, as to make us conclude they are the
same, were *I. anisátum* not a native of China, and the
other two natives of Florida. When the leaves and capsules of either of them are rubbed, they have a very strong
smell of anise; they grow very freely. (Soil No. 1.)

Indigófera; Indigo tree, about twenty species, belong
to the green-house, and are chiefly pretty free-flowering
shrubs. *I. denudàta, I. amæna, I. austràlis, I. angulàta,
I. càndicans,* and *I. filifòlia,* are very fine; flowers papi-

lionaceous, in long panicles; colour various, red, blue, yellow, and pink. (Soil No. 6.)

Jacksónias, a genus consisting of five species. The foliage is varied, and all natives of New South Wales. *J. scopária, J. hórrida,* and *J. reticuláta,* are the finest; the small flowers come out of the young shoots, are yellow and papilionaceous; the pots should be well drained. (Soil No. 6.)

Jambòsa vulgàris, or *Eugenìa jámbos,* is a splendid evergreen tree, producing a fruit of an agreeable odour and called rose apple. *J. austràlis* has a very neat habit, and produces purple fruit; they are of the earliest culture in soil No. 12.

Jasmìnum, Jasmine. A few species of this genus are celebrated either for the green-house or rooms. *J. odoratissimum,* Azorian, has very sweet-scented yellow flowers, blooming from April to November. *J. revolùtum* is the earliest flowering one, and of the same colour; it is apt to grow straggling, and should be close pruned as soon as done blooming, which will be in May. *J. pubigérum* is also yellow. *J. grandiflòrum* is frequently called Catalonian, and should be pruned early in spring to make it bloom well, especially old plants. *J. multiflòrum,* profuse flowering white. These plants are all perfectly hardy in the southern states. *J. officinàle* is a hardy climbing plant for arbours, walls, &c. There are several varieties of it. (Soil No. 3.)

Justicias. Only a few of these belong to the green-house, and are very simple-looking flowers. (The most beautiful of them belong to the hot-house.) *J. nigricans,* small striped flower; *J. orchioides* and *J. Adhátoda,* Malanut, are the only ones that are worth observation, and are very easily cultivated in any soil.

Kennèdias, about twelve species, all beautiful evergreen climbers, of the easiest culture, and flower abundantly. *K. monophylla,* blue-flowered, and *K. rubicúnda,* crimson-flowered, are common in our collections. *K. prostràta,* one-flowered scarlet, and *K. coccinea,* many-flowered scarlet, are very pretty. *K. Comptoniàna* has splendid purple flowers, *K. nigricans,* black flowers, and *K. spléndens* and *K. marryàtta* are thought the most superb. They have bright crimson flowers, and are yet rare in our collections.

21*

The pots should be well drained ; flowers are either in racemose spikes, or solitary, which is rather too much distinction for the same genus. (Soil No. 6.)

Lambértias, four species of very fine plants, natives of
New Holland. *L. formósa* is the finest of the genus that
we have seen ; flowers large and of a splendid rose colour.
L. echináta is said to be finer, but has not flowered in
cultivation. *L. uniflòra* has single red flowers, and *L.
inérmis* orange-coloured. They are rare plants in the
collections on this side of the Atlantic. Drain the pots
well; the foliage is narrow, and of a hard dry nature.
(Soil No. 1.)

Lasiopètalums, only two species. There were a few
more, but they are now *Thomàsias*, plants of no merit
whatever in regard to flower; foliage three-lobed, small,
rough, and rusty-like. *Thomàsia solanácea* and *T. quer-
cifòlia* are the best species ; foliage of the former is large,
cordate, and deeply indented ; they are all of the easiest
culture. (Soil No. 1.)

Laúrus. A few species are green-house plants. This
genus has been divided to *Cinnamòmum;* still there are a
few celebrated plants in the original. *L. nòbilis,* sweet
bay, though hardy, is kept under protection. It will bear
the winter with a little straw covering ; notwithstanding,
there should be a plant kept in the house in case of accident by frost or otherwise ; there is a variegated variety of
it. *L. indica,* royal bay, *L. fœtens, L. aggregàta,* and
L. gláuca, are favourites. There is a species known in
our collections as *L. scábra.* The Camphor tree, known
as *L. camphòra,* is *Cinnamomum camphora;* the wood,
leaves, and roots of this tree have a very strong odour of
camphor. It is obtained by distillation from the roots and
small branches, which are cut into chips, and put into a
net suspended within an iron pot, the bottom of which is
covered with water, having an earthen head fitted in it ;
heat is then applied, and the steam of the boiling water
acting upon the contents of the net, elevates the camphor
into the capital, where it concretes on the straws, with
which this part of the apparatus is lined. They are all
fine evergreens, (which the name denotes,) and easily cultivated. (Soil No. 10.)

Lavándulas, Lavender. About seven species belong to

the green-house, and a few of them very pretty soft-wooded, half shrubby plants, and, if touched, are highly scented. *L. dentàta* has narrow serrated foliage, very neat; *L. formòsa* and *L. pìnnata* are desirable; blue flowers on a long spike; should be kept near to the glass: they are of the easiest culture. (Soil No. 7.)

Lechenaùltia; four species of pretty dwarf blooming plants. *L. formòsa* is almost always a picture with its bright scarlet flowers and heath-like foliage, and ought to be in every collection; *L. bilòba* and *L. Drummóndii* are both blue, though very rarely seen in bloom; fine plants two years old, with us have not yet shown a flower; they must have an airy situation and near the front glass; otherwise they will be weak and spindling. (Soil No. 19.)

Leonòtis, Lion's-ear, four species. They have very fine scarlet tubular flowers, orifice-toothed. They come out in large whorls, and look elegant; but neither plant nor foliage has an agreeable appearance. They are of the easiest culture. *L. intérmedia* and *L. Leonùrus* are the best flowering species. (Soil No. 7.)

Leptospérmums, about thirty species, all pretty New Holland evergreen dwarf shrubs, with small white flowers. *L. baccàtum*, *L. péndulum*, *L. juniperìnum*, *L. ovátum*, *L. stellàtum*, *L. grandiflòrum*, and *L. scopàrium*, are the best of the species. The latter was used as tea by the crew of Captain Cook's ship. It is an agreeable bitter, with a pleasant flavour when fresh. When young plants are growing, they ought to be frequently topped to make them bushy, and kept in an airy situation, or they will be drawn and unsightly. They are of very easy culture. (Soil No. 1.)

Leucadéndrons, Silver tree, above forty species, all natives of the Cape of Good Hope. They are evergreens, with handsome silvery-like foliage. *L. argentéum* (once *Pròtas argentéa*) is a great beauty; foliage white, lanceolate and silky. It is a plant that has been long in cultivation, greatly admired, and much sought for, and is the finest of the genus. *L. squarròsum, L. stellatum,* (once *Pròtea stellàris,*) *L. tórtum, L. serviceum, L. marginàtum,* and *L. plumòsum,* (once *P. parviflòra,*) are all fine species. The pots must be well drained and the plants

never over-watered. They are very desirable in collections
for their beauty of foliage. (Soil No. 9.)

Leucospérmums, about eighteen species of Proteacous
plants, chiefly low growing, and are mostly downy or hairy;
flowers yellow, in terminal heads. *L. formósum, L. grandiflòrum, L. tomentósum,* and *L. candicans,* rose-scented.
These are fine species. For treatment, see *Próteas.* (Soil
No. 9.)

Lìnums, flax, two or three species are very fine, and
flower freely. *L. trigynum* has large yellow flowers in
clusters, and *L. ascyrifòlium,* whose flowers are large,
blue and white, and in long spikes. They bloom in February; the shape of them is very like the flower vulgarly
called Morning-glory. (Soil No. 4.)

Lipàrias, about five species, much esteemed for their
beauty of foliage; leaves ovate, lanceolate, downy or wool-
ly; flowers yellow, leguminose and capitate. *L. sphærica,
L. tomentósa, L. villòsa* and *L. sericea,* are the finest. *L.
vistìta* and *L. villòsa* are the same, although put in many
catalogues as different species. None of them ought to be
much watered over the foliage, as it adheres to the down,
and causes the young shoots to damp off. Drain the pots
well, and keep the plants in an airy situation. (Soil
No. 6.)

Lobèlias. Several of them, when well treated, form
pretty flowering plants; they are principally herbaceous.
The genus consists of about eighty species; seventy of
them are exotics; many of them natives of the Cape of
Good Hope, with little flowers of brilliant colours. *L. cœrùlea, L. Thunbérgii, L. corymbòsa, L. pyramidàlis, L.
érines,* and *L. illicifòlia,* are very fine species, of weak
growth, but flower freely. (Soil No. 4.)

Lonicera japónica. There is a plant in our collections
known by that name, which is now *Nintoóa longiflòra;*
flowers of a straw colour, but come out white. It has been
known to withstand the winter, but does not flower, and is
frequently killed entirely. (Soil No. 3.)

Lophospérmum scàndens. This is a magnificent climbing soft-wooded shrub, with rosy purple, campanulate flowers, which are produced from the axils on the young wood;
they bloom from May to September; leaves large, cordate,

and tomentose; grows rapidly, and flowers abundantly.
(Soil No. 3.)

Lychnis coronàta is an esteemed Chinese plant; flowers
in abundance, pentapetalous, large, and a little indented at
the edges; colour a red-like orange; flowers terminal and
axillary. A good method of treatment is to divide the
roots, and plant some of them in the garden; they will
flower well, and could be lifted in the fall, and put under
protection. If not done so, plant them in four-inch pots,
and repot them into those of six-inch in May. Do not expose them while in flower to the mid-day sun, for it will
deteriorate the fine orange colour. (Soil No. 9.)

Lysinèmas, four species, closely allied to *Epácris*. In
every respect treatment the same. *L. pentapítalum*, *L.
conspícum* and *L. ròseum*, are the best; the flowers of the
former two are white. (Soil No. 6.)

Magnòlias. There are four species that require the protection of our green-houses; all the others are hardy. *M.
fuscàta* and *M. annonæfòlia* are very similar in foliage and
flower: the young branches and leaves of *M. fuscàta* are
covered with a brown, rusty-like down; the other by some
is considered merely a variety; flowers small, brown, and
very sweet-scented. *M. pùmila* is very dwarf-growing;
leaves large and netted; flowers semi-double, white, pendent, and exceedingly fragrant. They are natives of China.
We have several others from the east, but being deciduous
are perfectly hardy. *M. odoratissima*, now *Talàuma Con-
dólii*, is a native of the Island of Java, and considered
odoriferous, but it is very rare even in Europe; said to have
a straw-coloured flower. (Soil No. 9.)

Manèttia; a genus of pretty climbing plants producing a
profusion of scarlet flowers, especially *C. glàbra*, (of Don,)
or *cordifòlia*, (of Paxton,) which is a complete mass of
flowers from July to October, and is a lovely object when
turned into the borders during summer. *M. bicólor*, red
and yellow, blooms throughout the winter, and is a charming climber in that dull period of flowers; they are of the
easiest culture in soil No. 17.

Melalèucas, above thirty species, and a beautiful genus
of New Holland plants, of easy culture; flowers come out
of the wood-like fringes. *M. ellíptica, M. fúlgens*, scarlet,
M. decussàta, M. hypericifòlia, M. squarrósa, M. linari-

fólia, M. incána, M. tetragonia, M. thymifólia, are all very fine species, and flower freely if they have been grown from cuttings ; the singularity of flower and diversity of foliage make them generally admired. (Soil No. 1.)

Melástoma nepalénsis is a good green-house species, flowering freely during winter, of a pale blush colour, and is of the easiest culture. As soon as done blooming, the plant should be well cut in to keep it into shape. (Soil No. 1.)

Menzièsia is a family of pretty dwarf British plants, very similar to the Erica in flower, and requiring the same mode of treatment: they bloom in July and August. (Soil No. 6.)

Méspilus. See *Eryabotrya.*

Metrosìdèros, about fifteen species. Many have been added to *Callistèmon. M. flòrida, M. umbellàta,* and *M. angustifòlia, C. salignum, C. lanceolàtum, C. semperflò- rens, C. glaùcum,* once *M. speciòsa,* and *C. formòsum ;* these are all beautiful plants, with scarlet flowers. Other two beautiful species with white flowers have been given to *Angophóra. A. cordifòlia,* once *M. hispida,* and *A. lanceolàta,* once *M. costàta ;* these genera are very easily distinguished from any other Australasian shrubs, by the peculiar character of having both sides of the leaves alike. The flowers consist of stamens, stiles, and anthers, coming in hundreds out of the young wood for the length of three or four inches, forming a dense cone crowned with a small twig, hence frequently called " bottle brush plant;" leaving capsules in the wood, which will keep their seeds perfect for a great number of years. They grow freely, and the pots should be well drained. (Soil No. 1.)

Myrsínes, Cape Myrtle, dwarf cape evergreen shrubs covered with small flowers from March to May. *M. retùsa* has purple flowers ; *M. rotundifòlia,* flowers white and purple. They will grow in any situation, and are of easy culture. (Soil No. 1.)

Myrtus, Myrtle, is a well-known and popular shrub, especially the common varieties, and was a great favourite (even to adoration) among the ancients. It was the mark of authority for Athenian rulers, and is among the moderns an emblem of pre-eminence. They are elegant evergreen shrubs with an agreeable odour. *M. commùnis multipléx,* double flowering, is a very neat shrub, and flowers abundantly. *M. commùnis, leucocárpa,* white-fruited myrtle. *M. itálica variegáta,* striped leaved ; *M. itálica maculàta,* blotch leaved, are very fine shrubs; and *M. tomentòsa,* Chinese myrtle, is a magnificent erect growing shrub, with a white down over the foliage ; the flowers are the largest of the genus. When they first expand they are purple, and afterward change to white, so that there are beautiful flowers of several shades of colour on the plant. We have not the smallest doubt but this species will become, in many instances, as plentiful as the common myrtle. It is more easily grown, but cannot stand much exposure to the sun in summer. *M. tenuifòlia* is a very fine plant, and a native of New South Wales. Myrtles in general should be sprinkled with water in the evening, to keep off the red spider. (Soil No. 11.)

Nandìna doméstica, the only species, and a popular shrub in the gardens of Japan, where it is called *Nandin.* It has supra-decompound leaves, with entire lanceolate leaflets, a kind of foliage that is very rare ; the flowers are small whitish green, in panicles, succeeded by berries of the size of a pea ; drain the pots well. (Soil No. 1.)

Nèrium (Oleander) is a genus of beautiful erect growing evergreen shrubs, of the easiest culture, and abundant in flower. *N. oleánder* is the common rose-coloured single flowering species, from which many varieties have originated. At present the most popular is *N. oleánder splendens,* which has a double rose-coloured flower, *N. o. striàta, fl. pl.,* has double striped flowers. *N. macròphyllum* has very large double pink flowers. *N. o. raginót,* or *tanglè,* has deep crimson flowers striped with white, though they are frequently of a pink colour. *N. o. purpùrea,* dark red. There is one that has got into our collections as double white, which is only semi-double. *N. oleánder elegantìssimum,* a most beautiful plant, with deep silver-edged foliage ; and the young wood is striped white and green. There are likewise single yellow, single white, and single blotched varieties of *N. oleánder.* They are subject to the small white scaly insect, and should be frequently washed, as has been directed, to keep it off. (Soil No. 12.)

Oleas, Olive, about twelve species and varieties. *O. Europæa longifòlia* is the species that is cultivated to such

an extent in the south of France, and Italy. *O. Europæa
latifólia* is chiefly cultivated in Spain. The fruit is larger
than that of Italy, but the oil is not so pleasant, which is
obtained by crushing the fruit to a paste, and pressing it
through a woollen bag, adding hot water as long as any
oil is yielded. The oil is then skimmed off the water, and
put into barrels, bottles, &c., for use. The tree seldom
exceeds thirty feet, and is a branchy, glaucous evergreen,
and is said to be of great longevity. Some plantations at
Turin, in Italy, are supposed to have existed from the time
of Pliny. It frequently flowers in our collections, but seldom carries fruit; flowers white, in small racemose axillary spikes. *O. capénsis* has thick large oblong foliage;
flowers white, in large terminal panicles. *O. verrucósa*,
foliage flat, lanceolate, and white beneath, branches curiously warted. *O. fragráns* blooms in winter; foliage and
blossoms are both highly odoriferous; the plant is much
esteemed in China, and is said to be used to adulterate and
flavour teas. Leaves are elliptic, lanceolate, and a little
serrated; flowers white in lateral bunches. It is subject to
the small, white scaly insect, and ought to be carefully
kept from them by washing. *O. rósea* has pink flowers.
O. paniculàta is also a fine species. They are all very
easily cultivated. (Soil No. 11.)

Oxylòbiums, seven species, plants very similar to *Cal-
listachys*, with ovate, cordate, light-coloured, pubescent
foliage, with papilionaceous flowers. *O. obtusifòlium* has
scarlet flowers; *O. retùsum*, orànge flowers; and *O. ellip-
ticum*, yellow flowers. They grow freely, and should be
well drained; flower from May to August. (Soil No. 6.)

Passiflóra; a celebrated genus of climbing plants, called
in common "Passion Vine." Those belonging to the
green-house flower during summer. Several of them are
both beautiful and profuse in bloom, especially *P. Kermó-
sine*, *P. princèps*, *P. hybrìda*, *P. fragrans*, and are very
distinct species; the former is of a beautiful rosy crimson
colour. (Soil No. 13.)

Pelargòniums, Stork's Bill. This genus, so universally
known among us as *Geçànium*, from which it was separated many years ago, is a family of great extent and variety
for which we are principally indebted to the Cape of Good
Hope. There are many hundred species, with upwards

of eight hundred beautiful and well-marked varieties, which have been obtained from seed. They are of every character, colour, and shade, of the most vivid description. The easy cultivation of the *Pelargònium* tribe, or *Gerà-niums*, as they are commonly called, has rendered them very popular; also the agreeableness of scent and fragrance, of which many of them are possessed, makes them favourites.

Their flowering season is also of considerable duration, especially the bright scarlet and crimson varieties, which bloom from March till August, rendering them quite indispensable in collections. Some growers complain of their straggling habits; but it is only those that do not know how to prune them : even some of the choice kinds of the present day could not be made to grow irregularly—such as *Perfection, King, Witch, Nymph, Sapphire,* and others; indeed, within these few years, the habits and beauties of the plant are improved a hundred-fold, and those who are only acquainted with the old sorts would be transported with a view of the dazzling and beauteous colony of the new kinds that have been procured by hybridizing those of good habit and character.

The best method to adopt in impregnating these is, to choose the female, one that has large flowers, of easy cultivation, and as nearly allied in character and other habits as possible. When a flower of the intended female is newly expanded, take a pair of very fine-pointed scissors, and cut off the anthers before the pollen expands ; then, as soon as the summit of the stile divides, apply the pollen taken from the anthers of the intended male plant on a very fine camel hair-pencil, or cut out the stigma entirely, and place the anther on the summit of the stile, which, if correctly done, will have the desired effect. As soon as the seed is ripe, sow it in light sandy soil; and when it has come up, take care not to over-water the soil, which would cause them to damp off. When they are about one inch high, put them into small pots, and treat as the other varieties. Have them all distinctly marked until they flower, which will be in the second year from the time of sowing.

The tuberous and fleshy stemmed species are very interesting to the discriminating inquirer. Their habit and

22

constitution are so peculiar, that we have frequently won-
dered that they have not been separated into distinct genera.
The cultivation of them is more difficult, water being very
prejudicial to them when they are inactive. If they are
well managed, they flower beautifully, and the colours are
very superior and peculiar, having frequently bright green
and purple in the same flower.

The following list comprehends the most desirable varieties that we have seen :

PURE WHITE,

MARKED OR STRIPED WITH
RED, PURPLE OR CRIMSON.

Alexandrina,
Annette,
Cecilia,
Grandis,
Madonna,
Mrs. Clay,
Una,
Witch.

BLUSH,

MARKED OR STRIPED WITH
RED, &c.

Alba multiflora, *early*,
Alicia,
Bridegroom,
Florence,
Lady Dillon,
Miss Percival,
Nymph.

PINK,

MARKED OR CLOUDED WITH
RED OR CRIMSON.

Aglaia,
Corrine,
Eliza,
Fanny Garth,
Lady Mayoress,
Mrs. Peck,
Mrs. Stiles,
Ophelia,
Priory Queen,
Sylph,
Victory.

ROSE,

WITH STRIPES OR SPOTS.

Conqueror,
Flash, *large spot*,
Flamingo, *large mark*,
Harrisonii,
Hebe,
Lady Douro,
Madeline,
Nonsuch,

President,
Siddonia,
Triumphant,
Vulcan,
Vivid.

Grand Monarch,
Jewess,
Perfection, (Dennis,)
King of Hanover,
Emperor.

RED OR SCARLET,

WITH STRIPES OR SPOTS.

Alarm,
Climax,
Comte de Paris,
Erectum,
Grand Sultan,
Gauntlet,
Goliah,
Henry Clay,
Isadorianum,
King,
Lifeguardsman,
Oliver Twist,
Sapphire,
Prince of Waterloo.

DARK RED,

WITH SPOTS OR STRIPES.

Conservative,
Grand Turk,

VERY DARK CRIMSON,
OR PURPLE,

MARKED WITH BLACK.

Ajax, (purple,)
Black Hawk,
Cassius,
Lenoxii, *very beautiful*,
Gipsey,
Mulatto.

VARIOUS, CURIOUS AND FINE
SORTS.

Bipinnatifidum,
Comptonianum,
Echinatum,
Maculatum,
Sanguineum,
Tricolor,
Tricolor major.

There are several others very recently introduced, which have not bloomed so as to allow us to judge of their merits; but their foreign characters are highly flattering. The repotting of the geranium tribe should be done as early in the month as possible, or even about the end of last month would be advisable in some seasons. (Soil No. 12, with a little more manure.)

Persoónias, about sixteen species of dwarf evergreen

shrubs; leaves oblong, or lanceolate, hairy or downy; flowers axillary and solitary; the pots should be well drained, and the plants in summer protected from the sun. *P. hirsùta, P. móllis, P. territifòlia,* and *P. lùcida,* are the most distinct, and grow freely. (Soil No. 6.)

Phórmium tènax, New Zealand flax lily, the only species; foliage resembling an *Iris,* and very thready. In New Zealand and Norfolk Island the natives manufacture from this plant a kind of stuff like coarse linen, cordage, &c.; the plant is very hardy, and we would be nowise surprised to see it stand the severity of our winters. It bears exposure to the open air in Europe in the fifty-sixth degree of north latitude. The flowers are said to be yellow and lily-like; of the easiest culture. (Soil No. 7.)

Phylicas, above twenty-five species. Several of them are very pretty growing evergreen shrubs, and of easy culture. *P. horizontális, P. squarròsa, P. imbricàta, P. myrtifòlia, P. callòsa, P. bicolor* and *P. ericoídes,* are all neat growing; flowers small white, in heads: drain the pots well, and keep them in an airy situation. The foliage of several of the species is downy. (Soil No. 6.)

Phaseólus caracálla, or snail-flower, is a very curious blooming plant, with flowers of a greenish yellow, all spirally twisted, in great profusion when the plant is well grown. (Soil No. 12.)

Phœnix dactylifera, common date palm; a plant that attains a large size, and of rather a rugged appearance; its fruit is the common well-known date. (Soil No. 12.)

Pimèleas, about fourteen species. Most of them are highly esteemed, and are not often seen in our collections. *P. decussàta* is the finest of the genus, both in foliage and flowers, which are red, and in large terminal clusters; *P. hispìda, P. ròsea, P. linifòlia, P. spicàta,* and *P. spectàblis,* are all fine species. The latter has very beautiful lanceolate foliage and of an elegant habit. They should be well drained. They are very small evergreen shrubs, with wihte, red, or pink flowers. (Soil No. 6.)

Pistàcias, seven species of trees, principally of the south of Europe. There is nothing particular in their appearance, except their productions in their native country. *P. terebinthus* is deciduous and produces the Cyprus turpentine. *P. lentíscus* is the true mastich tree, which is obtained by cutting transverse incisions in the bark. *P. vèra* and *P. reticulàta* are good species; leaves pinnated; leaflets ovate, lanceolate; easily cultivated. (Soil No. 2.)

Pittósporums, about nine species, with handsome foliage, and small white flowers in clusters, which are fragrant. *P. tobìra* is a native of China, and nearly hardy; leaves lucid, obovate, obtuse and smooth; there is a beautiful variegated variety of it. *P. undulàtum, P. coriàceum, P. revolùtum, P. fúlvum* and *P. ferrugineum,* are very ornamental evergreens, and will grow with the most simple treatment. (Soil No. 13.)

Platylòbiums, Flat Pea, four species of fine free-flowering plants; flowers leguminose; colour yellow. *P. formòsum, P. ovàtum* and *P. triangulàre,* are the best; the foliage of the former two is cordate, ovate; the latter hastate, with spiny angles. (Soil No. 6.)

Plumbàgos, Lead-wort. There are only two species of any consequence belonging to the green-house, *P. trístis* and *P. capénsis.* The former is a shy flowerer, but the latter flowers freely; colour beautiful light blue, and flowers in spikes; foliage oblong, entire, and a little glaucous; of very easy culture, and continues in bloom a considerable time. (Soil No. 1.)

Podalyrias, about fourteen species of pretty Cape shrubs; foliage oblong, obovate and silky-like; the flowers leguminose; colour blue or pink. *P. sericea, P. styracifòlia, P. corúscans, P. argéntea, P. liparioìdes* and *P. subiflòra,* are the finest and most distinct species, and flower abundantly. (Soil No. 6.)

Pròteas, about forty-four species. The foliage of this genus is very diversified; flowers very large, terminal; stamens protected by an involucrum; many-leaved and imbricated; which is very persistent. *P. cynaroídes* has the largest flower, which is purple, green and red. *P. speciòsa, P. umbonàlis,* once *P. longifòlia, P. melaleùca, P. grandiflòra, P. coccinea, P. cenocárpa, P. pállens, P. formòsa, P. magnifica, P. speciòsa rúbra,* and *P. mellifera,* will afford a very good variety. It is almost impossible to describe their true colour, it being so various; red, white, straw, brown, green and purple, are most predominant, and frequently to be seen in the same flower. The plants must be well drained; and during warm weather be careful that

.they are not neglected in water, for if they are suffered to droop, they seldom recover. For this reason the pots ought not to stand in the strong sun; the plants can bear it, but to the roots it is injurious. (Soil No. 9.)

Pultenæas, about forty species, pretty little dwarf grow-ing shrubs of New South Wales; flowers small, legumi-nose, all yellow, with a little red outside of the petals. *P. subumbellàta, P. villòsa, P. obcordàta, P. argéntea, P. plunòsa, P. flexilis*, shining leaved, fragrant; *P. cándida, and P. strìcta*, are all fine species, and esteemed in collec-tions. The leaves are all small; they require an airy ex-posure, and the pots drained. (Soil No. 6.)

Rhodochìton volùbile, or *Lophospérmum rhodochìton*: this is a very fine climbing plant, with large tubular dark brown flowers, blooming from July to October; it is of rapid growth, and is an excellent plant for the flower-gar-den. The plant must have frequent repottings to make it grow rapidly, for the finer it grows the more profuse will it flower. (Soil No. 12.)

Rhododéndrons, (Rose tree,) a magnificent genus, and contains some of the most superb and gigantic plants that adorn the green-house. At present the most admired is *R. arbòreum* with its varieties. It has deep crimson flow-ers, with dark spots and flakes campanulated, and in large clusters; leaves lanceolate, acute, rough and silvery be-neath. *R. arbòreum albúm* is very rare. *R. arbòreum supérbum*, flowers same shape as *arbòreum*, colour bright rosy scarlet; foliage one-third larger, but not silvery be-neath; grows freely, and generally thought the finest variety. *R. arbòrea álta-Clàrence* is also very .superb. *R. arbòrea Russeliánum, pictum, venùstum, guttátum, tigrìnum, nobleánum, grandiflòrum, spectábile*, are all very distinct; but there are so many other varieties from seed that they will soon be so much amalgamated, that the named sorts will not be distinguished. A green-house without some of the choice varieties of this plant, is defi-cient of a flower whose beauty and grandeur are beyond the highest imagination. It is a native of Nepaul, in India, and, when found by Dr. Wallach, awakened the ambition of every cultivator and connoisseur in Europe.* There

* Mr. Hogg, the eminent horticulturist of New York, raised the first plant of arboreum from seed in England.

are several other species lately brought from that country, which are highly valued: the species are *R. campanulà-tum*, *R. anthopògon* and *R. cinnamòmum*. They are rarely seen in our collections, but a few years will make them more plentiful. Their beauty of flower is beyond description. The pots should be well drained, and if they are large, put several pieces of sandy stone or potshreds around the side, for the fine fibres delight to twine about such, being mountainous plants. When growing, give copious waterings at the root. For young plants soil No. 6. And for blooming plants use one portion of leaf mould.

Roéllas, pretty leafy shrubs, with blue terminal funnel-shaped flowers, lip-spreading; *R. cilliàta*, *R. spicàta* and *R. pedunculàta*, are the finest of the genus. The pots must be well drained, and care taken that they are not over-watered. (Soil No. 6.)

Sálvia (Sage) is an extensive genus of soft-wooded, shrubby, or herbaceous plants; very few of them do well in the green-house, and many of them are very trifling, having no other attraction than the flower; and those of the tender species, when compared with *S. fúlgens*, crimson, *S. splèndens*, scarlet, *S. angustifòlia*, pale blue, *S. pátens*, dark blue, *S. involucrata*, pink, (which in artificial climates constitute the standard of the genus,) are not worth cultivation. The best method to adopt with the summer flowering kinds is, to plant them in the garden in May: they will grow strong and flower abundantly, and in the fall they can be lifted, and preserved during winter in pots. They neither grow nor flower so well as when planted out, and even a slip planted in the ground in moist weather will root in a few days, grow, and flower in a few weeks. *S. splèndens* is the best to select for the purpose. All will grow easily with encouragement. (Soil No. 12.)

Scòttias, three species of valuable plants; *S. dentàta*, with rosy leguminose blossoms; leaves opposite, ovate, acuminate, serrate; *S. angustifòlia* has brown flowers; *S. trapeziförmus*, leaves ovate, acute, serrulate. We do not know the colour of its flowers; the pots must be well drained, and the plants kept in the warmest part of the green-house, and near the light. (Soil No. 6.)

Senècios. Some species of this genus are pestiferous weeds all over the world. They are even found near the

limits of perpetual snow, where neither tree nor shrub is
able to rear its head, and yet there are a few species that
are neat little plants, and are worthy of a situation, namely
—*S. grandiflòrus, S. venústus*, and *S. cineráscens*, with
the double white, purple, and red variety of *S. élegans.*
The last three varieties are free flowering, but if allowed to
grow several years, they become unsightly.   Being very
easily propagated, a few cuttings of them should be put in,
in September, and in two weeks they will strike root, when
they may be put in pots to keep through the winter, and
then planted in the garden, continuing to renew them.
The other mentioned species should be frequently done
the same way.   Do not keep them damp during winter,
or they will rot off.   Give them an airy exposure. (Soil
No. 12.)

Sóllya heterophylla: a good climbing plant with bright
blue clusters of drooping flowers ; it is a native of N. Holland, and will prove a hardy plant south of latitude 36°.
(Soil No. 4.)

Sparrmánnias are strong-growing green-house shrubs.
S. africàna is a plant very common in our collections,
with large three-lobed cordate leaves, hairs on both sides ;
flowers from March to July.   *S. rugósa.*   The leaves are
rugged ; flowers of both are white, in a kind of corymb,
supported by a long footstalk ; buds drooping, flowers
erect.   There is a plant known in our collections as the
free-flowering *Sparrmánnia,* (which is *Entèlia arborés-
cens,*) and is easily distinguished from *Sparrmánnia* by
the leaves being cordate, acuminate, and otherwise, by all
its filaments being fertile, and the flowers more branching,
and blooming from November to June, profusely ; very
easily cultivated, and desirable. (Soil No. 12.)

Sphærolòbiums, only two species of leafless plants, with
yellow and red leguminose flowers, which proceed from
the young shoots.   *S. vimineum* and *S. médium.*   They
flower freely, and are easily cultivated.   The old wood
should be frequently cut out where it is practicable.
Drain the pots.   (Soil No. 6.)

Sprengélia incarnàta, the only species, a very pretty
plant, allied to *Epàcris ;* foliage acuminate, embracing the
stem; flowers small pink, bearded, and in close spikes;
grows freely.   The pots must be well drained, and the

plants, when dormant, watered sparingly; for if they get sodden about the roots, they very seldom recover. (Soil No. 6.)

Strelitzia, or queen plant: a genus of fine plants belonging to the natural order of *Musacea*. *S. regina*, *S. ovata*, and *S. humilis*, are the most free and beautiful flowering species, and are very similar, except in habit. The flower stalk is from one to two feet long, producing about five flowers of a bright yellow, having a large blue stigma, which forms a distinct contrast. *S. juncea* and *S. parviflora* are also desirable species, but are more rare than the former, which ought to be in every green-house. (Soil No. 19.)

Streptocarpus rhéxii, a free-blooming dwarf plant, of easy culture in soil No. 4.

Stylidium, six species of pretty little plants, with small linear leaves, and remarkable for the singular elasticity of the style or column, which, when the flower is newly expanded, lays to one side, and, on being touched with a pin, starts with violence to the opposite side. *S. graminifolium*, *S. fruticosum*, *S. lancifolium*, and *S. adnatum*, are all free-flowering; flowers in spikes, very small; colour light and dark pink; blooms from April to July. *S. adnatum* is half herbaceous, and should, when growing, be kept nigh the glass, or it will be drawn, and the flowers become of a pale colour. They are all of easy cultivation. (Soil No. 10.)

Styphelias, seven species of very showy flowers, with mucronate leaves; corolla in long tubular form, having several bundles of hairs in it; segments reflex and bearded. *S. tubiflora*, crimson, *S. triflora*, crimson and green, *S. adscendens*, and *S. longiflora*, are beautiful species. They grow freely, and should be well drained, as too much water is very hurtful to them. In summer they ought not to be much exposed to the hot sun, or the foliage will become brown. (Soil No. 6.)

Sutherlandia frutescens, very similar to *Swainsonia*; flowers fine scarlet. (Soil No. 2.)

Swainsonias, four species of free-flowering, soft-wooded shrubs, natives of New South Wales. *S. galegifolia*, *S. coronillæfolia*, and *S. astragalifolia*, are red, purple, and white; leguminose flowers in spikes from the axils, are of

easy culture, and deserving of a situation; the foliage is
pinnate; leaflets ovate, acute. (Soil No. 2.)

Tecòma is a genus of beautiful flowering plants, separated from *Bignònia*. They are of easy culture and desirable in all collections. *T. capénsis* has bright orange flowers
in large clusters, and very profuse on large plants. *T.
austrålis*, known as *Bignònia pandòra*, has white and
pink flowers in great profusion. *T. jasminóides* is quite
a new plant, producing very large clusters of white flowers
with a bright pink centre; it is a charming plant for climbing, and the foliage is of a very agreeable shining green.
The plants require encouragement. (Soil No. 10.)

Telopèa speciosíssimus is the only species, and was
once called *Embóthrium speciosíssimus*. It is now called
Telopèa, in allusion to the brilliant crimson flowers, which,
from their large size, are seen at a great distance, and
which render it one of the most conspicuous productions
of New South Wales. The leaves are oblong, deeply
toothed, veiny, and smooth; wood strong; flower ovate,
connate, and terminal, and of considerable duration. There
ought to be a specimen of it in every collection. The pots
must be well drained, and the plant in the extreme heat of
summer not too much exposed to the sun. Very scarce.
(Soil No. 19.)

Testudinària, Elephant's foot, or Hottentot's bread, two
species, remarkable for their appearance. The root or
bulb, if it may be so called, is of a conical shape, and
divided into transverse sections. Those of one foot diameter are computed to be one hundred and fifty years of
age. It is a climbing herbaceous plant, with entire reniform leaves of no beauty; flowers small; colour green.
The pots must be well drained, for when the plant is inactive, it is in danger of suffering from moisture, and ought
not to get any water. *T. elephántipes* and *T. montàna*
are the species, natives of the Cape of Good Hope, and
require the warmest part of the house. (Soil No. 10.)

Thea: a genus celebrated over the known world as fur-
nishing the domestic drug called *Tea. T. víridis*, and *T.
bohèa* are said to be the species which supply the tea.
Some have asserted that there is only one shrub used, but
by examination it may be easily perceived that there are
leaves of various shape and texture, some of them similar

to *Camellia sesanqua.* Dr. Abel gives an explicit detail
of the growing and manufacturing process of tea, from
which, in compliment to our fair patrons, we give a few
extracts :

"The tea districts of China extend from the twenty-
seventh to the thirty-first degree of north latitude. It
seems to succeed best on the sides of mountains. The
soils from which I collected the best specimens consisted
chiefly of sand-stone, schistus, or granite. The plants are
raised from seeds sown where they are to remain. Three
or more are dropped into a hole four or five inches deep ;
these come up without farther trouble, and require little
culture, except that of removing weeds, till the plants are
three years old. The more careful stir the soil, and some
manure it, but the latter practice is seldom adopted. The
third year the leaves are gathered, at three successive
gatherings, in February, April, and June, and so on until
the bushes become stunted or slow in their growth, which
generally happens in from six to ten years. They are
then cut in to encourage the production of fresh roots.

"The gathering of the leaves is performed with care and
selection. The leaves are plucked off one by one : at the
first gathering only the unexpanded and tender are taken ;
at the second those that are full growth ; and at the third
the coarsest. The first forms what is called in Europe
imperial tea ; but, as to the other names by which tea is
known, the Chinese know nothing ; and the compounds
and names are supposed to be made and given by the mer-
chants at Canton, who, from the great number of varieties
brought to them, have an ample opportunity of doing so.
Formerly it was thought that green tea was gathered ex-
clusively from *T. viridis;* but that now is doubtful, though
it is certain that there is what is called the green tea district and black tea district ; and the varieties grown in the
one district differ from those of the other. I was told by
competent persons that either of the two plants will afford
the black or green tea of the shops, but that the broad thin
leaved plant (*T. viridis*) is preferred for making the green
tea.

"The tea leaves being gathered, are cured in houses
which contain from five to twenty small furnaces, about
three feet high each, having at top a large flat iron pan.
There is also a long low table covered with mats, on which

the leaves are laid, and rolled by workmen, who sit round
it : the iron pan being heated to a certain degree, by a little
fire made in the furnace underneath, a few pounds of the
fresh-gathered leaves are put upon the pan ; the fresh and
juicy leaves crack when they touch the pan, and it is the
business of the operator to shift them as quickly as possible,
with his bare hands, till they cannot be easily endured.
At this instant he takes off the leaves with a kind of shovel
resembling a fan, and pours them on the mats before the
rollers, who, taking small quantities at a time, roll them in
the palm of their hands in one direction, while others are
fanning them, that they may cool the more speedily, and
retain their curl the longer. This process is repeated two
or three times, or oftener, before the tea is put into the
stores, in order that all the moisture of the leaves may be
thoroughly dissipated, and their curl more completely preserved. On every repetition the pan is less heated, and
the operation performed more closely and cautiously. The
tea is then separated into the different kinds, and deposited
in the store for domestic use or exportation.

" The different sorts of black and green arise not merely
from soil, situation, or the age of the leaf ; but after win-
nowing the tea, the leaves are taken up in succession as
they fall ; those nearest the machine, being the heaviest,
are the gunpowder tea ; the light dust the worst, being
chiefly used by the lower classes. That which is brought
down to Canton then undergoes a second roasting, win-
nowing, packing, &c., and many hundred women are
employed for these purposes." Kæmpfer asserts that a
species of *Caméllia* as well as *Olea Fràgrans* is used to
give it a high flavour.

Tacsònia pinnatistipula, a plant much resembling a
Passiflora, both in flower and habits. When planted into
the ground, and trained up the rafters of the green-house,
it makes a pretty appearance with its profusion of rosy
blush-coloured flowers. (Soil No. 13.)

Tropæólum, a genus of generally delicate growing
plants, principally from South America. They require
nicety of treatment to bloom them well, unless a large bulb
can be procured, when it may be planted in a seven-inch
pot, and will then flower without farther care by training
their delicate shoots on a wire trellis, or small twigs of

branches stuck in the pots. *T. tricolorùm, T. tricolorùm supérbum,* and *T. pentaphyllum,* have beautiful scarlet flowers marked with yellow and black, and are superb and lovely when in bloom. *T. brachyseras* and *T. tuberósum* have yellow flowers; the roots of the latter are considered a good vegetable. (Soil No. 10.)

Verbéna. The beauty of the green-house in spring, and the flower-garden in summer, is greatly augmented by the late introduction of this lovely family of perpetual flowering plants. There are among them every shade of colour, from the richest scarlet to the purest white, and, in addition to the beauty and profusion of their flowers, several of them are exquisitely scented. *V. chamædry-fòlia,* or *melindres,* was the first scarlet species introduced, and it is yet pretty. *V. bicolor grandiflora,* scarlet, crimson eye. *V. blue jay,* fine blue; *V. élegans,* rose; *V. Feaslii,* large white fading to lilac; *V. Julia,* beautiful large rose; *V. Mestonii,* bright scarlet; *V. queen,* pure white; *V. gazelle,* very dark purple crimson; *V. perfec-tion,* purple; *V. Wilsonii,* bluish purple; *V. Vesta,* beautiful pink; *V. Yarnellii,* very dark crimson.

These are principally new varieties of perfect formation, the flowers in many are as large as a dime, far outvieing those cultivated a few years ago. It is only seven years since I grew the first white, pink and crimson verbena, from seed received from Buenos Ayres. They created a very great excitement in the Floral world, both in this country and Europe. Now there are thousands produced from seed annually. In England, they bear the titled name of Ladies, Marquesses and Queens, commanding a very high price; but with all their titles, none of them excel a few of those named above. They require very little water during winter, and should be kept on a dry airy shelf till February, when the pots may be enlarged, except those intended for the garden, which can be planted out about the middle of April. Cuttings of the young shoots, placed in sandy soil and covered with a glass, will root in a few weeks. The whole family should be industriously collected and culti-vated; for truly we are not acquainted with a tribe of plants that will give as much satisfaction with as little cost and trouble: they naturally grow on hills and elevated plains, so that they must not be kept wet. (Soil No. 9.)

23

Verónica, an extensive genus of plants that are cultivated largely as ornaments for the Flower Garden. Within these few years some very beautiful species have been discovered in New Zealand. Among them is *V. speciósa,* a picture of a plant with foliage equal to a Camellia, producing spikes about three inches long, of bright purple flowers, fading to a pale blush. It is of the simplest culture—growing freely and symmetrically in soil No. 9.

Viminária denudàta, the only species. This plant is remarkable for its twiggy appearance, but it has no foliage, except when growing from seed. It has at the extremity of the twigs or shoots an ovate, lanceolate leaf, disappearing when the plant grows old; the flowers are small, yellow, coming out of the young shoots, to the astonishment of the beholder. It grows freely. (Soil No. 6.)

Vibúrnums. A few of these are very ornamental evergreen shrubs, and almost hardy. *V. tìnus* is the well-known Laurestine, (or what is commonly called Laurestinus,) is of the easiest culture; flowers small white, and in large flattened panicles ; blooming from February to May, and universally esteemed. It will stand the winter by a little protection, but the flower buds being formed in the fall, the intense frost destroys them; consequently, it will not flower finely, except it be protected from severe frost. *V. lùcidum* is a good species, and superior in flower and foliage to the former, but does not flower so freely when the plants are small. When they grow large, they flower profusely. There is a desirable variegated variety. *V. odoratissimum* has smooth, evergreen, oblong, elliptic, distinctly toothed leaves, and frequently a stripe in them, is sweet-scented, but not a free flowerer. *V. hirsùtum* has flowers similar to the above; foliage ovate, with rough brown hairs on both sides, and very characteristic. *V. strictum variegàtum* is a very fine variety, and upright growing. These plants are all very desirable, blooming early in spring, and continuing for several months; all easily cultivated. (Soil No. 17.)

Westríngias, a genus of four species, very like the common *Rosemary. W. rosmarinifòrmis,* leaves lanceolate, and silvery beneath ; *W. longifòlia* is similar ; both have small silvery white flowers, and are easily cultivated. (Soil No. 2.)

Witsènias, four species. *W. còrymbòsa* is a plant that
has stood in high estimation ever since it was known, but,
unfortunately, there is a very inferior plant. *Aristèa cyanea*
got into our collections under that name. The panicles of
W. corymbòsa are quite smooth; those of *Aristèa* are hairy,
which is itself sufficient to detect them; but otherwise the
appearance of *W. corymbòsa* is much stronger and more
erect growing, not inclining to push at the roots so much
as *Aristèa.* The foliage is lanceolate and amplexicaule,
the leaves having much the nature and appearance of *Iris.*
The plant is of easy culture, and blooms from July to
November; colour fine blue. *W. ramòsa* is a very fine
species, similar to the above; flowers yellow and blue;
plant branching. (Soil No. 8.)

Yúcca aloefòlia and its beautiful variety *variegàta* are
desirable plants. They do not bloom till they have grown
to considerable size; but still they make a decided contrast
among other plants; the flowers are white and produced
on terminal spikes. (Soil No. 11.)

Zàmias, about twenty species, eight of which belong to
this compartment. The foliage is greatly admired, and is
in large fronds, with oblique, lanceolate leaflets. Several
of them glaucous. They bear heads of flowers of a brown
colour in the centre of the plants, very like large pine cones.
Z. hòrrida, the finest, *Z. púngens, Z. spiralis,* and *Z. latifòlia,* are the most conspicuous. They must be kept in
the warmest part of the green-house; and give them large
well-drained pots, watering sparingly during winter. They
are imported from the Cape of Good Hope. (Soil No. 11.)

All the plants herein named requiring to be drained, in
preparing the pots, place first a piece of broken pot, oyster-
shell, or any similar substitute, with the convex side on the
hole of the pot, and then put in a few, or a handful, (according to the size of the pot,) of shivers of broken pots, or
round gravel about the size of garden beans. Those that
we have mentioned in this *Repotting,* as to be done in this
or beginning of next month, is not intended to apply to
plants in general, large and small, but to those that are
young, and require encouragement, or to those that were
not shifted last autumn. The roots must not be disturbed,
but the ball turned out entire; and put as much earth as
will raise the ball within about half an inch of the rim of

the pot. Press the earth down around it with a thin narrow piece of wood, called a potting stick, frequently shaking it that no vacancy may be left. If the roots are rotten,
or otherwise injured, take all such off. If this be the case,
the plant will be sickly. Give it a new pot of a smaller
size, administering water moderately until there are visible
signs of fresh growth. The plants must not be disturbed
while flowering; let the repotting be done afterward.
Plants are, at certain stages, if in good health, in a state
that no one can err in shifting them when desirous to
hasten their growth. Those plants that make two or more
growths during the summer may be repotted in the interim
of any of these growths, and all others just before they
begin to push in the spring; that is, when the wood buds
are perceptibly swelled. Never saturate with water fresh-
potted plants. There are many kinds that, without injury,
can be repotted when growing. When done potting, tie
all up neatly with stakes rather higher than the plant, that
the new shoots may be tied thereto during the summer, to
prevent them from being destroyed by the wind. There
may be many that do not require repotting, but would be
benefited by a top-dressing. This should be done by
probing off all the surface earth down to the roots, replac-
ing it with fresh compost, suitable to the nature of the
plant.

When the above is done, arrange all the plants in proper
order, and syringe them clean; but if there are any of the
green-fly, they must be fumigated previous to syringing.
The pavement of the house should be cleanly and neatly
swept every day, and washed at least once a week. Thus,
every part of the house will be in order before the hurry
of the garden commences.

OF ENARCHING OR GRAFTING BY APPROACH.

In this method of grafting the scion is not separated from
the parent plant until it is firmly united with the stock;
consequently, they must stand contiguously. We intend
the following method to apply directly to *Camellias*, as
they are the principal plants in the green-house that are
thus worked. The criterion for the operation is about the

first of March or June. Place the stock contiguous to the
plant where the graft or enarch is to be taken from. If
the branches, where the intended union is to take place,
do not grow at equal heights, a slight stage may be erected
to elevate the lower pot. Take the branch that is to be
enarched, (the wood of last year is the most proper,) and
bring it in contact with the stock; mark the parts where
they are to unite, so as to form a pointed arch. In that
part of the branch which is to rest against the stock, pare
off the bark and part of the wood to about two or three
inches in length, and in the side of the stock which is to
receive the graft do the same, that the inside rind of each
may be exactly opposite, which is the first part where a
union will take place. Bind them firmly and neatly together with strands of Russia matting, and protect the joint
from the air by a coat of close composition; clay of the con-
sistency of thick paint, turpentine, or wax, will equally
answer. Finish by fastening the grafted branch to the
head of the stock or a rod. Many practitioners make a
slit or tongue into the enarch and stock, but we find it
unnecessary, more tedious, and likewise more danger in
breaking. *Camèllias* are also grafted and budded, but
these two operations require great experience and continued attention, and seldom prove so successful as enarching. When they have perfectly taken, which will be in
from three to four months, begin to separate them by cutting the scion a little at three different periods, about a
week apart, separating it at the third time. If the head is
intended to be taken off the stock, do it in like manner.
By the above method, many kinds can be grown on the
same stock. The same plan applies to all evergreens.

23*

APRIL.

REGARDING the shifting or repotting of plants, the directions given last month may be followed. If the plants that require it are not shifted, get them done as soon as possible. Those that were repotted last month will have taken fresh root in the new soil, and the advantage will soon be perceptible. In order to strengthen the plants, and keep them from becoming drawn and spindly, admit large portions of air every mild day. Indeed there will be very few days in this month that a little air may not be given, always observing to divide the quantity regularly over the house, in cool nights closing in time. About the end of the month an abundance of air is indispensable, leaving the sashes and doors open every mild night, that the plants may be inured to the open exposure they will have in a few weeks.

WATERING.

As the season advances and vegetation increases, the waterings will require to be more copious and more frequent. Look over all plants minutely every day, and with judicious care supply their wants. Those that are of a soft shrubby nature, and in a free-growing state, will require a larger portion at one time than those of a hard texture, which may only want it every two or three days. The weather and situation, in some instances, may require a modification of these directions. Plants in general will not suffer so soon from being a little dry as from being over-watered. The health and beauty of the foliage of the plants may be much improved by syringing them freely three evenings in the week, except in moist weather, when it ought not to be done. The ravages of many insects also will be retarded, especially mildew and red spider, which will be entirely destroyed. If the red spider is on any of the plants particularly, take them aside evening and morning, and give them a good dashing with water through the syringe. Where there is mildew, after syringing the plant, dust it on the affected parts with flower of sulphur, and set them for a few days where they will be sheltered from the wind, after which wash off the sulphur. If the cure is not complete, renew the dose. Always sweep out and dry up the water in the house when any is spilt. The succulent plants will be in want of a little water about once a week, but do not over-water them, as there is not heat enough to absorb much moisture. If the soil is damp, it is quite sufficient.

ORANGES, LEMONS, &c.,

Will, in many instances, about the end of this month, be showing flowers or flower buds. They must, under these circumstances, have plenty of air to prevent them from falling off when entirely exposed. The reason that we see so much fine blossom falling to the ground where the trees are brought out of the house in May, is from the confinement they have had. Where there is a convenience of giving air from the back of the green-house, it should always be given in mild days, especially in those houses that have a recess back from the top of the sashes, for even if the sashes are let down every day, still the house will not be properly ventilated. Any plants that are sickly and intended to be planted in the garden next month to renovate their growth, may be cut back (if not already done) as far as is required to give the tree a handsome form, taking care not to cut below the graft or inoculation. Let the operation be done with a fine saw and sharp knife, smoothing the amputations that are made by the saw; and if they are large, put a little well-made clay over the wound, to prevent the air from injuring it. Bees'-wax and turpentine are preferable to clay, not being subject to crack or fall off by the weather.

If there are any *Lagerstrœmias, Pomegranate* or *Hydràngeas* in the cellar, they should be brought out about the first of the month, and planted in their respective situations. Give the *Hydràngea* a very shady spot. It does not require much sun, provided it has plenty of air, and do not plant it into soil that has been lately manured. A large plant must have great supplies of water in dry weather. If the plant is very thick, the oldest branches may be thinned out, but do not cut out any of the young shoots, as they contain the embryo of the flower. *Lagerstræmias* will flower abundantly without pruning, but, to have fine large spikes of flowers, cut in the wood of last year to about three eyes from the wood of the preceding year: by this they will be much finer. *Pomegranates* will only require a little of the superfluous wood cut out. Perhaps some of them may be desired to flower in pot or tubs during summer: the balls will admit of being much reduced, and by this a pot or tub very little larger will do for them. Do not give much water until they begin to grow.

MYRTLES AND OLEANDERS.

If any of these have grown irregularly, and are not headed down or otherwise pruned, as directed last month, it should now be done. Oleanders are very subject to the white scaly insect, and, before the heat of summer begins, they should be completely cleansed. This insect is likewise found on *Myrtles*, which are worse to clean, and ought to be minutely examined twice every year. We have observed the red spider on these shrubs, which makes the foliage brown and unsightly. If it is detected in time, syringing is an effectual remedy.

GERANIUMS.

These will now begin to flower, and the sun will greatly deteriorate their rich colours where they are near the glass with a southern aspect. The glass should be white-washed, or covered with thin muslin, which will cast a light shade over them, and prolong the duration of the bloom; but if they are above five feet from the glass, shading is not requisite. The strong kinds will be growing very luxuriantly, and require liberal supplies of water. When syringing, do not sprinkle the flowers, as it would make the colours intermingle with each other, and cause them to decay prematurely. If they have been properly attended to in that respect, it may be dispensed with after they have come in flower.

Cape Bulbs. Those that flowered late in autumn, as soon as the foliage begins to decay, may be set aside, and the water withheld by degrees. When the foliage is entirely gone, and the roots dry, clear them from the earth, and after laying exposed in the shade for a few days to dry, pack them up in dry moss, with their respective names attached, until August, when they may be again potted. Treat those that are in flower the same as directed in last month.

Dutch Roots. All the species and varieties of these that have been kept in the green-house during the winter, will now be done flowering; the water should be withdrawn gradually from them; and then the pots turned on their sides to ripen the bulbs. Or, a superior method is, where there is the convenience of a garden, to select a bed not much exposed. Turn the balls out of the pots and plant them; the roots will ripen better this way than any other. Have them correctly marked, that no error may take place. They can be lifted with the other garden bulbs.

FLOWERING PLANTS.

The best situation for most plants while in flower is, where they are shaded from the sun and fully exposed to the air. *Primroses*, both European and Chinese, flower best, and the colours are finest, when the plants are in the front of the house, and entirely shaded. The Chinese *Azaleas* and *Rhododéndrons* require, while in flower, a similar situation. Have all the shoots tied naturally to neat rods, and keep them clear from others by elevating them on empty pots, or any other substitute. See that there are no insects upon them; for they make a miserable contrast with flowers. The *Cálla æthiopica* should stand in water when in bloom, and even before flowering they will be much strengthened by it.

INSECTS.

Insects will, on some plants, be very perplexing. The weather may admit of those that are infected to be taken out of doors, and put into a frame in any way that is most convenient. Fumigating them about fifteen minutes, if the day is calm, will be sufficient; but if windy, they will take half an hour. When done, syringe them well, and put them in their respective situations. By the above method, the house will not be made disagreeable with the fumes of tobacco.

Tie up neatly all the climbing plants. Keep those that are running up the rafters of the house close to the longitudinal wires. As previously observed, running plants should not be taken across the house, except in some instances where it can be done over the pathway, otherwise it shades the house too much. Clear off all decayed leaves and all contracted foulness, that the house and plants may in this month have an enlivening aspect, as it is undoubtedly one of the most interesting seasons of the year in the green-house.

FLOWERING STOCKS.

Those that have been kept in the green-house, or in frames, should be planted into beds or the borders, where they will seed better than if kept in the pots. The method generally adopted is, to select the plants that are intended for seed; plant the different kinds distinctly and separately; then take a few double flowering plants of each kind, which plant round their respective single varieties that are to be kept for seed. Whenever any of the colours sport, that is, become spotted or striped with other colours, plant such by themselves, for they will soon degenerate the whole, and ought never to be seen in collections that have any pretensions to purity. Many have been the plans recommended as the best for saving and growing from seed the double varieties of German stock. In every method we have tried we have been successful and unsuccessful; although we generally practise planting the double kinds beside the single, where they are intended for seed. We have no scientific reason for it; not seeing what influence these monsters of flowers can have over a flower where the male and female organs are perfect; which in these are wanting. Some say that the semi-double sorts are best: we have likewise found them both abortive and fruitful in the desired results.

————

MAY.

ABOUT the first of the month all the small half hardy plants may be taken out of the green-house, and those that are left will be more benefited by a freer circulation of air, which will inure them to exposure. The *Geraniums* ought to stand perfectly clear of other plants, while in flower and growing, or they will be much drawn and spindly.

WATERING.

We have advanced so much on this subject, another observation is not necessary; except as to succulents, which are frequently over-watered about this period. Before they begin to grow, once a week is sufficient.

OF BRINGING OUT THE GREEN-HOUSE PLANTS.

Those trees or plants of *Orange, Lemon, Myrtle, Nerium,* &c., that were headed down with the intention of planting them into the garden, to renovate their growth, should be brought out and planted in the situations intended for them. A good light rich soil will do for either, and the balls of earth might be a little reduced, that, when they are lifted, they might go into the same pot or tub, or perhaps a less one. This being done, the plants, generally in a calm day from the 12th to the 18th of the month, should be taken out,

carrying them directly to a situation partially shaded from
the sun, and protected from the wind. In regard to a
situation best adapted for them during summer, see *hot-
house* this month, which will equally apply to green-house
plants. All Primroses and Polyanthus delight in shade.
The reason of so many plants of the *D. odóra** dying, is
from the effects of the sun and water. We keep them
always in the green-house.

The large trees may be fancifully set either in a spot for
the purpose, or through the garden. Put bricks or pieces
of wood under the tubs to prevent them from rotting, and
strew a little litter of any description over the surface of the
soil to prevent evaporation, or about one inch of well decayed manure, which will, from the waterings, help to
enrich the soil. A liberal supply of water twice or three
times a week is sufficient. A large tree will take at one
time from two to four gallons. We make this observation,
for many trees evidently have too limited a supply. Continue to syringe the plants through the dry season every
evening, or at least three times per week. All the tall
plants must be tied to some firm support, because the
squalls of wind frequently overturn them, and do much
harm by breaking, &c. Keep those that are in flower as
much in shade as will preserve them from the direct influence of the sun.

REPOTTING PLANTS.

After the following-mentioned plants, or any assimilated
to them, are brought out of the house, and before they are
put in their respective stations, repot them where they are
required to grow well. *Aloes.* These plants, so varied in

* On examining these plants, when the first appearance of decay
affected them, the decayed part was without exception at the surface of the soil, which was completely mortified, while the top and
roots were apparently fresh. This led us to conclude that the
cause was the effect of sun and water on the stem. We have since
kept the earth in a conical form round the stem, thereby throwing
the water to the sides of the pot, and kept them in the shade. Previously to doing this, great numbers perished every year, and now
no plants thus treated die with us.

character, have been divided into several genera. These
are, *Gastèria, Pachidéndron, Riphidodéndron, Howár-
thia,* and *Ápicra:* of these there are about two hundred
species and varieties; to enter into any specific detail
would be beyond our limits, especially with a tribe of
plants that as yet have but a few patrons. (Soil No. 10.)

Chamærops. There are about seven species of these
palms: four of them belong to this department, and are the
finest of those that will keep in the green-house. They all
have large palmated fronds, and require large pots or tubs
to make them grow freely, and are tenacious of life if kept
from frost.

Gardènia. This is an esteemed genus of plants, especially for the double flowering varieties, which are highly
odoriferous, and have an evergreen shining foliage. *G.
flòrida flore plèno,* Cape Jasmine, is a plant universally
known in our collections, and trees of it are frequently seen
above seven feet high, and five feet in diameter, blooming
from June to October. *G. rádicans,* dwarf Cape Jasmine,
G. longifòlia, G. multiflòra, and *G. latifòlia,* are also in
several collections, but not so generally known; the flowers
are double, and all equally fragrant. We are inclined to
think they are only varieties of *G. flòrida,* of which *multiflòra* is one of the finest. Any of the above will keep in
the coldest part of the green-house, and even under the
front of the stage is a good situation for them, where the
house is otherwise crowded during winter. They must
be sparingly watered from November to March. Much
water, while they are dormant, gives the foliage a sickly
tinge, a state in which they are too frequently seen. *G.
rothmànnia* and *G. Thunbérgia* are fine plants, but
seldom flower; the flowers of the former are spotted, and
are most fragrant during night. (Soil No. 10.)

Mesembryánthemum, a very extensive genus, containing upward of four hundred and fifty species and varieties,
with few exceptions, natives of the Cape of Good Hope.
They are all singular, many of them beautiful, and some
splendid; yet they have never been popular plants in our
collections. The leaves are almost of every shape and
form; their habits vary in appearance. Some of them are
straggling, others are insignificant, and a few grotesque
When they are well grown, they flower in great profusion;

24

the colours are brilliant and of every shade; yellow and
white are most prevalent. Each species continues a considerable time in flower. The flowers are either solitary,
axillary, extra-axillary, but most frequently terminal; leaves
mostly opposite, thick, or succulent, and of various forms.
They are sometimes kept in the hot-house, but undoubtedly the green-house is the best situation for them. They
must not get water above twice a month during winter, but
while they are in flower, and through the summer, they
require a more liberal supply, and they seldom need to be
repotted; once a year is sufficient. (Soil No. 18.)

CAMELLIAS.

These plants, when they are brought from the green-
house, (which should be about the end of June,) ought to
be set in a situation by themselves, that they may be the
more strictly attended to in watering and syringing. An
airy situation, where the sun has little effect upon them, is
the best. They should be syringed every evening when
there has been no rain through the day. After heavy
rains examine the pots, and where water is found, turn the
plant on its side for a few hours to let the water pass off,
and then examine the draining in the bottom of the pots,
which must be defective.

CAPE BULBS.

As soon as these are done flowering, and the foliage
begins to decay, cease watering, and turn the pots on their
sides, until the soil is perfectly dry; then take out the
bulbs, and preserve them dry until the time of planting,
which will be about the end of August or first of September.

JUNE AND JULY.

The plants being out of the house, there need be little. added under this head. Their treatment is in the general, and the required attention is in giving water according to their different constitutions and habits. Where there is no rain nor river water, it should stand at least one day in butts or cisterns, to take the chilly air from it, and become softened by the surrounding atmosphere. This is more essential to the health of the plants than is generally supposed. The small plants in dry weather will need water evening and morning. Continue regular syringings as directed last month. There are frequently rains continuing for several days, which will materially injure many plants if they are not turned on their sides, or defended by sash or shutters, until the rain is over, especially small plants. The syringings should never be done till after the waterings at the roots, and they should never be more seldom than every alternate evening. Turn all the plants frequently, to prevent them from being drawn to one side by the sun or light. Carefully look over them at these turnings, to detect any insects; and observe that the tuberose-rooted or deciduous geraniums, such as *Ardéns, Bicólor, Comptònia, Echinàtum, Tristum,* &c., are not getting too much water, they being now dormant.

AUGUST.

ANY of the *Myrtles, Oranges, Lemons, Oleanders,* &c., that were headed down in April or May, will be pushing many young shoots. The plant must be carefully examined, to observe which of the shoots ought to be left to form the tree. Having determined on this, cut out all the others close to the stem with a small sharp knife; and if the remaining shoots are above one foot long, pinch off the tops to make them branch out.

The trees that were entirely headed down should not have above six shoots left, which will, by being topped, make a sufficient quantity to form the bush or tree.

GERANIUMS.

These plants, about the first of the month, require a complete dressing. In the first place collect them all together, and, with a sharp knife, cut off the wood of this year to within a few eyes of the wood of last year. *Citriodórum* and its varieties do not need pruning. The plants grown from cuttings during the season, that have flowered, cut them to about three inches from the pot. This being done, have the earth all prepared, and potsherds or fine gravel at hand, for draining the delicate kinds. Choose a cloudy day for the operation, and turn the plants progressively out of the pots they are in, reducing the balls of earth so that the same pots may contain them again, and allow from half an inch to two inches, according to the size of the pot, of fresh soil around the ball, carefully pressing it with the potting-stick. Finish by leveling all neatly with the hand. Give very gentle waterings from a pot with a rose mouth, for a few weeks, until they have begun to grow. The tuberous-rooted and deciduous species must be very moderately supplied. Be careful, when watering, that the new soil does not become saturated with water, for, though allowed to dry again, it will not be so pure. When they grow afresh, expose them fully to the sun, turn them regularly every two weeks, to prevent them growing to one side.

ORANGES, LEMONS, &c.

As it is frequently very inconvenient to shift these trees into larger tubs in the months of March and April, this month is a period that is suitable, both from the growth of the trees and their being in the open air. It would be improper to state the day or the week, that depending entirely on the season. The criterion is easily observed, which is when the first growth is over, these trees making another growth in autumn. When they are large, they require great exertion, and are frequently attended with inconvenience to get them shifted. Where there is a quantity of them, the best plan that we have tried or seen adopted is as follows: Have a strong double and a single block trimmed with a sufficiency of rope; make it fast to the limb of a large tree, or any thing that projects and will bear the weight, and as high as will admit of the plant being raised a few feet under it. Take a soft bandage and put around the stem, to prevent the bark from being bruised; make a rope fast to it, in which hook the single block. Raise the plant the height of the tub, put a spar across the tub, and strike on the spar with a mallet, which will separate the tub from the ball. Then with a strong pointed stick probe a little of the earth from among the roots, observing to cut away any that are affected by dry rot, damp, or mildew, with any very matted roots. Having all dressed, place a potsherds over the hole or holes in the bottom of the tub; measure exactly the depth of the ball that remains around the plant, and fill up with earth, pressing it well with the hand, until it will hold the ball one inch under the edge of the tub. If there is from two to four inches of earth under it, it is quite enough. Fill all around the ball, and press it down with a stick, finishing neatly off with the hand. Observe that the stem of the tree is exactly in the centre. This being done, carry the tree to where it is intended to stand, and give it water with a rose on the pot. The earth will subside about two inches, thus leaving three inches, which will, at any time, hold

24*

enough of water for the tree. Trees thus treated will not require to be shifted again within four or five years, having in the interim got a few rich top-dressings.

Frequently, in attempting to take out of the tubs those that are in a sickly state, all the soil falls from their roots, having no fibres attached. When there are any such, after replanting, put them in the green-house, and shut it almost close up, there give shade to the tree, and frequent sprinklings of water, until it begins to grow, when admit more air gradually until it becomes hardened. Sickly trees should be put in very small tubs, and a little sand added to the soil. Give very moderate supplies of water, merely keeping the soil moist. Tubs generally give way at the bottom when they begin to decay, and in the usual method of coopering after this failure they are useless, the ledging being rotten, and will not admit of another bottom. The staves should be made without any groove, and have four brackets nailed on the inside, having the bottom in a piece by itself, that it can be placed on these brackets, and there is no necessity of it being water tight. Then when it fails, it can be replaced again at a trifling expense. A tub made in this way will last out three or four bottoms, and is in every respect the cheapest, and should be more wide than deep. When made in this manner they are easier shifted; you have only to set the tub on a high block of wood, and drive the tub off with a mallet, when the tree can be easily replaced into another tub. *Large Myrtles* and *Oleanders* may be treated in the same manner as directed for the above.

OF PRUNING ORANGES, LEMONS, &c.

These trees will grow very irregularly, especially the *Lemon*, if not frequently dressed or pruned. Any time this month look over them all minutely, and cut away any of the small naked wood where it is too crowded, and cut all young strong straggling shoots to the bounds of the tree, giving it a round regular head. It is sometimes necessary to cut out a small limb, but large amputations should be avoided. Cover all large wounds with clay, turpentine, or bees'-wax, to prevent the bad effects of the air.

OF REPOTTING PLANTS.

Any of the plants enumerated in March under this head may be now done according to directions therein given, and which apply to all sizes. This is the proper period for repotting the following:

Cálla, a genus of four species. None of them in our collections, and in fact not worth cultivation, except *C. æthiopica*, Ethiopian Lily, which is admired for the purity and singularity of its large white flowers, or rather spatha, which is cucullate, leaves sagittate. It is now called *Richardia æthiopica*. The roots, which are tubers, should be entirely divested of the soil they have been grown in, breaking off any small off-sets, and potting them wholly in fresh earth. When growing they cannot get too much water. The plant will grow in a pond of water, and withstand our severest winters, provided the roots are kept at the bottom of the water.

Cyclamen. There are eight species and six varieties of this genus, which consists of humble plants with very beautiful flowers. The bulbs are round, flattened and solid, and are peculiarly adapted for pots and the decorating of rooms. *C. còum*, leaves almost round ; flowers light red; in bloom from January to April. *C. pérsicum*, with its four varieties, flower from January to April; colour white, and some white and purple. *C. hederæfòlium*, Ivy-leaved; colour lilac; there is a white variety; flowers from September to December. *O. Europæum*, colour lilac, in bloom from August to October. *C. neapolitànum*, flowers red, in bloom from July to September. These are all desirable plants. When the foliage begins to decay, withhold the accustomed supplies of water, keeping them in a half dry state; and, when growing, they must not be over-watered, as they are apt to rot from moisture. Keep them during the summer months in partial shade. The best time for potting either of the sorts is when the crown of the bulb begins to protrude. If the pots are becoming large, every alternate year they may be cleared from the old soil, and put in smaller pots with the crown entirely above the ground. When the flowers fade, the pedicles twist up like a screw, enclosing the germen in the centre, lying close to the ground until the seeds ripen, from which plants can be grown, and will flower the third year.

Lachenàlia, a genus of about forty species of bulbs, all natives of the Cape of Good Hope, and grow well in our collections. The most common is *L. tricolor*. *L. quadricolor* and its varieties, are all fine; the colours yellow, scarlet, orange and green, very pure and distinct; *L. rùbida*, *L. punctàta*, *L. orchoides* and *L. nervòsa*, are all fine species. The flowers are on a stem from a half to one foot high, and much in the character of a hyacinth. The end of the month is about the time of planting. Five-inch pots are large enough, and they must get very little water till they begin to grow.

Oxàlis, above one hundred species of Cape bulbs, and, like all other bulbs of that country, they do exceedingly well in our collections, in which there are only comparatively a few species, not exceeding twenty. *O. hirta*, branching, of a vermilion colour; *O. flabifòlia*, yellow; *O. elongàta*, striped; and *amæna*, are those that require potting this month. The first of September is the most proper period for the others. (Soil No. 11.)

This genus of plants is so varied in the construction of its roots, that the same treatment will not do for all. The root is commonly bulbous, and these will keep a few weeks or months out of the soil, according to their size. Several are only thick and fleshy; these ought not to be taken out of the pots, but kept in them, while dormant; and about the end of this month give them gentle waterings. When they begin to grow, take the earth from the roots, and put them in fresh soil. In a few months the bulbs are curiously produced, the original bulb near the surface striking a radical fibre downright from its base, at the extremity of which is produced a new bulb for the next year's plant, the old one perishing.

Ornithógalum, Star of Bethlehem, about sixty species of bulbs, principally from the Cape of Good Hope. Many of them have but little attraction. The most beautiful that we have seen are, *O. lactéum* which has a spike about one foot long, of fine white flowers; *O. peruviàna*, blue flowered, and *O. aùreum*, flowers of a golden colour, in contracted racemose corymbs. These three are magnificent. *O. maritimum* is the officinal squill. The bulb is frequently as large as a human head, pear-shaped, and tunicated like the onion. From the centre of the root arise several shining glaucous leaves a foot long, two inches broad at base, and narrowing to a point. They are green during winter, and decay in the spring; then the flowerstalk comes out, rising two feet, naked half-way, and terminated by a pyramidal thyrse of white bowers. The bulb ought to be kept dry from the end of June till now, or it will not flower freely.

GENERAL OBSERVATIONS.

Watering, and other practical care of the plants, to be done as heretofore described. Frequently the weather at the end of this month becomes cool and heavy. Dew falling through the night, will, in part, supply the syringing operation, but it must not be suspended altogether. Once or twice a week will suffice. Any of the plants that are plunged should be turned every week. In wet weather observe that none are suffering from moisture.

SEPTEMBER.

During this month every part of the green-house should have a thorough cleansing, which is too frequently neglected, and many hundreds of insects left unmolested. To preserve the wood-work in good order, give it one coat of paint every year. Repair all broken glass, white-wash the whole interior, giving the flues two or three coats, and cover the stages with hot lime, white-wash, or oil-paint; examine ropes, pulleys, and weights, finishing by washing the pavement perfectly clean. If there have been any plants in the house during summer, be sure after this cleansing that they are clean also, before they are returned to their respective situations.

OF WATERING.

The intensity of the heat being over for the season, the
heavy dews during night will prevent so much absorption
among the plants.   They will, in general, especially by the
end of the month, require limited supplies of water comparatively to their wants in the summer months.   Be careful
among the *Geraniums* that were repotted in August, not
to water them until the new soil about their roots is becoming dry.   Syringing in this month may be suspended in
time of heavy dews, but in dry nights resort to it again.

The herbaceous plants and those of a succulent nature
must be sparingly supplied.   The large trees that were
put in new earth will require a supply only once a week,
but in such quantity as will go to the bottom of the tubs.

PREPARING FOR TAKING IN THE PLANTS.

About the end of the month all the plants should be examined and cleaned in like manner as directed for those of
the hot-house last month, which see.   From the first to
the eighth of October is the most proper time to take them
into the green-house, except those of a half hardy nature,
which may stand out till the appearance of frost.   Always
endeavour to have *Geranium* plants short and bushy, for
they are unsightly otherwise, except where a few very
large specimens are desired for show.   All Myrtles and
Oleanders that were headed down, if the young shoots are
too crowded, continue to thin them out, and give regular
turnings, that all the heads may grow regularly.

STOCKS AND WALL-FLOWERS,

That are wanted to flower in the green-house, (where
they do remarkably well,) and are in the ground, have
them carefully lifted before the end of the month, and
planted in six or seven inch pots, with light loamy soil.
Place them in the shade till they take fresh root, and give
them frequent sprinklings of water.   As soon as the foliage

becomes erect, expose them to the full sun, and treat as green-house plants.

CHRYSANTHEMUMS.

These very ornamental plants blooming so late, and at a period when there are few others in flower, one of each variety (or two of some of the finest) should be lifted and put in eight-inch pots, in light loamy soil, and treated as above directed for stocks, &c. These will flower beautifully from October to December; and, when done blooming, the pots may be plunged in the garden, or covered with any kind of litter until spring, when they can be divided, and planted out.

CAPE AND HOLLAND BULBS.

About the end of this month is the period for all of these that are intended for the green-house to be potted. We specified some of the former last month, and will here enumerate a few others.

Babìana, a genus of small bulbs, with pretty blue, white, red, and yellow flowers. *B. distíca*, pale blue flowers in two ranks. *B. strícta*, flowers blue and white. *B. tubiflòra*, beautiful bright blue. *B. plicàta* has sweet-scented pale blue flowers. *B. villosa*, red; *B. sulphurea*, sulphur colour; *B. rubro-cyanea*, dark purple with crimson centre. There are about twenty species of them, and they grow from six to twelve inches high. Five inch pots are sufficient for them. (Soil No. 11.)

Gladìolus, Corn-flag, a genus of above fifty species. There are several very showy plants among them, and a few very superb. *G. floribúndus*, large pink and white flowers. *G. cardinális*, flowers superb scarlet, spotted with white. *G. byzantìnus*, purple. *G. blándus*, flowers of a blush rose colour, and handsome. *G. cuspidàtus*, flowers white and purple. *G. racemòsus*, flowers beautiful rose and white. *G. psittácinus*; the flowers are striped with green, yellow, and scarlet, about four inches in diameter, in great profusion, on a stem about two feet high,

G. formosissimus, beautiful bright scarlet, the three upper petals having a spot of white, a very profuse bloomer. *G. Queen Victoria, G. Lafayette,* and several others are of very similar character. They all do perfectly when kept dry all winter, and planted in the open ground early in March. The beauty of this genus is all centered in the flowers. (Soil No. 10.)

Ixia, a genus containing about twenty-five species of very free-flowering bulbs. *I. monadélpha,* flowers blush and green. *I. leucántha,* flowers large white. *I. capatàta,* flowers in heads, of a white and almost black colour. *I. cònica,* flowers orange and velvet. *I. columelàris* is a beautiful shaded rosy purple. *I. kermosìna,* a fine vermilion colour. *I. squallida,* shaded rosy lilac; *I. viridiflòra,* green; *I. longiflòra,* buff. The flower stems are from six to twenty-four inches high. (Soil No. 11.)

Lilium. The Chinese species of this emblem of purity is everywhere esteemed, and the fine Chinese sorts are very splendid, such as *L. longiflòra, L. longiflòra suavèolens,* and *L. japónicum,* are all pure white; *L. lancifòlium,* white, petals reflexed; *L. lancifòlium punctatum,* white spotted with rose ; *L. lancifòlium speciosum,* rose, spotted with crimson. *L. lancifòlium* and its varieties, are all delightfully scented with the odour of vanilla ; noble specimens of the family from Japan, growing from four to six feet high ; a full grown bulb producing from ten to twenty flowers, and perfectly hardy south of Philadelphia.* They should be potted in seven or eight-inch pots, and kept in a cool part of the green-house ; give the pots at least one inch of drainage. (Soil No. 11.)

Oxális. All the varieties and species may now be potted ; the whole are pretty spring flowers, requiring to be kept near the glass : among the many the following are very deserving of attention : *O. laxùlus,* or *rosàcea,* bright rose. *O. Bòwii,* bright rose red, a large and profuse bloomer, and one of the finest. *O. florabùnda,* pink ; a pretty free-flowering tuberous species. *O. luxula alba,* blush white ; *O. multiflòra,* profuse flowering white. *O. versícolor,* striped. *O. dippii,* lilac, which blooms in summer. *O. caparina,* yellow ; there is also a double yellow variety, though not pretty ; for a few others see last month. There should be three or four bulbs planted in a five-inch pot, giving very little water till they begin to grow. They will all keep in good pits, as well as in the green-house. (Soil No. 11.)

Sparáxis. We are enraptured with this beautiful genus of small bulbs, closely allied to *Ixia*, but more varied in colour. *S. grandiflòra striàta* is striped with purple and white. *S. versicolor*, colours crimson, dark purple, and yellow. *S. tricolor*, yellow, black, and scarlet. *S. albída*, large white, with black spots. *S. cælestis*, bluish purple. *S. sulphùrea*, yellow. *S. purpùrescens*, purple. Treat as *Oxális.* (Soil No. 11.)

Tritònia, a genus of about twenty-five species. Few of them deserve culture in regard to their beauty. *T. crocàta* is in our collections as *I. crocàta*, which is among the finest, and *T. zanthospìla* has white flowers, curiously spotted with yellow. (Soil No. 11.)

Watsònia, a genus containing several species of showy flowers, several of which are in our collections under the genus *Gladiolus*, but the most of the species may be distinguished from it by their flat shell-formed bulbs. *W. iridifòlia* is the largest of the genus, and has flowers of a flesh colour. *W. ròsea* is large growing, the flowers are pink, and on the stem in a pyramidal form. *W. humilis* is a pretty red flowering species. *W. fúlgida*, once *Antholyza fúlgens*, has fine bright scarlet flowers. *W. rùbens* is an esteemed red flowering species, but scarce. (Soil No. 11.)

These genera of bulbous plants are in general cultivation. There are, no doubt, some splendid species that have not come under our observation, and others which may be obtained from the Cape of Good Hope and China that are not known in any collection, all of which would be perfectly hardy in our southern states. Bulbs generally require very little water until they begin to grow ; then supply moderately, and keep them near the light. Of the Holland or Dutch bulbs, the *Hyacinth* is the favourite to bloom in the green-house. A few of the *Tulip, Narcissus, Iris* and *Crocus*, may, for variety, be also planted with any other that curiosity may dictate. When these are grown in pots, the soil should be four-eighths loam, two-eighths leaf mould, one-eighth decomposed manure, one-eighth sand, well compounded ; plant in pots from five to seven inches, keep the crown of the bulb above the surface of the soil,

25

except of the tulip, which should be covered two inches. When these roots are potted, plunge them in the garden about three inches under ground; mark out a space sufficient to contain them; throw out the earth about four inches deep, place the pots therein, covering them with earth to the above depth, making it in the form of a bed. Leave a trench all round to carry off the rain. By so doing, the bulbs will root strongly, the soil will be kept in a congenial state about them, and they will prove far superior than if done in the common method. Lift them from this bed on the approach of frost, or not later than the second week of December; wash the pots and take them into the green-house.

OCTOBER.

OF TAKING IN AND ARRANGING THE PLANTS.

As observed in the previous month, let the housing of green-house plants now be attended to. Have all in before the eighth of the month, except a few of the half hardy sorts, which may stand until convenient. Begin by taking in all the tallest first, such as *Oranges, Lemons, Myrtles, Oleanders,* &c. *Limes* ought to be kept in the warmest part of the house, otherwise they will throw their foliage. In arrangement, order is necessary to have a good effect; and in small houses it ought to be neat and regular, placing the tallest behind, and according to their size graduating the others down to the lowest in front. Dispose the different sorts in varied order over the house, making the contrast as striking as possible. Having the surface of the whole as even as practicable, with a few of the most conspicuous for shape and beauty protruding above the mass, which will much improve the general appearance, and greatly add to the effect. All succulents should be put together. In winter they will do in a dark part of the house, where other plants will not grow, studying to have the most tender kinds in the warmest part, and giving gentle waterings every three or four weeks. When all are arranged give them a proper syringing, after which wipe clean all the stages, *benches*, &c., sweeping out all litter, and wash clean the pavement, which will give to all a neat and becoming appearance.

Let the waterings now be done in the mornings, as often and in such quantities as will supply their respective wants, examining the plants every day.

During the continuance of mild weather, the circulation of air must be as free as possible, opening the doors and front and top sashes regularly over the house. But observe in frosty nights to keep all close shut. Be attentive in clearing off decayed leaves and insects.

Any plants of *Lagerstræmia, Sterculia, Hydrángea, Pomegránate*, and others equally hardy, that are deciduous, may be kept perfectly in a dry, light, airy cellar: give frequent admissions of air, and one or two waterings during winter.

OF REPOTTING.

Anemònes. Where *A. nemoròsa flòre plèno* and *A. thalictròides flòre plèno* are kept in pots in the greenhouse, they should be turned out of the old earth, and planted in fresh soil. They are both pretty, low growing, double white flowering plants, and require a shaded situation. The latter is now called *Thalictrum anemonoides*. (Soil No. 11.)

Dáphne is a genus of diminutive shrubs, mostly evergreens, of great beauty and fragrance. Very few species of them are in our collections. *D. odòra*, frequently called *D. indica*, is an esteemed plant for the delightful odour of its flowers, and valuable for the period of its flowering, being from December to March, according to the situation; leaves scattered, oblong, lanceolate and smooth; flowers small white in many flowered terminal heads: there is a variety equally as fine with marginated foliage. *D. odòra rubra*, the buds are red, and the flowers rose white, of a delightful spicy fragrance. *D. hybrida* is a species in high estimation at present in Europe, but little known here,

being only in a few collections, flowers rosy purple, in
terminal heads, and lateral bunches in great profusion;
blooms from January to May, and is of a peculiar fragrance. *D. oleoides* is what may be termed " ever-bloom
ing:" flowers of a lilac colour; leaves elliptic, lanceolate,
smooth. *D. lauréola*, Spurge laurel; *D. póntica*, *D. al-
pìna*, and *D. Cneòrum*, are all fine species, and in Europe
are esteemed ornaments in the shrubbery, but they are not
hardy in our vicinity. (Soil No. 15.)

Primula. There are a few fine species and varieties
in this genus, adapted either for the green-house or rooms.
All the species and varieties will keep perfectly well in a
frame, except the China sorts. Having previously observed a few of the other species and varieties, we will
observe the treatment of these. *P. sinénsis*, now *præni-
tens*, known commonly as China Primrose; flowers pink,
and in large proliferous umbels, flowering almost through
the whole year, but most profusely from January to May
—there is a double variety of it. Keep them in the shade,
and be careful that they are not over-watered during summer. As the stems of the plant become naked, at this repotting a few inches should be taken off the bottom of the
ball, and placing them in a larger pot, will allow the stems
to be covered up to the leaves. *P. p. albiflòra*, colour
pure white and beautiful. *P. p. dentiflòra.* There is
also a white variety of this, both similar to the former two,
only the flower indented or fringed. All these require the
same treatment. As they live only a few years, many
individuals, to propagate them, divide the stems, which in
most cases will utterly destroy them. The best, and we
may say the only method to increase them is, from seed,
which they produce every year. (Soil No. 2.)

Pæonia móután : this magnificent plant and its varieties
are quite hardy with us, but most of them require the green-
house in northern latitudes. These are *P. moután*, Tree
Pæony; the flower is about five inches in diameter, of a
blush colour, and semi-double. *P. M. Bànksii* is the common Tree Pæony, and called in our collection *P. moután ;*
it has a very large double blush flower, and is much admired. *P. M. papaverácea* is a most magnificent variety ;
has large single white flowers, with purple centres. *P.
M. ròsea* is a splendid rose-coloured double variety, and is

scarce ; there are also in China several other varieties, such as purple, scarlet and crimson, which we have not seen in cultivation, and within these few years, many varieties have originated in Europe, *said to be* very magnificent. These plants ought not to be exposed to the sun while in flower, as the colours become degenerated, and premature decay follows.

If the Dutch bulbs intended for flowering during winter are not potted, have them all done as soon as possible, according to directions given last month.

CAMELLIAS.

These plants ought to have a thorough examination, and those that were omitted in repotting before they commenced growing, may be done in the early part of this month; but it is not advisable, except the roots are all round the ball of earth, which should be turned out entire. Examine all the pots, stir up the surface of the earth, and take it out to the roots, supplying its place with fresh soil. Destroy any worms that may be in the pots, as they are very destructive to the fibres. Look over the foliage, and, with a sponge and water, clear it of all dust, &c. Frequently the buds are too crowded on these plants, especially the *Double white* and *Variegated*. In such case pick off the weakest, and where there are two together, be careful in cutting, so that the remaining bud may not be injured.

This is the best period of the year to make selections of these, as they now can be transported hundreds of miles without any material injury, if they are judiciously packed in close boxes. In making a choice of these, keep in view to have distinctly marked varieties, including a few of those that are esteemed as stocks for producing new kinds, which are undoubtedly indispensable, and will reward the cultivator in a few years with new sorts. Besides, it will afford unbounded gratification to behold any of these universally admired ornaments of the green-house improving by our assistance and under our immediate observation. There is nothing to prevent any individual from producing splendid varieties in a few years. Mr. Hogg correctly observes, "It is very probable in a few years we shall have

25*

as great a variety of Camellias as there are of Tulips, Hyacinths, Carnations, Auriculas, &c." This shrewd remark is likely to be verified much earlier than we anticipated.

It has been often said that these plants are difficult of cultivation. This is unfounded; indeed they are the reverse if put in a soil congenial to their nature. When highly manured soils are given, which are poisonous to the plants, sickness or death will inevitably ensue; but this cannot be attributed to the delicacy of their nature. We can unhesitatingly say, there is no green-house plant more hardy or easier of cultivation, provided they are kept at an even temperature, say from 40° to 45° during night, and 45° to 50° during day, and they are equally so in the parlour, if not kept confined in a room where there is a continuance of drying fire heat, their constitution not agreeing with an arid atmosphere.

SOWING CAMELLIA SEED.

These seeds ripen generally during September and October, and must be sown as soon as ripe; plant them about one inch under ground into pots filled with leaf mould, loam, and white sand, in equal portions; if the pots after sowing can be placed in a hot-house, they will vegetate in about six weeks, and be ready to pot into single pots in February. Many of them will bloom in the second year; but if heat is not accessible, keep the pots in the warmest part of the green-house, and give an occasional watering, and the plants will appear some time in May and June: they will be ready to pot into single pots in September, and after doing so put them into a close frame, and shade from the sun for a few weeks; use at this potting only about one-fifth of sand.

NOVEMBER.

OF AIR AND WATER.

AIRING the house should be strictly attended to. Every day that there is no frost it may be admitted largely, and in time of slight frosts in smaller portions, never keeping it altogether close when the sun has any effect on the interior temperature of the house, which should not be allowed to be higher than fifty degrees.

Water must be given in a very sparing manner. None of the plants are in an active state of vegetation, consequently it will be found that looking over them thrice a week and supplying their wants will be sufficient. Succulents will need a little once in three weeks or a month. Give very moderate supplies to the *Amaryllis* that are dormant, and keep all these bulbs in the warmest part of the house.

OF TENDER BULBS.

Where there are tropical bulbs in the collection, and there is not the convenience of a hot-house, they may be very well preserved by shaking them clear of the soil. Dry them properly, and place them in a box of very dry sand or moss, and put them in a situation near the furnace, where they will be free from damp. These can be potted about the first of April. Give no water till they begin to grow, then plant them in the garden about the middle of May, where they will flower during the summer season, if they are mature.

GENERAL OBSERVATIONS.

If there are any of the half hardy plants exposed, have them taken into the house, or under the requisite protection, in frames, pits, cellars, &c. The autumn flowering

Cape bulbs should be placed near the glass, and free from
the shade of other plants. Cleanliness through the whole
house and among the plants ought at all times to be attended to.

DECEMBER.

THE weather may probably be now severe, and it is at
all times advisable to keep the temperature as steady and
regular as possible. The thermometer should be kept in
the centre of the house, and free from the effects of reflection. As noticed last month, sun heat may be as high as
50° in the house, and would not be hurtful, but it should
not continue so for any considerable time without admission of air. The fire heat should not exceed 45°, and never
below 35°. It ought not to continue at that point—36° is
the lowest for a continuation that with safety can be practised, and where a collection of Cactii are kept, 40° should
be the lowest. So that no error may occur, the temperature ought to be known in the coolest and warmest parts
of the house, and the variation remembered; then whatever part of the house the thermometer is placed, a true
calculation of the heat of the whole interior can be made.
We would recommend to the inexperienced to keep the
thermometer in the coldest part of the house. A green-
house compactly and closely built, and the lowest row of
top sash all covered with shutters, (which no house ought
to be constructed without,) will seldom require artificial
heat; but by being long kept close, the damp will increase.
In such case give a little fire heat, and admit air to purify
the house. In fresh mild weather give liberal portions of
air all over the house; and though there is a little frost,
while mild, and the sun shining, the plants will be benefited by a small portion of air for the space of an hour, or
even for half of that time..

Whatever state the weather may be through the winter,
never keep the house long shut up. Thirty-six hours

should be the longest time at once ; rather give a little fire heat.

We are no advocates for keeping plants in the dark, and never think that our plants are receiving justice if kept longer in darkness than one night.

BULBOUS ROOTS.

Those that were plunged in the garden, if not lifted and brought under cover, this should now be done without delay. Clean the pots, and stir up the surface of the soil. Hyacinths grow neatest by being kept very close to the top glass ; the flower stems are thereby stronger and shorter. Water moderately until they begin to grow freely.

AMERICAN FLOWER GARDEN

DIRECTORY.

ROOMS.

PLANTS IN ROOMS.

To TREAT on the proper management of plants in windows is a subject of considerable difficulty: every genus requiring some variation both in soil, water and general treatment. However, a great part of the labour will be abridged by referring to these subjects in the green-house culture, which is quite applicable to the parlour, green-room, or veranda. If the room where the plants are kept is dark and close, but few will ever thrive; if, on the contrary, it is light and airy, with the windows in a suitable aspect to receive the sun, plants will do nearly as well, and, in some instances, better, than in a green-house. This is a well-known fact, and may be observed every day. We have seen as fine plants of Cactus, Daphne, Roses, Geraniums, Callas, Laurestinus, Carnations, Azaleas and Myrtles, grown in a window from year to year, as ever could be grown in a green-house. Indeed, when there is a failure, it can be traced to one of the following three causes:

1st. *Want of proper light and pure air* is, perhaps, the most essential point of any to be considered; for, however well all other requisites are attended to, a deficiency in either of these will cause the plants to grow weak, yellow, and sickly. Therefore, have them always placed as near the light as possible, and receive as much air as can be admitted, when the weather will allow, and occasionally, in fine days, carry them out of doors, and give them a sprinkling of water all over.

2d. *Injurious watering* does more injury to plants in rooms than many persons imagine; and it is very often to be observed, that some individuals destroy all with too much, and others kill all with too little of that nourisher of health. To prevent the soil ever having a dry appearance, is an object of great importance in the estimation of many: they, therefore, water to such an excess, that the soil becomes sodden, and the roots consequently perish. Others, as we have said, run to the opposite extreme, and do not give sufficient to sustain life, and this is a more common practice than that of too much. The best plan is, always to allow the mould in the pot to have the appearance of dryness, but never sufficient to make the plant droop before a supply of water is given, which should then be copious and thoroughly going to the bottom of the pot; but always empty it out of the saucer or pan in which the pot stands: the water used should always be of about the same temperature as that in which the plants grow; avoid using it fresh from the pump.

3d. *Being over-potted in unsuitable soil.* This is also a crying evil, and large pots invariably given to weak plants, with the view of causing them to grow; but such practitioners are like the unskilful physician who gluts the weakly stomach of his patient, only hastening on what they are trying to prevent. With weak plants the very reverse should be practised, giving small pots to encourage their roots outward: whereas, the earth in a large pot to a small plant, with frequent waterings, soon becomes sour and stagnated, and utterly obnoxious to the roots of even the strongest growing plants. If the directions and table of soils, in this work, are properly followed up, *unsuitable* soils will rarely occur, especially when each genus is separately treated.

In fact, we have yet to be convinced why all plants, with the exception of a few tropical, and those belonging to *Ericeæ* and *Epacrideæ*, will not grow and bloom well in rooms and windows. With the following monthly instructions, and executing them properly, failure will seldom occur; but where failure should occur, we would call par-

ticular attention to the tribe of Cactii, which are varied,
beautiful and truly interesting, and grow admirably in dry
rooms, with or without full exposure to the sun, and in any
temperature from 45° to 85°, requiring only small portions
of water once a week in winter, and twice or thrice a week
during summer: they also only require fresh soil once a
year, or even once in two years, for large plants will be
found sufficient. The variety now cultivated is truly astonishing, and we doubt not, but in a few years, large horticultural buildings will be erected for their express culture;
and, to the inexperienced amateur, there is not a family of
plants that will give more satisfaction, or, when properly
studied, will afford greater interest and amusement.

JANUARY.

Plants that are kept in rooms generally are such as require a medium temperature, say from 40° to 60°. Sit-
ting rooms or parlours, about this season, are, for the most
part, heated from 60° to 70°, and very seldom has the air
any admittance into these apartments; thus keeping the
temperature from 10° to 15° higher than the nature of the
plants requires, and excluding that fresh air which is requisite to support a vegetative principle. Therefore, as far
as practicable, let the plants be kept in a room adjoining
to one where there is fire heat, and the intervening door
can be opened when desirable. They will admit sometimes
of being as low as 38°.

If they be constantly kept where there is fire, let the
window be open some inches, once a day, for a few minutes,
thereby making the air of the apartment more congenial,
both for animal and vegetable nature.

WATERING, &c.

All that is necessary is merely to keep the soil in a moist
state, that is, do not let it get so dry that you can divide the

particles of earth, nor so wet that they could be beat to clay. The frequency of watering can be best regulated by the person doing it, as it depends entirely upon the size of the pot or jar in proportion to the plant, whether it is too small or too large, and the situation it stands in, whether moist or arid.   Never allow any quantity of water to stand in the flats or saucers.   This is too frequently practised with plants in general.   Such as *Cálla Æthiòpica*, or African Lily, will do well, as water is its element; (like *Sagittària* in this country;) the *Hydrángea* and *Hyacinths*, when in a growing state, will do admirably under such treatment. Many plants may do well for some time, but it being so contrary to their nature, causes premature decay; a fetid stagnation takes place at the root, the foliage becomes yellow, the plant stunted, and death follows.

OF CAMELLIA JAPONICA.

In rooms, the buds of Camellias will be well swelled, and on the double white and double variegated sorts perhaps they will be full-blown.   While in that state the temperature should not be below 40°; if lower, they will not expand so well, and the expanded petals will soon become yellow and decay.   If they are where there is fire heat, they must have plenty of air admitted to them every favourable opportunity, and water freely given, or the consequence will be, that all the buds will turn dark brown, and fall off. It is generally the case, in the treatment of these beautiful plants in rooms, that, through too much intended care, they are entirely destroyed.   They do not agree with confined air, and to sponge frequently will greatly promote the health of the plants and add to the beauty of their foliage, as it prevents the attacks of the red spider.

When the flowers are expanded, and droop, tie them up neatly, so that the flower may be shown to every advantage.

OF INSECTS, &c.

Insects of various kinds will be appearing on your plants.   For method of destruction, see *Hot-house, Janu-*

26

ary. It will not be agreeable to fumigate the room or rooms, or even to have the smell of tobacco near the house from this cause.

Take a tub of soft water, (if the day is frosty, it had better be done in the house,) invert the plant, holding the hand, or tying a piece of cloth, or any thing of the kind, over the soil in the pot, put all the branches in the water, keeping the pot in the hand, drawing it to and fro a few times; take it out and shake it. If any insects remain, take a small fine brush, and brush them off, giving another dip, which will clean them for the present. As soon as they appear again, repeat the process—for nothing that we have found out, or heard of, can totally extirpate them.

OF BULBOUS ROOTS IN GENERAL.

If you have retained any of the *Cape bulbs* from the last planting, let them be put in, in the early part of the month. For method, see *September*. Those that are growing must be kept very near the light, that is, close to the window, or they will not flourish to your satisfaction. The fall-flowering oxalis may be kept on the stage, or any other place, to give room to those that are to flower.

Hyacinths, Jonquils, Narcissus, Tulips, &c., will keep very well in a room where fire heat is constantly kept, provided that they are close to the window. A succession of these, as before observed, may beautify the drawing-room from February to April, by having a reserved stock, in a cold situation, and taking a few of them every week into the warmest apartment.

Wherever any of the bulbs are growing, and in the interior of the room, remove them close to the light, observing to turn the pots or glasses frequently to prevent them from growing to one side, and giving them support as soon as the stems droop, or the head becomes pendent. The saucers under the Hyacinth and Narcissus may stand with water, and observe to change the water in the glasses once or twice a week.

Every one that has any taste or refinement in their floral undertakings, will delight in seeing the plants in perfection: to have them so, they must be divested of every leaf that has the appearance of decaying—let this always be attended to.

FEBRUARY.

At this season the plants call for the most assiduous attention. If the stage has been made according to our description in September, in very cold nights it should be drawn to the centre of the room, or at least withdrawn from the window, observing every nights to close the window tight by shutters, or some substitute equally as good. And, if the temperature begins to fall below 40°, means should be adopted to prevent it from lowering, either by putting a fire in the room, or opening any adjoining apartment where fire is constantly kept. This latter method is the best where it is practicable, and ought to be studied to be made so.

Some very injudiciously, in extreme frosts, put into the room, where there is no chimney, among the plants, a furnace of charcoal, in order to heat the room. The effect is, that the foliage becomes dark brown and hardened like, and many of the plants die, the rest not recovering until summer.

Watering may be attended to according to the directions of January, only observing that those that begin to grow will absorb a little more than those that are dormant.

Roses, especially the daily, if kept in the house, will begin to show flower. Use means to kill the green-fly that may attack them.

Hyacinths and other bulbs must have regular attendance in tying up, &c. Take care not to tie them too tightly, leaving sufficiency of space for the stem to expand. Give those in the glasses their necessary supplies, and keep them all near the light. Never keep bulbous roots, while growing, under the shade of any other plant.

Camellias, with all their varied beauties, will, in this month, make a splendid show. Adhere to the directions given in the previous month, and so that new varieties

may be obtained, (see *green-house*, *February*, under the
head of *Camellia*,) which directions are equally applicable
here.   When the flowers are full-blown, and kept in a
temperature between 40° and 50°, they will be perfect for
the space of four, five, and frequently six weeks, and a
good selection of healthy plants will continue to flower
from December to April.

Be sure that there is a little air admitted at all favourable opportunities.

MARCH.

If the plants in these situations have been properly attended to by admitting air at all favourable times, and when
the apartment was below 40°, a little fire heat applied to
counteract the cold, keeping the heat above that degree,
your attention will be rewarded by the healthy appearance
of your plants.   The weather by this time has generally
become milder, so that air may be more freely admitted,
especially from ten to three o'clock.   They will require a
more liberal supply of water, but always avoid keeping
them wet.   Pick off all decayed leaves, and tie up any
straggling shoots ; give the pots a top-dressing with fresh
soil, which will greatly invigorate the plants, and will allow
the fresh air to act upon the roots, which is one of the principal assistants in vegetation.   For those that require shifting or repotting, see *green-house, March;* the plants enumerated there equally apply here, if they are in the collection, with this difference, that well-kept rooms are about two
or three weeks earlier than the green-house.   After the
end of this month, where there is a convenience, plants
will do better in windows that look to the east, in which
the direct rays of a hot sun are prevented from falling upon
them, and the morning sun is more congenial for plants in
this country than the afternoon sun.   Where there is any
dust on the leaves of any of them, take a sponge and water,
and make the whole clean ; likewise divest them of all insects.   The green-fly is perhaps on the roses ; if there are

no conveniences for fumigating, wash them off as previously
directed.   Where there are only a few plants, these pests
could be very easily kept off by examining the plants every
day.   For the scaly insect, see *January*.   If they have
not been cleared off, get it done directly; for by the heat
of the weather they will increase tenfold.

FLOWERING PLANTS.

Hyacinths, Tulips, Narcissus, Jonquils and *Crocus*,
will be generally in flower.   The former require plenty of
water, and the saucers under the pots should be constantly
full until they are done blooming.   The others need only
be liberally supplied at the surface of the pot.   Give them
neat green painted rods to support their flower stems, and
keep them all near the light.   The spring flowering *Oxalis*
will not open except it is exposed to the full rays of the
sun.   The *Lachenàlia* is greatly improved in colour with
exposure to the sun, though when in flower, its beauties
are preserved by keeping it a little in the shade.

Primulas, or Primrose, both Chinese and European, delight in an airy exposure ; but the sun destroys the beauty
of their flowers, by making the colours fade.

Caméllias.   Many of them will be in perfection.   See
green-house this month for a description of the finest varieties.   Do not let the sun shine upon the blooms.   Those
that are done flowering will, in small pots, require to be
repotted.

The Hyacinths that are in glasses must be regularly supplied with water.   The roots will be very much reduced
by this method; therefore, when the bloom is over, if possible, plant them in the garden, or bury them in pots of
earth, to ripen and strengthen the bulbs.   They cannot
satisfactorily be again flowered in glasses, and, properly,
they ought not to be allowed to bloom in the garden next
year.   Those that are done flowering in pots can be set
aside, and the usual waterings gradually withdrawn.   Treat
all other Dutch bulbs in a similar manner.

APRIL.

WE remarked last month that, about this season, where it is convenient, an eastern window is more congenial to plants than a southern. The sun becomes too powerful, and the morning sun is preferable to that of the afternoon. West is also preferable to south. Some keep their flowering plants in excellent order at a north window. But the weather is so mild after this, that there is no difficulty in protecting and growing plants in rooms. They generally suffer most from want of air and water; the window must be up a few inches, or altogether, according to the mildness of the day. And as plants are liable to get covered with dust in these apartments, and not so convenient to be syringed or otherwise cleaned, take the first opportunity of a mild day to carry them to a shady situation, and syringe well with water such as are not in flower; or, for want of a syringe, take a watering-pot with a rose upon it; allowing them to stand until they drip, when they may be put into their respective situations; or expose them to a shower of rain, but avoid allowing them to be deluged, which would be very injurious.

DIRECTIONS FOR PLANTS BROUGHT FROM THE GREEN-HOUSE.

Any plants that are brought from the green-house during the spring months ought to be as little exposed to the direct rays of the sun as possible. Keep them in airy situations, with plenty of light, giving frequent and liberal supplies of water. Plants may be often observed through our city during this month fully exposed in the outside of a south window, with the blaze of a mid-day sun upon them, and these, too, just come from the temperate and damp atmosphere of a well-regulated green-house. Being thus placed in an arid situation, scorched between the glass and the sun, whose heat is too powerful for them to withstand, the transition is so sudden, that, however great their beauties may have appeared, they in a few days become brown, the

flowers tarnish or decay, and the failure is generally attributed to individuals not at all concerned. From this and
similar causes many have drawn the unjust conclusion,
viz., that "plants from green-houses are of too delicate a
nature to be exposed in rooms or windows at this early
season." But every year gives more and more proof to
the contrary. There are ladies in Philadelphia, and those
not a few, whose rooms and windows at this period vie
with the finest of our green-houses, with respect to the
health, beauty and order of their plants, and we might
almost say in variety. Some of them have got above twenty
kinds of Camellias in their collections, which afford a continual beauty through the winter, with many other desirable and equally valuable plants. The plants generally are
now growing pretty freely, and are not so liable to suffer
from liberal supplies of water, observing never to give it
until the soil in the pot is inclining to become dry, and administering it in the evenings or mornings.

FLOWERING PLANTS.

Our directions last month under this head will equally
apply now. The Chinese *roses* and geraniums that are
now coming plentifully into flower should be kept near the
light, and in airy exposures, to brighten their colours,
otherwise they will be very pale and sickly.

BRINGING PLANTS OUT OF THE CELLAR, &c.

All or most of the plants that have been in the cellar during winter, such as *Pomegranates, Lagerstrœmias, Hydrángeas, Oleanders, Sweet-bay, &c.*, may be brought out
to the open air any time about the middle of the month. If
any of them stand in need of larger pots or tubs, have them
turned out, the balls reduced, and put them in others a little
larger, or where convenient, they may be planted in the
ground. Be sure to keep the *Hydrángeas* in shady situations. It will not be advisable to expose entirely the
orange and lemon trees until the end of this or first of next
month. Where there is any scale or foulness of any

kind collected on the foliage or wood, have it cleaned
directly before the heat increases the one, and to get clear
of the disagreeable appearance of the other.

MAY.

ALL the plants will be able to withstand exposure, in the
general state of the seasons, about the tenth of the month.
Begin about the first, to take out the hardiest, such as *Lau-
restínus, Hydrángeas, Roses, Primroses, Polyanthus,*
&c., and thus allow the others to stand more free and become hardened to exposure. The reason that plants are
so often seen brown, stunted, and almost half dead during
summer, is from the exposed situation they are placed in,
with the direct sun upon them, and too frequently from
being so sparingly watered. There are no shrubby plants
cultivated in pots that are benefited by full exposure to the
hot sun from this period to September. A north-eastern
aspect is the best for every plant except *Càctus, Aloe, Me-
sembryànthemum,* and such as go under the name of succulents, which may be fully exposed to the sun, but not to
long and continued rains. Where there only a few plants,
they should be conveniently placed, to allow water from a
pot with a rose mouth to be poured frequently over them,
which is the best substitute for the syringe. *Dáphne,
Coronílla, Fúchsia, Caméllia, Primrose* and *Polyánthus,*
do not agree with bright sun through the summer. There
has been a general question what is the cause of the death
of so many of the *Dáphne odòra.* It may be observed,
that the first place that shows symptoms of decay is at the
surface of the soil, and this takes place a few weeks before there are evident effects of it. The cause is from the
effect of heat or sun and water, acting on the stem at least.
If the soil is drawn in the form of a cone round the stem,
to throw off the water to the edges of the pot, that the
stem may be dry above the roots, mortification does not take
place, neither do they die prematurely when thus treated.
For farther remarks, see green-house this month.

CAPE BULBS.

Any of these that are done flowering, such as *Ixia, Oxalis, Lachenàlia*, &c., as soon as the foliage begins to decay, turn the pots on their sides, which will ripen the roots, and, when perfectly dry, clear them from the soil, wrap them up in paper, with their names attached, and put them carefully aside until the time of planting.

REPOTTING.

Where it is required, repot *Cáctus, Àloe, Mesembryánthemums*, and all other succulents, with any of the *Amaryllis* that are required to be kept in pots; also, Cape Jasmines. For description of the above, see hot-house and green-house of this month, under the same head.

JUNE AND JULY.

THE only attention requisite to *these* plants is, in giving water, keeping them from being much exposed to either sun or high winds, and preventing the attack of insects. Water must be regularly given every evening, when there has not been rain during the day. Where they are in a growing state, they are not liable at this season of the year to suffer from too much water, except in a few instances, such as the Lemon-scented Geranium, and those kinds that are tuberose-rooted, as *Ardèns, Bicólor, Tristúm*, &c., which should have moderate supplies.

All the plants ought to be turned round every few weeks to prevent them from growing to one side, by the one being more dark than the other, and keep those of a straggling growth tied neatly to rods. Wherever insects of any description appear, wash them off directly. Give regular syringings or sprinklings from the rose of a watering-pot.

Be particularly attentive in this respect to the *Caméllias*, which will keep the foliage in a healthy state.

If the foliage of *Lilium longiflòrum* or *Japónicum*, has decayed, do not water them while dormant, as they are easily injured by such treatment.

AUGUST.

For the kinds of plants that require potting, we refer to the green-house for this month. All that are therein specified are peculiarly adapted for rooms, and we would call attention to the genus *Cyclamen*, which has not been generally introduced into the collections of our ladies; as, from the character and beauty of the flowers, they are very attracting and highly deserving of culture. Attend to the Geraniums as there directed, and be particular in having them cut down and repotted, as there fully described. The *Oranges, Lemons, Oleanders* and *Myrtles*, that are kept in cellars or rooms, should have the same attention in this month as directed in the green-house, which to repeat here, would be occupying space unnecessarily.

Réseda odoráta, or Mignonette, is one of the most fragrant annuals. To have it in perfection during winter, the seed should be sown about the end of this month, or the beginning of next, into pots of fine light earth, and sprinkled with water frequently. When it comes up, the plants must be thinned out or transplanted: the former method is preferable. Keep them from frost during winter, and always near the light.

This will equally apply to the green-house.

Cape bulbs, such as *Sparaxis, Ixia, Oxalis* and *Lachenália*, should now be planted. For method and sorts, see green-house in August and September.

SEPTEMBER.

WHERE there is a quantity of plants to be kept in these apartments, they should be disposed of to the best effect, and, at the same time, in such a manner as will be most effectual to their preservation. A stage of some description is better than a table, and, of whatever shape or form, it ought to be on castors, that it may, in severe nights of frost, be drawn to the centre of the room. The shape may be either concave, a half circle, or one square side. The bottom step or table should be six inches wide and five inches deep, keeping each successive step one inch farther apart, to the desired height, which may be about six feet. Allowing the first step to be about two feet from the floor, there will be five or six steps, which will hold about fifty pots of a common size. A stage in the form of half a circle will hold more, look the handsomest, and be most convenient. We have seen them circular, and, when filled, appeared like a pyramid. These do very well, but they must be turned every day, or the plants will not grow regularly. With this attention it is decidedly the best. Green is the most suitable colour to paint them.

GENERAL OBSERVATIONS.

The directions given for the green-house this month are equally applicable here. The late blooming *Chrysanthemums* are particularly adapted for rooms. The colours are so varied, and many of them are dwarf-growing, and even neat in their habit, especially the new hybrid sorts.

OCTOBER.

Have a stage or stages, as described last month, in the situations where they are intended to remain all winter ; place the plants on them from the first to the eighth of this month, beginning with the tallest on the top, graduating to the bottom. It is desirable to place flats or saucers under each, to prevent the water from falling to the floor, and the water should be emptied from the flats of all except those of *Cálla* and *Hydrángea.* The latter, while dormant, should be kept only a little moist.

Previous to taking in the plants, they should be divested of every decayed leaf, insects, and all contracted dust, having their shoots neatly tied up, and every one in correct order. Every leaf of the *Caméllias* ought to be sponged, and the plants placed in an airy exposure, and from this period till they begin to grow, have them exposed to the sun. If the flower buds are too crowded, picking off the weakest will preserve the remainder in greater perfection, and prevent them, in part, from falling off. Do not on any occasion, keep them in a room where there is much fluctuating fire heat, as the flower buds will not expand, except they are kept in an even temperature. See green-house, this month, more largely on this subject.

OF BULBOUS ROOTS.

Those that are intended to flower in glasses should be placed therein this month, and kept in a cool room. After the fibres begin to push a few shoots, the glasses may be taken to the warmest apartments to cause them to flower early. Bring a few from the coldest to the warmest every two weeks, and thus a succession of bloom may be kept up from January to March. Hyacinths and other Dutch bulbs should now be planted in pots. See green-house for full directions.

Cape Bulbs. All that are unplanted and offering to grow, should be put in pots forthwith. Ample directions are given for the planting of these in the two preceding months.

Repot. *Rùbus rosæfòlius,* or Bramble-rose. They should have pots one size larger than those they are now in. To make them flower profusely, when done blooming in May, divide them and put only a few stems in one pot, and repot them in this month, as above directed.

GENERAL OBSERVATIONS.

Any herbaceous plants in the collection ought to be set aside, and the water in part withheld. When the stems and foliage are decayed, the plants may be put in a cool cellar, where they will not be in danger of frost, and be permitted to remain there until they begin to grow ; then bring them to the light, and treat as directed for these kinds of plants. Deciduous plants may be treated in a similar manner.

NOVEMBER.

GENERAL OBSERVATIONS.

THE remarks and instructions that are given last month for these apartments will equally answer here. Where the Dutch bulbs were omitted to be placed in glasses, they ought not to be longer delayed.

Oxàlis. The autumn-flowering species will now be in bloom, and must be kept in the sun to make them expand freely. The neglect of this is the principal reason that these do not flower perfectly in rooms.

Caméllias. These plants, where there is a collection. flower from this period till April; and the general desire to be fully acquainted with the method of their culture has induced us to be liberal in our observations on every point and period through the various stages of their growth and

27

flowering. We will here only remind the inquirer, that a
pure air and plenty of water, giving the plants frequent
sprinklings, are the present necessities, which only are
conducive to their perfection.

Attend to the turning of Geraniums and other rapidly
growing plants, that all sides of them may have an equal
share of light.

DECEMBER.

As the trying season is now approaching for all plants
that are kept in rooms, especially those that are desired to
have a flourishing aspect through the winter, a few general
instructions (although they may have been previously
advanced) will, perhaps, be desirable to all those who are
engaged in this interesting occupation, which forms a
luxury through the retired hours of a winter season, and
with very little attention many are the beauties of vegetative nature that will be developed to the gratification of
every reflecting mind. The following is a routine of
every-day culture:

Do not, at any time, admit air (except for a few moments) while the thermometer is below 35°, exposed in
the shade.

In time of very severe frosts the plants ought to be withdrawn from the window to the centre of the room during
night.

Never give water until the soil in the pots is inclining to
become dry, except for Hyacinths and other Dutch bulbs
that are in a growing state, which must be liberally supplied.

Destroy all insects as soon as they appear: for the means
of destruction, see next month.

Give a little air every favourable opportunity, (that is,
when the thermometer is above 35°, exposed in the shade,)
by putting up the window one, two, or three inches, according to the state of the weather.

Clean the foliage with sponge, and water frequently

to remove all dust, &c. The water thus used must not exceed 80°, but 60° is preferable.

Turn the plants frequently, to prevent them growing to one side.

Roses of the daily sort may be obtained early by having them in a warm room, that has a south window, and as soon as they begin to grow, admit air in small portions about noon every day that the sun has any effect. Such must be well supplied with water.

Bulbs in glasses must be supplied with fresh water at least once a week, in which period they will inhale all the nutritive gas that they derive from that element, if they are in a growing state.

Caméllias, when in bud and flower, should never be allowed to become the least dry, neither confined from fresh air. The effects would be, that the buds would become stinted, dry, and drop off. Therefore, to have these in perfection, attend strictly to watering. Give frequent airings, and wash the leaves occasionally with water. Never keep them in a room where there is a strong coal fire. The most of *Caméllias* will bear 3° of frost without the smallest injury, so that they are easier kept than *Geraniums*, except when they are in bloom. In that state frost will destroy the flowers. The air of a close cellar is also destructive to the buds.

The reason that the Camellia does not bloom perfectly in parlours or other heated rooms, is owing to their being too warm and arid, destroying the vital vegetative principle of the plant, and it soon perishes. There is one way in which these plants can be kept perfect even in such dry places when the recess in the windows is of sufficient depth as to allow plants to stand within it, enclosing them from the apartment by another sash : in such a situation, water could be placed, which would keep the atmosphere between the windows perfectly moist. The verdure would be rich and the flowers brilliant; and they would be completely protected from dust—the whole would have a very pleasing effect. Attention will be requisite to give them air during the mild part of the day. There are several Camellias not proper for room culture; those which have dry brown scaly buds, are to be avoided, such as *anemoneflora, egertonia, cleviana, fulgens, atrorubens;* also avoid *woodsii, chandlerii* and *dorsetia*, as being difficult of expanding—they are so very full of petals. Those most proper for room culture, are *double white, conchiflora, eclipse, fimbriata, florida, imbricata, maliflora, pæoniflora, punctata, Colvillii, rossii, speciosa, variegata* and *incarnata.* Such will be found to bloom freely and fully: many others might be added, but these will give an idea of those sorts that agree best with room culture. We cannot conclude our subject without giving our readers some hints on the effect of plants in household apartments. It has been proved that the leaves of plants absorb carbonic acid gas by their upper surfaces, and give out oxygen by their under ones, thereby tending to purify the air in as far as animal life is concerned, because carbonic acid gas is pernicious to animals, and oxygen is what that life requires. It is in the light, however, that these operations are carried on, for in the dark, plants give out carbonic. It does not appear that any of the scentless products given out by plants are injurious to human beings, because those who live among accumulated plants are not less healthy than others, but rather enjoy more uninterrupted health, which, of itself, is a sufficient recommendation for all to spend their leisure moments in so healthful and rational an employment.

THE

AMERICAN FLOWER GARDEN

DIRECTORY.

ON THE CULTURE OF THE GRAPE.

WE are not aware of any vegetable production that is
more conducive to the luxurious gratifications and pleasures of man than the vine. In fact, there is no fruit so
delicious, applicable to so many purposes, nor any that is
so agreeable to all palates: from the remotest ages the vine
has been celebrated as the emblem of plenty and the
"symbol of happiness." Its quickness of growth, its great
fertility, and astonishing vegetative powers, with its un-
known age, has rendered it one of the most fruitful bless-
ings bestowed by Providence; a blessing which almost
every inhabitant of this union may enjoy, and we see no
occasion to doubt but that thousands of acres of our fertile
uplands will be converted into vineyards, producing the
finest fruits and richest wines in the world. Indeed, with
very little care and attention, our unsightly post and rail
fences may be converted into grape espaliers, and fine
wines produced at as little cost as spruce beer; every square
foot of surface might be made to produce a pound of
grapes, and every post, at least, round our gardens afford
ample space for one vine, which would yearly produce
from three to nine pounds of fruit, fit either for the table or
the wine-press. But the small space allotted in this volume
will not allow us to dilate on this fruitful subject. Our
object is to give a few hints on the aspect, soil, propagation, and culture of the vine, so as to produce an extra

27*

crop in the smallest given space. We will then consider, first, the

ASPECT.

As our climate gives us plenty of heat for the maturation of the vine, we have, therefore, more scope in aspect than any other country. However, the most preferable is one from south to east, or west. Shelter from high and often recurring winds is a prime consideration. Our western and south-western gusts of wind are very destructive to the vine when it is in the full vigour of growth: it dissipates all the accumulated secretions of the foliage, and closes its pores, thereby totally deranging the vital functions of the plant, which (although in the height of the growing season) has been known to be suspended for weeks. There are frequently many local circumstances affecting the shelter of walls and other buildings, which, where they exist, must determine the best aspect for training the vine. But if there be no such local circumstances, we have no hesitation in stating that an eastern aspect is the best. On such the sun shines with full force during the morning, at which time there is something highly favourable to vegetation in his rays, which seems to stimulate the energies of plants in an extraordinary degree, and to excite them to a vigorous exertion of all the functions appertaining to vegetable life.

ON SOIL.

The soil most congenial to the growth of the vine and the maturity of its fruit is a rich, sandy, turfy loam, about two feet deep, on a dry, gravelly, rocky, or sandy bottom; the roots run with avidity into such sub-soils, lying secure from the excess of moisture, which always accumulates in clayey or compact soils. The excrementitious matter discharged from the roots of a vine is very great, and if this be given out in close and retentive soils, they quickly become deleterious, and a languid and diseased vegetation ensues: this is the great reason that so many failures exist.

It may hence be inferred that vines will not thrive in a
cold wet soil, nor composed of stiff clay, which is easily
accounted for from the fact that they delight only in soils
easily rendered dry by evaporation, and free from excess
of moisture, and are always more warm, which is so genial
to the growth of this plant. To elucidate this, we can
record an instance that occurred a few years ago in this
vicinity:—A vine border was dug out to the depth of three
feet and a half, in a cold retentive clay soil; twenty inches
of stone, brick, and lime rubbish were put in the bottom,
and the remainder filled up with good compost for the
vines, in which they were planted, and grew well for two
years, and produced some fruit; finally, they languished,
and almost died, and it was at once pronounced that fine
foreign grapes would not do in this country. But, on examining the roots of the plants, it was discovered that they
were rotten from the excess of moisture which was retained
in this pit; for though it had been partially filled with a
dry bottom, no provision was made to carry off the water,
therefore it proved to be a complete water pail: a drain
was necessarily dug to th. full depth to carry off the water,
and the soil generally renewed; the vines were cut to
within two feet of the ground; they now (four years after
the operation) grow luxuriantly, and produce abundant
crops every year. Therefore, if the sub-soil is not naturally dry, it must be made so by draining, which is the
basis of the work, filling up the bottom with a sufficient
quantity of dry materials, such as stones broken moderately
small, brick-bats, lumps of lime rubbish, oyster-shells, &c.,
which will keep them dry and warm by the free admission of air and solar heat, and to admit of heavy rains passing quickly through without being retained sufficiently
long to saturate the roots or injure the tender extremities;
having thus furnished a dry bottom, cover to the desired
height with turf taken about three inches deep from a rich
pasture; and to every four loads of turf add one load of
thoroughly decomposed manure, at least one year old, interspersing it with bones of any description, oyster-shells,
or any other enriching material that undergoes slow decomposition: the whole must be repeatedly turned, and
allowed to settle before the vines are planted. Extreme
caution has to be exercised in administering bone-dust,

slaughter-house offal, and other over-rich manures, especially if the vines are to be planted the same or even the
following season. Soils glutted with instant enriching
manures are destructive to the vine. The surface of the
border should have a gentle descent from the wall or fence:
never crop your vine borders, and be careful of treading
much upon them; a board trellis should be laid for walking upon when the operation of pruning, tying, &c., takes
place, which is almost daily during summer. The border,
after it has been once made, ought never to be stirred,
except at intervals, to keep it from becoming hard and
impervious to heat or moisture; and, when necessary, it
should only be forked up about two inches deep, at all
times taking care not to injure the roots.

In dry sandy soils all that is wanted for the full perfection of the grape is, to take out about one foot of the poorest
of the ground, and replace it by turf from a meadow, adding
thereto a portion of well-decomposed manure. Sweepings
from turnpike roads, where there is much travel, is an excellent article for incorporating with such soils; it is of an
enriching quality, its component parts consisting chiefly of
sand, pulverized stones, dung, and urine, which is of a
more lasting nature than can be found in almost any other
compost; it ought to be thoroughly incorporated with the
other soil soon after it has been collected from the road, as
all its valuable qualities will then be entirely preserved.
The foregoing remarks in the preparation of soil, if followed, will ensure the luxuriant growth of vines and the
yearly production of fine crops of grapes, and, when circumstances will permit, should be practically adopted at
all times. But it must not be supposed that vines will not
grow and mature fine crops unless thus encouraged in
extra prepared soils. Such is not the fact, for vines will
do well in any soil that is not adhesive, and has a dry
bottom; but they grow finer and bear greater crops of fruit
within a given space of time, when planted in ground that
has been properly prepared for their reception. For instance, if two cuttings be planted, the one in a soil fully
prepared, and the other in that of the latter description, it
will be found at the end of three years that the vine in the
former soil is double the size of the latter; consequently,
the strong vine will produce two-thirds more fruit, and of

a better quality, than the weak vine. This difference occurring every year, and even greater as the age increases, is sufficient to amply repay for all the trouble and expense incurred in making a suitable compost. However, the disadvantage of a poor soil may in part be compensated for by planting the vines closer together. If, indeed, vines could not be planted with any prospect of success, except in borders purposely prepared, only a very small quantity of grapes would be grown, compared with what this rich and fertile country is capable of producing.

Many instances occur in towns and cities, around dwellings and other descriptions of brick and stone erections, which present very favourable situations for the training of vines, but which, nevertheless, are so situated as to admit of little or no soil being placed at their roots. In such cases, if an opening can be made, twenty inches deep, and as many wide, it will be sufficient to admit of the roots of a young vine, which will support it till its rambling roots have found their way under the pavement, or along the walls to some more distant nourishment; if a wider space can be made, it will, of course, be better: loosen the sides and bottom as much as possible, and fill up with compost, as previously directed, and therein plant the vine. The surface covering, whether of brick or stone, may be replaced after the soil has fully settled, leaving a hole about six inches square to allow the stem of the plant to swell in its future growth. The roots soon find their way under the paving or along the foundation walls, and, indeed, in every direction in search after food, and will extract nourishment from sources apparently *barren*. The fact is, that the roots of the vine possess an astonishing power of adapting themselves to any situation in which they may be planted, *provided it be a dry one*.

ON THE PROPAGATION OF VINES.

Vines are generally propagated in the open ground by cuttings and layers.

By cuttings. At the general pruning provide cuttings or the preceding summer's growth; choose such as are of a medium size, well ripened, and short-jointed, cut them

into lengths of about eighteen inches each, leaving at the
ends not less than two inches of wood to protect the eye,
place these temporary cuttings about three-fourths of their
length in the ground, in a warm and sheltered situation,
where they can be protected with a little litter from the
severity of frost during winter.   The best time for planting
them is about the 25th of March in this latitude, earlier or
later if more south or north: if intended to plant the cutting where the plant is to remain, which is the most preferable method, prepare them in the following manner:

By cutting them into lengths of tree buds each, and letting
the uppermost bud have an inch of blank wood remaining
to protect it, the extremity of which must be cut in a slanting manner, and the slanting side opposite to the buds, to
throw off the moisture: the end that is to be inserted in the
ground cut transversely just under the bud, and the cutting will be complete; the cuttings being thus prepared,
plant them forthwith; if intended to remain, place two in
each space, inserting them in the ground so as the second
eye may be about half an inch under the soil, which must
be pressed close, when it will, most frequently, be found
that the eye thus placed will grow first and strongest, when
the upper eye can be displaced; if both the cuttings grow,
cut off the weakest.   During May, June, and July, care
must be taken to keep the cuttings constantly moist; soap-
suds or drainings of the dung-hill can be used for the purpose once a week, but not oftener, using rain or river water
for general waterings.   If the soil should sink down and
leave the buds higher than above mentioned, more must be
added to keep them as directed.   To prevent the ground
from becoming hard by repeated waterings, and also to
retain a regular moisture about the cutting, cover the soil
with shells, litter, or any such substitute, which will greatly
promote the vegetating powers of the scion.   As soon as
they have made shoots six inches long, water may be more
sparingly applied, and the shoots must be carefully tied to
some support, and their tendrils and lateral shoots should
be cut off, the latter to within one eye of the main stem:
about the first of November cut every plant down to within
two eyes of the cutting.   But if the plants are intended to
be removed, they should be planted in such a situation as
to be shaded from the mid-day sun; from four to six hours

a day of sun is quite sufficient. A spot sheltered from severe winds is also most desirable. When transplanted, be careful of their small roots, and choose a mild day, (about the first of April, or earlier, is a good season,) for the operation.

By layers. This is a very expeditious mode of growing young vines, provided the shoots be laid in pots; but vines raised from shoots, laid down in the open ground, should be avoided as the worst of all plants: they make but few roots, and, when removed, these nearly all die off from being cut at the extremities in lifting, and the second year of such a plant is not much in advance of a good cutting. To grow vines by laying the shoots in pots, the following directions, if followed, will ensure success: For each intended layer procure a seven-inch pot, or a small box of a similar, or even larger size, prepare some fine rich sandy mould, containing a great portion of decayed leaves, then take the shoot and run it through the hole in the bottom of the pot till you come to the last three buds; close up the aperture round the shoot with moss, cotton, or any elastic substance, and then fill up the pot or box to within half an inch of the top with the prepared soil, having previously secured it in a safe and level position; and, where it can be conveniently watered during the season, this must be attended to at least once a day. When there is not time for this attendance, the pot or box should be plunged under ground, and the layer placed thereon, and firmly secured, so that its own force will not raise it up, then cover up the shoots at least three inches, leaving space for occasionally holding some liquid nourishment. Shoots may be thus laid any time from the first of March to the first of April. It must be clearly understood that the success of the operation depends entirely on keeping the mould in the pots moist, treating it as directed for watering cuttings. The plant may be separated from the vine about the first of September, and instantly planted into its desired locality, or put into a larger vessel, and there remain till planting season; the following year displace the tendrils and laterals as directed for cuttings, and in pruning cut it down to within three eyes of the ground. We may safely assert, that it is a species of strangling to a vine in the first three years of its growth, to be sparing of the knife, allowing, at once,

small weak shoots to be laid in to form in a day (comparatively) a plant that is expected to withstand the vicissitude
of ages, and produce yearly its quantum of fruit; but more
of this when treating of pruning.

By eyes. This is our most favourite method of propagating plants of this most valuable fruit. Early in the
month of March we cut the shoots into eyes, leaving about
an inch of wood on each extremity, and plant those with
their eyes uppermost into pots, and place them in a hot or
cold frame, prepared for the purpose; plants from a single
eye may easily be made to grow twelve feet in one season,
by constant repotting and nourishing. The plants thus
growing are decidedly the best rooted, forming more capillary fibres; consequently more nutritious support to the
vine is absorbed in the same given period of time; they
also form shorter joints, and are capable of producing more
fruit on a plant of the same size. We are aware that some
start at this idea, and say that in a few years it is not
observed. It reminds us very much of the son of the
"Isle of the Ocean," when asked how old his brother was,
replied, he was so much, but in two years he would be
"the same age." Nevertheless, this method of propagating may not be generally accessible, the former two plans
being at the command of every one.

ON ERECTIONS FOR THE SUPPORT AND PROTECTION OF THE VINE IN OUT-DOOR CULTURE.

To limit the proper height for training grapes would be
a preposterous idea, for they can be perfectly cultivated in
this country on any height from four to forty feet: indeed,
on a wall of the former, we have thirty sorts of grapes
growing luxuriantly, and fruiting in the most profuse
manner. Some of the vines, four years old, which have
produced from six to nine bunches of fine fruit, which
only occupy, after pruning, a space of about eighteen
inches square.

Walls of brick are decidedly the most preferable for the
perfection of the grape; and if they be built for the express
purpose, the most judicious distribution of materials would
be in the erection of several low walls, not more than seven

feet high. For the purpose of pruning, training, &c., walls of this height are far preferable to those of a greater, and if built to run directly south or north, the entire surface of both sides may be judiciously covered. The eastern aspect would render a sure and abundant early crop: those on the western side would not be so productive, and more liable to be affected by our frequent severe westerly gales. When in bloom, or when the fruit is ripening, would be the period that they would be most liable to suffer. However, as they would frequently produce a full crop, an astonishing quantity of fruit may be produced on a very small space of ground by erecting walls of this description, built parallel to, and not far distant from, each other—say, at the nearest, from twenty to twenty-five feet. If from local causes bricks cannot be had, a good substitute will be found in strong ranges of plank fencing made of well-seasoned wood, and closely jointed, having three or four good coats of oil paint: grapes raised in this way will be nowise inferior to those produced on walls: indeed we would prefer such to any wall of stone that could be erected, it being of a more even surface and more convenient for training, and not giving harbour for insects, &c. A very great advantage will be derived by having a coping on the wall or fence, projecting eight or ten inches, turning on a pivot, so as it can be used in time of heavy dashing rains while the vines are in bloom, or when the fruit is ripening, which are the only periods that it will be of actual service, for all dews and light rains are indispensable to the health and maturity of the vine; and if the fence is north and south, the light and heat excluded by it would be a serious drawback on the ripening of the fruit. We say, therefore, if it is not on a pivot, the plants will be better without it, unless it have only one or two inches of a projection, the dripping from the coping will fall on the foliage, and that will carry it entirely free from the fruit; but we urge the great utility and even necessity for movable coping. Espaliers or trellises are in common use for the training of the vine, also arbours: the former suit admirably in small gardens where it is not desirable to go to expense, but the latter should be avoided as the worst possible construction for growing grapes; the interior is always filled with a current of cold air highly prejudicial to the maturity of fine fruits; but for coarse

28

grapes it is a matter of little consequence, as they are at
best only fit for producing shade.   Upright trellises in city
gardens may be made eight feet high, with the spars not
more than six inches apart, and these should be made of
the very best materials, and supported every three feet by
uprights: strong wire makes an elegant substitute for the
cross slats, which, if kept well painted, will not suffer by
corrosion.   We have seen an elegant new erection by a
tasteful grape amateur, and think it will answer a very
good purpose : it consists of an upright double trellis, about
one foot wide at the bottom, tapering to one bar at the top,
running north and south, which is about eight feet high ;
from which, on each side, there is fixed a small projecting
sash at an angle of about 48°, which keeps the vines perfectly secure from deluging rains, and even concentrates
more solar heat for their maturity.   The whole has a light
and rather imposing effect; its practical utility remains to
be tried, as it is but lately finished : there is no apparent
doubt but it will prove very beneficial in its results.

ON TRANSPLANTING THE VINE.

The best period of the year for transplanting is during
the months of October or March.   The longer its removal
is postponed after these periods, the more injurious will be
the effects of transplanting.   Admitting the ground has
been prepared according to directions formerly given, dig
a hole about twenty inches deep, and as wide as will admit
of the roots, if possible, to their full extension, without crip-
pling in any manner.   If any of them are injured in lifting, they must be cut back to soundness: fill up the hole
to within twelve inches of the top, set the vine in the hole
thus made, with its stem about six inches from the wall or
fence, and let the plant be cut even with the ground, or,
where there is plenty of space, and the plant two or more
feet long, plant the root at a distance from where the stem
of the vine is desired, and then disbud the young shoot,
except the uppermost three, lay it down its full length,
bringing the terminal buds to where the plant is wanted;
by this method the whole extent of the shoot will make
roots, and be of infinite service for the farther growth and

support of the plant. When the eyes thus left grow, displace the weakest two, leaving the strongest for the permanent plant. We have seen old vines laid down in this manner for the distance of thirty feet, and, in two years, formed plants of most astonishing vigour and production. If the vine has been grown in a pot, shake the ball of earth from the roots, among which place, with care, new and fresh soil, taking the plant and giving it several shakes to settle it well about the roots, which will encourage the plant to put forth new roots for its farther support. Transplanting should always be done in dry and mild weather, and when the soil is mellow and free. During the removal the roots must be carefully kept from exposure; the atmosphere would dry up their tender extremities, and cause much injury; and, when vines are brought from a distance, this precaution ought to be carefully put in practice. Its first season's growth should be confined to one stem only, carefully cutting off all lateral shoots within one eye of the main shoot, as directed on the subject of propagation.

ON PRUNING.

The first year's growth of a transplanted vine should, in November, be cut down within four inches of the ground, and, on the appearance, cover the plant with about three inches of stable litter, allowing it to remain in this state till the middle of March. The plant will now push strongly, and two of the best shoots should be trained their full length during summer, carefully nipping off tendrils and laterals, and, at all times, securing the shoots from the effects of high winds. If walls are used for training, there should be slats fixed about one inch from the wall to tie the shoots thereto, using soft material for the purpose of tying: if the vines should show fruit, cut it off.

Having the previous season retained two well-grown shoots from near the surface of the ground, you will now, in November, tie these in a horizontal position, about six or eight inches above the surface, cutting them at nearly two feet distance from the main stem. In the following month, February, when the weather is mild, displace

every alternate bud, observing that it is those on the under
side of the shoot. If every thing has been attended to in
soil, planting, and pruning that we have advanced, there
may be expected to arise four shoots from each of these
horizontal branches, which, if any show fruit, it must be
cut off: these young shoots must be trained upright during
summer, being careful to displace every other as they
appear. Some approve of training these young upright
shoots in a serpentine form, which, in our opinion at present, is of little consequence; but top them about the end of
August, or earlier if they are to the desired height. In
November of the third summer's growth, you may now
prune for fruit as above stated. Your horizontal branches
will have fully matured four luxuriant upright shoots. Cut
two of these alternately within one eye of the horizontal
shoot, which will produce wood to be fruited the following
year, and lay in the other two, in a serpentine form for
fruit, to about three feet in length. The vine has now
assumed the form in which it is permanently to remain,
and it may be considered as the foundation of a system of
alternately fruiting four shoots, and training four out their
full length every year, which method may be continued
every year without any alteration. After several years, if
it is thought proper, the arms may be lengthened by the
training in of a shoot at their extremities, and managing it
in the same manner as when the arms were first formed;
but it is not advisable that the branches should be far extended, which would ultimately prove injurious to those
branches arising from the bosom of the vine. This system
of pruning and training the vine we do not advocate as
something *new or original*, but one which we have seen
in full and successful practice twenty years ago. By procuring well-grown plants in pots, one year may be gained
on the above calculation; for you can prune, and at once
take two shoots to prepare for laying the foundation of
your future plant; but more than this cannot be accomplished. We are aware that many of our readers are
already startled at this tedious method of fruiting vines,
and have almost concluded to have fruit the *first year* or
none. Such are too frequently the conclusions of many;
but, as sure as they practice it, they as invariably meet
with a failure, and that in a very few years. The practice

of training vines to get them up to the top of arbours, &c., cannot be done with fine vines without risk. As we have already said, it may and will do with our native kinds, but no other. The general system of spur-pruning has many advantages in in-door culture, but does not at all agree with growing grapes in the open air. Our limits do not admit of giving in detail our reasons for so saying, but those who doubt may go on in the old way, giving the system herein advised a trial. with one plant *only*, and we guarantee that in less than five years their old vines are headed down to the stump, to begin on a system that yearly renews itself, and can be perpetuated for ages on the same vine, which may be said to "renew its youth every year." In fact, it recommends itself by simplicity—by the small number of wounds annually made—by the clear and handsome appearance of the vine, and by the great ease with which it is managed—its occupying but a small space. We therefore conclude this subject with the following few general rules : Use a knife of the best description, and let it be perfectly sharp; cut always upward and in a sloping direction, always leave about an inch of blank wood beyond a terminal bud, and let the cut be on the opposite side of the bud. In pruning out an old branch, cut it even with the parent limb, that the wound may quickly heal. Never prune in frosty weather, nor in the months of March, April, or May. Let the general fall pruning take place about the end of October or first of November; after which, stir up the ground, and let a good coating of fresh stable manure be laid thereon, which will both protect the roots that are near the surface, and also enrich the soil; but if stable manure cannot be procured, leaves from the woods are an excellent substitute, which, after decomposition, form a vegetable manure very enriching, and one very congenial to the vine; this being done, nothing more is required till the first of March, when the roughest must be removed, and the decomposed particles forked into the borders. It may be proper to state, that in more northern latitudes and greater altitudes than Philadelphia, it will be necessary to lay down the vines after pruning, during winter, and give them a light covering of litter, straw, leaves, or mats, which will completely protect them from the severest frost; although it is not altogether the severity

28*

that destroys, but the alternate frost and sun acting on the plant every twenty-four hours, which overcomes the vitality of the plant; and another fell-destroyer is, when we have a mild February and a severe March. When such occurs, which is but rarely, the vines must all be protected by mats while there is danger.

ON MANURE.

This subject has been very recently indulged in to a destructive extent. We could record instances of soils strongly impregnated with very enriching manures, being almost death to the plant; very rich soils are adhesive and retentive of moisture, which is destruction to the roots of the vine. The celebrated Brassin, conductor of the royal vinery of France, used to practise enriching his vine borders with exciting manures: he now finds that cleansing of ditches, grass-turf, and road sweepings, mixed well together and allowed to ferment for a year, is far preferable. He now uses it entirely as an annual dressing; but, in our opinion, this cannot be continued for any length of time, unless the border is also yearly reduced; consequently, manures that are of slow decomposition are preferable, and nothing that we are acquainted with excels bones of every description; but these are not always at hand in quantity. When to be·obtained, they should always be put to a good purpose—an annual winter top-dressing of manure of a few inches, and the roughest removed in the spring, digging in the remainder not over four inches deep, which will encourage the roots to the surface, where they will be greatly benefited by solar heat and air. Liquid manures are highly valuable where immediate effect is required: they contain all the soluble parts of manure in such a state as to admit of being taken up by the plant as soon as applied. These are *urine*, which may be used pure any time from the first of November to February when the ground is not frozen; but if used at any other period, must be diluted with its equal quantity of water. *Drainings of manure-heaps and soap-suds* can be used at all times, but not too frequently. *Soot* dissolved in water, in the proportion of one to twelve, is an exceedingly strong manure, and very stimulating; *Guano* dissolved in water at the rate of 20 lbs. to 100 gallons is a first rate manure; where great growth is required, they may be safely watered once a week, during the growing season, with the enriched liquid; but all these exciting manures must be cautiously applied, as excess is very injurious to the fertility of the vine; and although one of the grossest feeders in nature, even possessing the appetite of a glutton, it can be satiated and destroyed.

DESCRIPTIVE CATALOGUE OF GRAPES MOST SUITABLE FOR OPEN AIR CULTURE.

Golden Chasselas, Chasselas de Fontainbleau, D'Arboyce, or *Royal Muscadine.* Bunches medium size, with very small shoulders, berries of a moderate size, round when ripe, turning to a bright amber colour, having a thin skin, a soft flesh, and a rich juice. This is an exceedingly fine grape, a free bearer, is very hardy, and ripens early; it may be considered one of the best white grapes for outdoor culture.

White Chasselas or *White Muscadine.* Bunches medium size, shouldered, and well formed. Berries round and of a good size, juicy, rich, and well flavoured; it ripens about the middle or toward the end of September, and is an excellent hardy grape, and fully equal to the former. We consider this grape the same as the *Malmsey Muscadine.*

White Sweet Water, (early.) Bunches rather large; berries of a good size, round, of a white colour, and, when perfectly ripe, especially when exposed, they are shaded with a light russet colour; they grow close on the bunches, and when desired to have large berries, the bunches must be well thinned, the juice very saccharine and luscious. We consider this the very best white grape for walls; it is an excellent bearer, makes good short-jointed wood, and is very early. We have had it perfectly ripe on a south wall the first day of September.

White Muscat of Alexandria, Jerusalem Muscat, Malaga. Bunches large, but short and well shouldered; berries large, oval, and, when perfectly ripe, (which will not be till October), are of a pale amber colour, often without

stones, skin rather thick, the flesh firm, juice not plentiful,
but of a sweet, highly musky, delicious and peculiar flavour. It is an extra fine grape, and requires a warm situation. It does not bear so freely as the former two.

White Frontignac or *Frontignan.* Bunches long and
narrow, without shoulders, rather closely set, of a dull
white or greenish yellow, and covered with a powdering
bloom, juice very sugary and rich, with a delightful spicy
flavour. It ripens in September, and delights in a dry
soil.

White Hamburg, White Lisbon, White Portugal.
Bunches very large, short, and loosely formed: berries
large and oval, skin thick, of a greenish white colour, flesh
firm, juice sweet, slightly mixed with acid, one of our latest
white grapes. The plant is of a strong robust habit, and
an excellent bearer.

Austrian Muscat. Bunches large and tapering: berries
round, of a russet white colour, skin thin, juice rich and
musky, and of excellent flavour. It ripens about the second
week of September, and is an excellent bearer.

Black Frontignac, Violet Frontignac, Muscat Noir.
Bunches small and short: berries round, and grow close in
bunches, skin black, covered with a fine light bloom, flesh
tender and juicy, of a rich vinous spicy flavour.

Black Hamburg. Bunches tolerably large, with short
compact shoulders, tapering to a point: berries large, of an
oval form, skin rather thick, very nearly black, and covered
with a blue bloom; flesh tender, sweet, and of a rich vinous
flavour: ripens about the first of October, but will hang on
the vine till frost. This is, in every respect, one of the
finest black grapes that can be grown in the open air: it is
also a constant bearer. The leaves in the fall are mottled
with green and yellow.

Black Prince. Bunches rather long and generally
shouldered: berries oval, and of a good size, skin rather
thick, of a dark purple, and covered with a thick bloom;
flesh white, sweet, juicy and well flavoured: ripe about the
first of October.

Black Lombardy, West's St. Peter's. Bunches long
and well shouldered: berries large, round, and of a regular size; skin thin and very black, juice plentiful and of a

very high flavour; is perfectly ripe about the middle of October, and will keep on the vines till frost.

Black Muscadine, Black Chasselas, Violet Chasselas. Bunches about the size and shape of the *Golden Chasselas*: berries perfectly round and covered with a blue bloom: flesh juicy and of a very rich flavour: ripens about the first of October.

Frankendale. Bunches large, with small shoulders, and rather longer than the Black Hamburg: berries round and closely set; skin deep purple, approaching to black, covered with a thin blue bloom; flesh tender, sweet, rich, and of a luscious flavour: it is a great bearer, and fully ripe about the end of September or first of October.

Grizzly Frontignac, Muscat Gris. Bunches of a medium size, with small shoulders: berries round, of a light brown colour, intermixed with red and yellow; the *juice* is exceedingly rich, and possesses a high spicy flavour: it ripens about the middle of September.

Hansteretto. Bunches large and well formed: berries also large and perfectly round, of a jet black colour when perfectly ripe; flesh rather juicy and of a rich flavour; leaves deeply lobed and a little downy underneath. An excellent hardy grape, but inferior in quality to the Black Hamburg: ripe about the first of October.

GENERAL INDEX.

LIST OF HARDY SHRUBS.

SEE PAGE 56.

Those marked thus*, require protection in winter, and those marked thus†, shade during summer.

AMORPHA,	Bastard indigo.	Dutzia scàbra,	red, white and purple.
fruticòsa,	shrubby. .	EUONYMUS,	Japan Burning
AMY'GDALUS,	Almond.	japonica,	Bush.
nàna,	dwarf.	argentea,	silver edged.
pùmlia,	double-flowering.	GORD'ONIA,	Franklinia.
aérsica,	peach-leaved.	pubèscens,	downy.
ANDRÓMEDA,		HALESIA,	snow flake.
all the species.		diptera,	winged do.
AZ'ZALEA,	American honey-	tetraptera,	
	suckle.	HIB'ISCUS,	Althæa.
all the hardy species.		syriacus,	Althæa frutax.
AUCU'BA,	Gold tree.	var. var.	
† japònica,	Japan.	HYDR'ANGEA,	
B'ERBERIS,		all the varieties.	
all the species.		†* hortensis,	garden.
BU'XUS,	Box tree.	HYPERICUM,	profuse flowered
two species.		kalmianum,	St. Johnswort.
CALYC'ANTHUS,	Sweet-scented	ILEX,	Holly.
	shrub.	var. var.	
flòridus,	purple-flowered.	JASM'INUM,	Jasmine.
þrecòx,	early.	fruticáns,	shrubby.
var. var.		officinàle,	climbing white.
CASTI'NEA,	Chestnut-tree.	JUNIP'ERUS,	Juniper.
pùmila,	dwarf.	suècica,	Swedish.
CE'RCIS,	Judas tree.	virgínicus,	Virginian.
canadénsis,		KA'LMIA,	American laurel.
CHIONA'NTHUS.	Fringe tree.	glàuca,	glaucous.
virgïnica,	common.	latifòlia,	broad-leaved.
CLE'THRA,		KŒUTREUTERIA,	yellow-flowered.
all the hardy species.		paniculata.	
CÓRNUS,	Dogwood.	LA'URUS,	Laurel.
flòrida,	large flowered.	nòbilis,	sweet-bay.
sangùinea,	bloody.	var. var.	
Crat'ægus,		LAVEND'ULA,	Lavender.
several species.		spíca,	spike-flowered.
Cotonéaster,		MAGN'OLIA,	
all are fine.		purpùrea,	purple.
Cy'tisus,		Kòbus,	slender.
all the species.		grácilis,	
DA'PHNE,		grandiflòra,	large-flowered.
mezerium,	red.	var. var.	
var. var.	white flowering,	Thomsoniùna,	hybrid.
	fine.		

conspícua,	zoulan.
soulangeàna,	hybrid.
PHILAD'ELPHUS,	mock-orange.
grandiflòra,	large-flowered.
màna,	dwarf.
variegàtus,	variegated.
P'INUS,	Pine or Fir tree.
balsàmea,	balm of Gilead.
PINCKNE'YA,	Georgia bark tree.
pùbens,	downy.
PRU'NUS,	Cherry.
* lusitànica,	Portugal laurel.
* laurocérasus,	English laurel.
P'YRUS,	
all are very fine.	
RHODODE'NDRON,	Rose-bay.
catawbiènse,	Catawba.
daùricum,	daurian.
var. var.	
pónticum,	pink.
var. var.	
máximum,	common.
RH'US,	Sumach.
cotìnus,	mist tree.
RI'BES,	
áureum,	fragrant.
sanguíneum,	bloody.
ROBÍNIA,	Locust tree.
hìspida,	rose-acacia.
SHEPHERDIA,	buffalo-berry.
argentea,	
SÓRBUS,	

h'ybrida,	mountain ash—a beautiful shrub.
SPIR'ÆA,	
toment'osa,	tomentose.
bélla,	red-flowered.
frùtex, &c.	showy.
SYMPH'ORA,	Snow-berry.
racem'osa,	white-berried.
glomeràta,	red-berried.
SYR'INGA,	Lilac.
all the species.	
TA'MARIX,	
Germanica,	Tamarisk tree.
TAX'US,	Yew.
baccàta,	
hibérnica,	a handsome erect, growing ever-green.
THU'JA,	arbor-vitæ.
occidentàlis,	American.
orienta'lis,	Chinese.
THUJA,	Norway arbor-vitæ.
plicata,	
THILLIA,	Lime or Linden tree.
parvifolia,	small-leaved.
coccínea,	scarlet.
VIBURNUM,	
opùlus,	guelder-rose.
var.	
rósea,	rose-coloured.

LIST OF VERONICAS.

SEE PAGE 46.

VERÓNICA,	Sweed-well.
officinàlis,	officinal.
cham'ædrys,	Germander.
mèdia,	long-spiked.
incàna,	hoary.
élegans,	elegant.
spícàta,	spiked.
grándis,	large white.

incarnàta,	flesh-coloured.
cárnea,	pale red.
leucántha,	white flowered.
bellidioídes,	daisy-leaved.
vérna,	vernal.
am'œna,	fine-blue.
pulchélla,	neat.

TABLE OF SOILS.

THE following compound of soils are adapted to the nature of the Plants contained in this work :

NUMBER.	Savanna.	Loam.	Leaf.	Sand.	Manure.
1	2	1	–	–	–
2	–	3	2	1	–
3	–	4	–	1	1
4	–	2	1	¼	–
5	all	–	–	–	–
6	3	1	–	–	–
7	–	3	1	1	–
8	4	1	–	–	–
9	–	2	2	¼	–
10	1	1	1	–	–
11	–	3	2	1	–
12	–	3	1	1	1
13	2	2	1	¼	1
14	–	4	–	1	–
15	–	4	2	1	–
16	4	–	1	–	–
17	–	5	1	1	1
18	–	1	1	1	1
19	1	1	–	–	–

REMARKS ON THE NATURE OF SOILS USED IN THE ABOVE TABLE.

Peat or Savanna soil—is of a dark colour, with a large portion of white sand incorporated with it, and is found frequently in New Jersey. A mixture of two-thirds black earth from the woods and one-third of pure white sand will be similar to it, and may be used as a substitute, but is not exactly of the same nature.

Loam—is of a light brown colour, and is that from the top of old pastures or commons, which should lie one year, and be frequently turned before using. It ought not to be from a clay bottom, and merely three inches of the turf taken.

Leaf mould—is that which is to be found on the surface of the ground in woods, and is the decomposed leaves. It may be termed nearly of first rate importance in vegetation.

Sand—is a substance that is generally known, and that which is found on the surface is decidedly the best. If it is from a pit, it must be spread out, and frequently turned, that it may assimilate with the atmosphere before using; four months will be sufficient.

Manure—before using, must be decomposed to very fine particles. It will require two years, during which time it must be often turned, and the longer it lays it will be the finer and more congenial.

THE END.

ERRATA.

ROBERT BUIST,

NURSERYMAN, SEEDSMAN, AND FLORIST,

NO. 140 SOUTH TWELFTH STREET, PHILADELPHIA,

Cultivates and has for Sale, on the very lowest cash terms, an extensive assortment of the Rose, Camellia, Pelargonium and other foreign Plants, and is constantly introducing those new sorts worthy of the attention of either amateur or cultivator. He also has a select assortment of all the choice Fruits, with several thousand fruiting plants of foreign Grape Vines in pots. He invites personal inspection to his stock, which is not excelled by any in the United States. His green-house department occupies 18,000 square feet of glass, which enables him to fulfil the most extensive demands. Flowers and Vegetable Seeds, Hyacinths, Tulips and other Dutch bulbs.

All orders must be accompanied with cash or responsibility. Every article carefully packed and forwarded at the risk of the purchaser.

Priced catalogues mailed to order.

BUIST'S PRIZE SEEDLING STRAWBERRY.

This new American Seedling Strawberry is offered to the public as one of the very best in cultivation. The fructifying organs of the plants are all perfect, thereby ensuring a full crop. It is of very high flavour and rich crimson colour, large size and great bearer, and, when brought before a Committee of the Pennsylvania Horticultural Society, in comparison with others, was pronounced "decidedly the best."

CPSIA information can be obtained
at www.ICGtesting.com
Printed in the USA
BVHW042101100323
660195BV00003B/22